Sing
the Lord's Song
in a Strange Land

Dear Howard and Elsa —

I thought that you might like to see the end of the quest on which Howard helped us so much.

Love,

Betty Bandel

May 1981

"Verona"

Also by Betty Bandel:

Walk into My Parlor
Margaret Lane Cooper

Sing the Lord's Song in a Strange Land

The Life of Justin Morgan

Betty Bandel

With a Musical Appendix Compiled and Edited
by James G. Chapman

Rutherford • Madison • Teaneck
Fairleigh Dickinson University Press
London and Toronto: Associated University Presses

©1981 by Associated University Presses, Inc.

Associated University Presses, Inc.
4 Cornwall Drive
East Brunswick, N.J. 08816

Associated University Presses Ltd.
69 Fleet Street
London EC4Y lEU, England

Associated University Presses
Toronto Ontario, Canada M5E 1A7

Library of Congress Cataloging in Publication Data

Bandel, Betty, 1912-
    Sing the Lord's song in a strange land.

    "The music of Justin Morgan": p.
    "Accounts of the origin of the 'Justin Morgan
Horse'": p.
    Bibliography: p.
    Includes index.
    1. Morgan, Justin. 2. Composers—United States
—Vermont—Biography. 3. Choruses, Sacred (Mixed
voices, 4 parts), Unaccompanied. 4. Anthems.
5. Morgan horse. I. Morgan, Justin. Works . 1981
II. Chapman, James G. III. Title.
ML410.M779B3 [(M2092.4)] 783'60924 [B] 78-73309
ISBN 0-8386-2411-1

Printed in the United States of America

Dedicated to
Dorothy Bandel Dragonette
and
Helen Pease Long,
and to the memory of
Charles Angoff

Contents

Acknowledgments

The persons and institutions that have given aid and comfort during the years when this study has been evolving stretch from the coast of Maine to Ann Arbor, Michigan, and from the Canadian border to the District of Columbia. If one attempted to name each person who has courteously and efficiently helped to unearth the records on which this study is based, he would be obligated to name half the town clerks in Vermont and a third of those in other New England states, along with a good number of county and court clerks. There would also, of course, be dozens of librarians in the University of Vermont, the Vermont State Library, the Vermont Historical Society, Middlebury College, the American Antiquarian Society (Worcester, Massachusetts), The Boston Public Library, the Forbes Library in Northhampton, Massachusetts, the Harvard and Yale libraries, the University of Michigan's William L. Clements Library, the Connecticut and Massachusetts state libraries and historical societies, and a host of smaller collections. The staff of Vermont's Public Records Office in Montpelier has been unfailingly helpful, as has the staff of the National Archives (War Department Collection of Revolutionary War Records) in Washington, D.C.

Special thanks are due to: The late Reverend Dr. Charles H. Atkins of Merrimack, New Hampshire, for his expert assistance in analyzing the texts employed by Morgan; Professor James G. Chapman of the University of Vermont Department of Music, for his invaluable aid in analyzing Morgan's music, and to Professor-Emeritus Howard Bennett of the same department for similar aid; Professor Richard Crawford of the University of Michigan, for assistance in determining Morgan's place among musicians of his era in the United States; Mrs. Robert Whitelaw Wilson (Janet Morgan Mahony Wilson) of Washington, D.C., and her sister, Mrs. Leland Scott Brown (Mary Murray Mahony Brown) of Mt. Kisco, New York, great-great-great-granddaughters of Justin Morgan, for their help in following the Morgan line down to the present day; Mrs. Carleton Craig of Brookfield, Vermont, for her assistance in tracking down many Morgan descendants; Mr. Wesley Herwig of Randolph Center, Vermont, for aid in straightening out the Randolph side of Morgan's story; Mrs. Henry Aschenbach of West Springfield, Massachusetts, and Miss Florance Wight, also of West Springfield, for their help in determining how Morgan lived during his Massachusetts years; the late Mrs. Henry Edson of West Lebanon, New Hampshire, for information regarding the Morgan legend in Vermont; Professor Emeritus Marine Leland of Smith College for aid in finding Massachusetts elements of the Morgan story; Mrs. Marion Moore Coleman of Cheshire, Connecticut, for assistance in locating Connecticut records; Mrs. Erma Shepherd Griffith of Binghamton, New York, for aid in pursuing Morgan descendants who settled in the state of New York; Mrs. Raymond E. Fontaine (Marie V. Fontaine) of Wilbraham, Massachusetts, for research in the Connecticut Valley Historical Society's library at Springfield, Massachusetts; Dr. D. F. Musto, historian and psychiatrist at Yale University, for help in determining the significance of medicines that appear in the inventory of Morgan's estate; the Honorable John Powers, Clerk of the Supreme Judicial Court, Suffolk County, Massachusetts, for assistance in locating supreme and other court records of Massachusetts that have a bearing on the Justin Morgan story; Mrs. Betty Lovell, Special Collections, Bailey Library, University of Vermont; Miss Margaret Gardiner of Kennebec Morgan Horse Farm, South Woolwich, Maine; Mrs. Leon Webster (Geneva Carpenter Webster) of Randolph, Vermont, a descendant of Morgan; Miss Dorothy Mozley, head of the genealogical and local history division, Springfield (Mass.) City Library; Mrs. Laura Abbott and Mrs. Maude Legru, librarians of the Vermont Historical Society (Montpelier); Miss Marguerite Olney of Springfield, Vermont; the late Helen Harkness Flanders (Mrs. Ralph E. Flanders) of Springfield, Vermont, authority on Vermont folk music; the late Mildred Shampeny (Mrs. Worth Shampeny) of Rochester, Vermont, historian of Rochester and its environs. Finally a special debt of gratitude is owed to my sister, Dorothy Bandel Dragonette of Riverside, California, and to Helen Pease Long of Keeseville, New York, both of whom brought to bear expert research techniques, sharpened by the reading of many detective stories, on the problem of ferreting out Morgan and allied records in the basements and attics of town halls and similar unlikely places.

By the rivers of Babylon; there we sat down: yea, we wept, when we remembered Zion.

We hanged our harps upon the willows in the midst thereof.

For there they that carried us away captive required of us a song; and they that wasted us required of us mirth, saying, Sing us one of the songs of Zion.

How shall we sing the Lord's song in a strange land?

If I forget thee, O Jerusalem, let my right hand forget her cunning. . . .

Psalm 137

Introduction

1

If one needs evidence that artistic creativity is as natural to man as is eating or sleeping or renewing the species, there is no clearer proof of that fact than the dogged persistence with which men living on the rocky, cold, formidable New England frontier of the 1790s composed music. Anyone who has attempted to weed a New England garden and has watched the forest creep back, minute elm tree by minute elm tree, to correct man's presumption that he has tamed nature, will have some inkling of what work must have been involved in clearing a patch in the wilderness and creating a farm. In historical museums one peers at rows of marvelous hand-made and hand-wielded tools that seem toothpick-size when measured against the great elm and oak and maple trees of the forest that covered New England when Englishmen arrived at Plymouth. With the roar and whine of chain saws and diamond drills in mind try to imagine walking through that silent forest, axe and hoe in hand, and deciding which clump of forest giants to attempt to fell. How did they get the first tree down, this young man of thirty with his boy of twelve, who had come out to the frontier in the spring of 1783, say, to make a clearing and build a cabin to which the young woman of twenty-nine and the brood of younger children could move the following spring? There are old journals and diaries to tell something of how the pioneers achieved these miracles, although naturally they do not tell just how a man wielded an axe, or burned off brush, or reduced logs to timber before the first sawmill moved in. One does learn from even the barest accounts, however, of unending, back-breaking toil by men, women, and children. One reads of privation so great, in the early uncertain years before crops were well established, that a man, faint with hunger, had to stop cultivating a field and catch, cook, and eat a fish from a neighboring stream before he could go on with his labors.[1]

In post-Revolutionary days, Vermont, northern New Hampshire, and northern Maine were the last remaining frontier areas in New England. Boston and Salem, Plymouth and Charlestown, New Haven and Hartford, even Springfield in western Massachusetts—these had been settled cities or large towns, with substantial frame and brick buildings along sometimes cobbled streets, for a century or longer when the Revolution ended. Indeed, well established towns were flourishing in Vermont by 1791, when "the New State"'—the fourteenth—entered the Union. Bennington, the first town chartered in Vermont (its charter having been granted as early as 1749 by Benning Wentworth, governor of New Hampshire, during those years when New Hampshire and New York were jockeying for possession of the wilderness that lay between them), had 2,377 inhabitants by 1790.[2] Such towns as Bennington were, however, few and far between in the 157 miles that stretch from Vermont's southern border to Canada, and in the 90 miles that lie between Lake Champlain on the west and the Connecticut River on the east at Vermont's widest point, its Canadian border. Men were still making clearings and erecting log huts in parts of Vermont when the nineteenth century dawned.

This book tells the story of Justin Morgan—composer, horse breeder, and Vermont settler. Morgan lived in Vermont during the last decade of the eighteenth century, or the first

half of the score of years (1790-1810) that lay between the time
when towns grew big enough to support considerable musical activity and the time when a change in religious and
musical fashions gradually drove the Yankee singing master
out of his central position in the life of New England communities. Morgan was one of a number of Vermont singing
masters of the eighteenth century who were also composers of
music. Eight of these men compiled, edited, and published
tunebooks that contained much of their own music, as well as
much music by other "psalmodists," as the New England
writers who comprised the first school of distinctively American composers were called.[3] Do not let the word *psalmodist*
suggest a narrow field of musical activity. The tunes composed and arranged by these pioneer composers were, as
Irving Lowens has pointed out in his definitive study of early
American music,[4] sung and whistled as men followed the
plow, and as women worked at the great wheel that spun the
wool, or the small wheel that spun the flax. They were used in
the "singing schools" that, as one song relates, provided the
"only joy"[5] in many an isolated village during the long
winter months. They were sung also, of course, in the churches, and in the revivals and camp meetings that became
increasingly popular as the early years of the nineteenth
century witnessed the "Great Revival," or second "Great
Awakening" of religious enthusiasm that had swept across
young America. They were, in a word, probably the most
widely known songs in post-Revolutionary New England.
Other music was known, of course,—dance tunes, folk songs,
music for the fife and drum,—but because of their connection, even when tenuous, with the church, the psalm tunes
held a special place in the hearts of New Englanders, and
therefore of New England composers.

   In recent years many persons have come to recognize the
richness and originality of the psalmodists' compositions,
and the importance of this art form to the composers' fellow
townsmen and to later generations of Americans. Books,

Ph.D. theses, and articles have been written about the prominent members of the groups, such as William Billings and
Oliver Holden of Massachusetts, and Daniel Read and Andrew Law of Connecticut. The final proof of the significance
of the school, both musically and socially, may rest, however,
in the extent to which it flourished not in cities like Boston or
New Haven, but in such new rugged towns as Justin Morgan's Randolph, Vermont.

At every hand there is evidence of widespread and deep
interest in psalmody on the part of Vermont settlers, and
there is evidence of care to make the writing and singing of
such music excellent. In 1786 music was so important to the
inhabitants of Tinmouth, for instance, that at the March
town meeting it was voted "that such psalm tunes be sung on
the Sabbath in the former part of the day, as the Elderly people
are acquainted with." At that same meeting two men were
chosen "choristers" to lead the singing in the church. There
are a few other Vermont towns that, prior to the final separation of town and parish in 1807, evidently believed a chorister
to be as necessary a town officer as a leather-sealer, a tything-
man, or a hog-reeve. In 1785, as the ninety-second work to be
published in what is now Vermont, Haswell and Russell of
Bennington brought out *A Compleat Gamut, or Scale of
Music, for the instruction of youths in that delightful study,
psalmody.*[6] Newspapers of the 1790s and early 1800s carried
frequent announcements for singing schools. There were
advertisements for tunebooks, as companions to the psalm-
and hymn-books that contained the religious poetry popular
in Protestant and largely Puritan New England. Although
local news was kept at a minimum, the newspapers rarely
failed to mention excellent choir performances when they
reported the great doings that surrounded an "election sermon" or a college commencement.

So widespread was musical activity and apparent interest
in music during the first decades of Vermont's history that
one attempting to ferret out information on this activity is

inclined to wonder at the lack of attention to music in most accounts of the early period now available in libraries. Of the men who stubbornly wrote music while they were farming or working as coopers or house-wrights in the Vermont of 1800, even Simeon Pease Cheney, a well known Vermont singing master of the mid-nineteenth century, fails to mention in his useful *The American Singing Book* of 1879 three of the eight Vermonters who published tunebooks of psalmody prior to 1810. If one consults the card catalog of Vermont's largest library, that of the University of Vermont, he finds perhaps an inch of cards labeled "Vermont—poetry," but not one card labeled "Vermont—music." If he turns to the principal source of the detailed history of Vermont's towns and their inhabitants, Abby Hemenway's *A Vermont Historical Gazetteer* (1868-91), nowhere in its five bulky volumes will he find mention of six of the eight musicians who compiled tunebooks; and of Justin Morgan nothing is said of his musical activities.

Wonder at this neglect abates, however, when consideration is given to how rapidly life styles and intellectual fashions have changed in recent times. What would today's college students make, for instance, of the idea of a program dance? Yet a substantial portion of the population under seventy years old has attended program dances. By 1810, sufficient numbers of European music masters had appeared on the American scene to begin to create the impression that music could best be taught by Europeans, and had certainly been written best by Europeans. The organization of Boston's Handel and Haydn Society in 1815 provided the first foreshadowing of an era nearly a century later in which American singers would give their names an Italian flourish before attempting an operatic debut. It is perhaps not surprising that when Handel's *Messiah* was first heard by American composers of psalm tunes, the Americans, sensitive musicians that they were, stopped writing in order to listen. If one remembers that this musical revolution coincided with a

growing secularity and complexity in American life as most
citizens turned their attention to the War of 1812, political
upheaval, and westward expansion, one begins to understand why the psalmodists faded from view, or at least ceased
to occupy a portion of center stage.

By the time that the first extensive histories of Vermont
towns were being written, in the prosperous years that followed recovery from the exhaustions of the Civil War, the
notion was firmly fixed in most historians' heads that the
important men were the soldiers and the politicians. Their
story was dramatic. So was the story, already legendary and
fast becoming mythical, of the struggle to conquer a wilderness—the third great theme in most town histories. The
grandchildren of the men and women who had survived the
first winter, killed the first bear, escaped the first real or
imaginary Indian, would read with zealous attention to
possible errors the stories that they had heard many times
from the very men and women who had lived through, and
had brought about, the conquest of the frontier. With such
dramatic fare at hand, why read about the farmer's, the
mechanic's, the housewife's, or the musician's essential but
hardly crisis-ridden work? Of course, being New Englanders,
the writers and readers of these histories could not fail to give
some attention to the learned professions, and to learning for
its own sake. Therefore, the preacher, the teacher, the doctor,
the lawyer,—even the poet, along with other writers—found
their way into the histories. The musician, together with that
backbone of any Vermont community of the last century, the
farmer, stayed out.

A few nineteenth-century town histories are notable excep-
tions to this rule of thumb. The history of Newbury by
Frederick P. Wells, that of Pawlet by Hiel Hollister, and that
of Woodstock by Henry Swan Dana[7] give detailed accounts of
the rich musical life of the authors' towns at the dawn of the
last century. It is obvious, however, in the cases of Dana and
Hollister, that the authors are themselves musicians and

lovers of music, as well as historians and lovers of history. Given a powerful assist by these writers, and by Simeon Pease Cheney and a few other early students of New England music, one must proceed to pick his way among town and county records, land deeds, probate accounts, wills, newspapers of the early period, and similar primary source material if he hopes to reconstruct the life stories of Vermont's first composers.

The story that emerges from such a hunt is, however, so rich in artistic and particularly in human values, so significant with regard to the development of the United States, that it deserves to be known. The story is still fragmentary. It is hoped that the telling of Morgan's story in this form will bring to the surface diaries, letters, and other material that will shed further light upon Vermont's musical heritage.

2

In order to take the shortest path to this quarry, it seems advisable to avoid certain thickets of misconception that have grown up about frontier life in Vermont and about the Yankee singing masters. First and most important of these misconceptions is the notion that actual frontier life resembled the stereotype dear to the modern "western" film—a hard-breathing, mindless existence of rough, tough customers fast on the draw who liked their liquor raw and neat and their women big-bosomed and available. The classic prototype of "westerns," Owen Wister's *The Virginian*, with its emphasis on a witty, intelligent hero who learns to love Russian novels because of the influence of the schoolteacher-heroine, shows how false the modern stereotype is even to the fictionalized West of the late nineteenth century.

No one, surely, has ever imagined the New England frontier in terms of the film stereotype of the West. As Lucy Lockwood Hazard has remarked in *The Frontier in Amer-*

ican Literature, the New England Puritan who traveled, usually with fellow townsmen, to found a new community on the frontier, was unlike the later western frontiersman, who is often pictured as a solitary wanderer, a lover of the wilderness and of adventure. The Puritan frontiersman, says Miss Hazard, "was not a primitive pathfinder, but a land-hungry 'nester.'"[8] He wanted to build a new and substantial farm as soon as possible, and he wanted to own his own land, just as his father had done before him in Massachusetts or Connecticut. Even writers who have the Puritan frontiersman firmly in mind, however, tend to assume that life on the Vermont frontier must have been reduced to the raw necessity of keeping alive, that life in a log hut must have been a matter of eating, sleeping, producing offspring, and going out each morning with gun and axe, or staying indoors with flax-wheel and doing endless chores. There were chores in plenty in and around every pioneer cabin, but, as Irving Lowens points out,[9] people tend to forget that it was the land that was uncivilized, not the pioneers. The men and women who came to Vermont from the close of the French and Indians Wars in 1763 on to the end of the pioneering period had, by and large, been reared in the old and civilized towns of Massachusetts and Connecticut. Whether they had gone to Harvard or had had three years of village schooling, they brought with them the not-inconsiderable intellectual interests of their home towns. If families had settled far apart on isolated farms, such interests could, of course, have dwindled and died within a generation. New England did not, however, pioneer by set-tling on isolated farms.

When one examines an early map or town plan of Ran-dolph, for example, or Newbury, in Vermont, one discovers the essential ingredient of the New England way of coloniz-ing—the ingredient that made the New England village, clustered around church and school and often common, the central fact in the development of new communities settled by New Englanders, not only in Vermont but on into Ohio and beyond.[10] There in the middle of the map of the six-mile-square township of a Randolph or Newbury are certain small lots, often from two to five acres, called "home lots." Almost before a tree had been felled in the township, the proprietors to whom the town had been granted by charter hired a surveyor to lay out the "rights" within the town. To each proprietor would go one home lot and as many larger, usually 100-acre lots, as his purse and optimism could afford. Sometimes one finds a home lot, a thirty-acre pasture, and a hundred-acre lot of arable land, all in different parts of the town, marked off to a given proprietor. Some proprietors moved into Vermont and settled on their land; others, acting as speculators, sold the land to someone who could not possibly afford to buy land in Massachusetts, but who wished to try his luck and realize the dream of all agrarian workers of English heritage—the ownership of his own land—by buying the relatively inexpensive land on the frontier. When the settler arrived, he found exactly the situation developing that he had known in his home in Massachusetts or Connecticut.

Here in the center of things was laid out a broad street such as runs down the middle of tiny Randolph Center to this day. Here along the street was the settler's home lot, ready to be cleared for his log hut (to be replaced by a frame house when the first saw mill arose), his barn and sheds, his vegetable garden, and his orchard. Out there perhaps quite some distance away were the hundred acres that he was to clear and farm, driving his oxen from the barn to the "farm" every morning.

This arrangement had of course been modified in many of the older communities, as parents with numerous children divided their land among the children, or as someone who had to wade through a swamp to get to his farm from his home lot petitioned the town to allow him to build a house on his farm. By and large, however, the arrangement contained and shaped New England life, as Thomas Jefferson Wertenbaker has pointed out in *The Puritan Oligarchy*.[11]

Wertenbaker explains that the arrangement was an inheritance of the pattern developed on English manors, minus the manor house. It suited exactly the desire and need of the first Puritan settlers for mutual protection and for centralization of the people under the eyes of the minister, the elders, and the deacons. There along the straight, wide street that had first been laid out were the narrow, deep home lots.[12] There also were the meeting house; the school that was built almost as soon as the meeting house; the houses and workshops of shoemaker, blacksmith, tanner, cooper, wheelwright, and other specialists who multiplied as the first settlers became affluent enough to buy necessities difficult for farmers to make at home. In the early seventeenth century many towns farmed the arable lands in common, thus adding one more impetus to collaboration; but even after the great fields had been divided into individually owned farm lots, the system tended to prevent what Wertenbaker calls "the intellectual stagnation which isolation breeds."[13]

Jacob Abbott, writing in 1835 of *New England and Her Institutions,* declares that "you can hardly find a dwelling in New England, be it a framed house or a log cabin, in which some periodical print is not taken."[14] He tells of staying overnight in a log house in which he found the tenant "well acquainted with the various subjects which were then agitating the political and religious world." He describes how his host picked up a novel of Walter Scott's that Abbott had with him, and read it through the night.

Although some Vermont towns were laid out in individual, self-contained farms, many followed the older pattern characteristic of the towns of southern New England. The system seems to have promoted the same advantages for Vermont that it had for Massachusetts and Connecticut. One looks in vain in the history of nineteenth-century Vermont for the development of widespread isolation and its attendant "intellectual stagnation." When jobs were lacking, young men moved westward in search of new opportunities, but they carried with them sound educations and knowledge of and interest in the world.

That Vermont towns began at once to guard and perpetuate the cultivated life that many of the settlers had known in the older towns is apparent from accounts of life written by men and women who were living through the pioneering phase of the state's development, and by those of the next generation who heard the story from the lips of the pioneers themselves. Some accounts stress the wildness of the land and the primitive nature of the huts, roads, and villages that were encountered wherever pioneers had just arrived. Such an account is the perhaps too-well-known *A Narrative of A Tour through The State of Vermont,* written by the Reverend Nathan Perkins of civilized Hartford, Connecticut in 1789.[15] Mr. Perkins spent so much time regretting the miserable food while he mourned the absence of his wife's splendid dinners, and deploring the presence of fleas in chaff-beds and the "nasty, stinking rooms" in which he had to huddle with entire families, that one wonders how he had time for his missionary activities.

Often the stress laid on primitive conditions seems to result from pride in what the pioneers were able to overcome. Thus the Reverend Grant Powers, writing in 1840 of the settlement of towns along the northern stretches of the Connecticut River in pre-Revolutionary days,[16] devotes four pages to the exploits of one Richard Wallace of Thetford, and more particularly of his wife, when Burgoyne's campaign of 1777 on the shores of Lake Champlain alarmed people in all parts of Vermont. Settlers in Thetford, Strafford, and other communities on or near the Connecticut River who felt themselves isolated gathered up whatever household goods they could carry and hurried down to the more thickly settled regions along the river bank. Wallace enlisted for service against Burgoyne; and Mrs. Wallace, alone and six miles from her home, trudged to the cabin day after day to scythe and mow the oats ripe for harvesting, to use her axe in cutting poles to fence the bound bunches of oats, to harvest her corn and potatoes, and to clear and sow an acre of wheat. When her husband returned after the surrender of Burgoyne's army in October, he found that his wife had traveled seventy-two miles, to and from the river, in order to harvest and make secure their crops. Mr. Powers calls upon his readers in 1840, sitting in "broadcloth, silks, and satins," to think long and well of this feat, accomplished "without steam, rail-road, or piano forte."[17]

In contrast to such accounts, however, is the booklet published in 1797 by John Andrew Graham, a young Rutland lawyer and aide-de-camp to Vermont's first governor, Thomas Chittenden. Graham, an Episcopalian who in 1794 went to London on business of the Episcopal Church in Vermont, improved the hours during his stay in England by writing *A Descriptive Sketch of The Present State of Vermont, One of The United States of America* and publishing his book for the edification of the British public.[18] The book gives one of the most detailed pictures now available of Vermont towns of the post-Revolutionary period. If Graham's Episcopalian, lawyer's, and possibly slightly Tory sympathies lead him to deplore strongly Calvinistic tendencies in parts of the state and to list as the "leading people" in each town the lawyers and holders of political office, those same sympathies may be responsible for the fact that Graham avoids chauvinism. He is frank to say that the meeting house in Bennington makes a "mean appearance," and that the church in Windsor—the town on the Connecticut River where Vermont's first constitution was written in 1777—is "a disgrace." One can, therefore, put considerable reliance on his insistence that a number of towns already possess many of the amenities.

In Bennington Graham finds that "the houses are magnificent and elegant," and that the town has not only "corn" (grist) and saw mills and iron works, but also several day schools and an academy, as well as the county courthouse and jail. Castleton has handsome main street; Fairhaven is a "flourishing manufacturing town," with its furnace for casting hollow iron ware, its two forges, its slitting mill for making nail rods, its paper mill, its printing press, its grist and saw mills. Westminster, on the Connecticut River, has several "superb houses." At Windsor there are some fine wooden houses and a good courthouse and "gaol"; and there a 520-foot bridge has just been completed, the first of its kind to span the Connecticut River. Also in Windsor there are large works and furnaces for the manufacture of pot and pearl ashes not only by the old method but also by the new one recently "pointed out by Mr. Samuel Hopkins of Philadelphia." Burlington is already building a house for the president of the University of Vermont, which, although chartered in 1791, has yet to admit its first student. Of his own town, Rutland, Graham says that there is much to praise in the "handsome houses" that line the large square—but that the courthouse, in which sessions of the General Assembly and many other important affairs take place, shows architectural "bad taste." Woodstock has a handsome bridge over the "Waserqueechy" (Ottauquechee) River, and Newbury has "the most elegant church in the State, with a large bell, and the only bell in the state."

It was in Newbury that one of the Vermont psalmodists, Jeremiah Ingalls, settled; and if another, Hezekiah Moors, settled in Mount Holly, described by Graham simply as "a mountain town," at least he had the consolation of knowing that "the great road" from Rutland to Boston ran nearby. Both Newbury and Mount Holly, and all towns between, were interested in religion, in education, and in other civilized and civilizing forces. They were prepared to greet good singing masters, if not with open arms (perish the thought, in New England), at least with the warm welcome that they accorded to good shoemakers, doctors, and other useful men.[19]

Yet, whether in Newbury with its 873 people in 1790, or

Mount Holly with nobody in 1790 and 668 by 1810, all these men—the shoemaker and the doctor as well as the singing master—had to farm it to some extent if they and their families were to survive. Justin Morgan did not have to make a clearing and build a log house—but two psalmodists, Ebenezer Child and Hezekiah Moors, may have helped to do even that. The life that enfolded the psalmodists when they entered Vermont was both demanding and challenging: they found themselves living under frontier conditions, but in closely knit towns in which most people shared what Lucy Lockwood Hazard calls "the mood of the eternal pioneer— turning from the frontier as it is to the frontier as he is going to make it, forgetting cold, hunger, danger, in plans 'of the great progresse they would make.' "[20] In fact, the pioneers did make over the frontier with surprising speed, so that by 1810 Vermont's frontier era had ended, and a singing master who settled in one of the larger towns might reasonably expect to devote most of his time to music—and to make a living thereby.

A composer, however, did not need to wait for the era of professional musicianship to begin to make his mark. In the twenty years preceding 1810, a man who was moved to compose music in Vermont could look with confidence toward performance of his music by choir and singing-school and toward appreciation and approval of his efforts by his fellow townsmen. He would, however, have to make up the fire, rule his paper, and sharpen his pen after a long day of farming or working as a cooper or housewright or inn-keeper. It is doubtful if he knew that he had an illustrious predecessor in Geoffrey Chaucer, who, four hundred years before Vermont became one of the United States, returned home from his duties as controller of customs in the port of London and proceeded to write poetry until he made his "hed to ake."[21] What they did know, the psalmodists as well as Chaucer, was that they had to write what they had to write, regardless of obstacles.

3

The obstacles, fortunately, were in the frontier rather than in the settlers. Writing in the 1880s and recalling the early years of the century, Henry Swan Dana in his *History of Woodstock, Vermont* (p. 221), declares that "good singing was esteemed as a main source of enjoyment, and furthermore an indispensable part of church worship." He adds, "Everybody went to the singing-school . . . for the people thought their children should all be taught to sing, just as much as they should be taught the arithmetic." This statement should alert us to a second widespread misconception about life in early New England. For years it was assumed by historians of Puritan life that colonial and early federal New England was indifferent or hostile to the arts—especially to music—and was most certainly not productive of them.

Just as frontier life in New England was frontier life with a difference, so artistic activity was artistic activity with a difference. They might call plays "dialogues" when presented at college commencement exercises; they might describe a concert of sacred music as a "singing lecture"—but plays were presented and concerts were given. Furthermore, plays were written and music was composed.

Museums such as Sturbridge in Massachusetts or Shelburne in Vermont today bear graphic witness to how widespread was artistic creativity in New England, once settlements had been established. The museums are crammed with the fine handwork, the wall-paintings, the beautifully designed silver and furniture, the portraits that have graced New England houses since at least the eighteenth century. In the field of music, a constantly growing number of sound recordings is bringing to one's attention the original, fresh, and often fine music of William Billings, Oliver Holden, Samuel Holyoke, Daniel Read, Andrew Law, and many another "psalmodist."

As long ago as 1942 Constance Rourke pointed out that if

the theory of Puritan suppression of the arts were correct, one would expect painting to develop first in the South.[22] Actually, she says, it developed first in Pennsylvania and New England. One form of art—the drama—Miss Rourke believes can claim a special link with Puritanism, despite the official Puritan abhorrence of the theater. She remarks that Puritanism is itself a highly dramatic form of faith.[23] The conflict between Good and Evil was dramatically set forth in sermon after sermon. Miss Rourke sees the seventeenth-century Puritan dress, with its repetition of dark grays, as "a theatrical device." In the popular *New England Primer* of 1735 there appeared "A Dialogue between Christ, Youth and the Devil," which Miss Rourke suggests might be considered the first American play.[24]

If the peculiar situation of New England encouraged a kind of dramatic writing, it also encouraged the writing of one type of vocal music. From the days of Calvin in the sixteenth century, the Protestant church and particularly its Puritan wing had stressed the singing of psalms by the congregation as a religious privilege and obligation. It is true that hymns of "human composure" were discouraged; but this restriction merely magnified the place in the religious life of the psalms, which were viewed, even in the metrical form into which they had to be transformed if they were to be set to music, as the word of God. Calvin's insistence on banishing from the church instrumental music and such ornate vocal music as seemed to him worldly, as well as his requirement that psalm tunes be sung in unison, has created the impression that Puritans disapproved of music and discouraged its cultivation. Percy Scholes, however, in *The Puritans and Music in England and New England* (1962) has demonstrated not only how many Puritans on both sides of the ocean owned, used, and apparently loved musical instruments, but also what efforts were made in the seventeenth and eighteenth centuries to provide New England churches with an adequate repertory of psalm tunes.

Henry Ainsworth's *Book of Psalmes,* published in 1612 in Amsterdam and brought to America by the Pilgrims, included thirty-nine tunes, among them some of the fine tunes from the Dutch and French psalters that the Pilgrims had evidently learned during their long stay in Holland.[25] The famous *Bay Psalm Book,* published by the Puritans of the Massachusetts Bay Colony in 1640 in order to provide a more literal version of the psalms than that afforded by the old standard English version, "Sternhold and Hopkins,"[26] did not include tunes until the ninth edition came out in 1700; but from the beginning of the book's long history the compilers recommended the use of Thomas Ravenscroft's *The Whole Book of Psalmes . . . Composed into 4 parts* (London, 1621) as a source of music to accompany the words of the psalms.[27] The forty-eight tunes in the Ravenscroft psalter, a copy of which Governor John Endicott brought with him across the sea, gave to New Englanders the music popular in the homeland as a fit accompaniment to the psalms. The very fact that the *Bay Psalm Book* was the first book printed in New England—indeed, printed anywhere in the Americas north of Mexico[28]—speaks for the importance of the singing of psalms in the Puritan world. By 1773 the *Bay Psalm Book* had run through seventy editions, not to speak of its eighteen English and twenty-two Scottish editions.

It would be strange indeed if the early Puritans, contemporaries of Shakespeare, living and being educated in the golden age of English music, had been either musically illiterate or uninterested in music. They were, after all, bent on purifying the Church of England, not on either eradicating it or altering those aspects of its worship that seemed to them essential to the religious life. Congregational singing of psalms was one of the essentials on which the Puritan wing of the church could agree with the Establishment. Even the queen, the great Elizabeth, in 1559 had enjoined the clergy to begin and end common prayer, either morning or evening, with a hymn to the praise of God, "in the best melody or music that may be devised, having respect that the sentence of the hymn may be understood and perceived."[29]

Much has been made of the fact that by the end of the seventeenth century many New England congregations could no longer keep their balance as they picked their way through the difficult tunes in Ainsworth, and even many of the Ravenscroft airs. Psalters were published with fewer and fewer tunes, and these tunes were drawn from John Playford's *Brief Introduction to the Skill of Musick* (eighth edition, 1679), which provided music of a style more familiar to the people of 1700 than was the music gathered into psalters three-quarters of a century earlier. The inability to maintain a high standard of musical literacy and competence during three generations of pioneering in a wilderness stemmed, surely, not from lack of interest in music but from lack of opportunity for adequate training. In England the nurturing of highly developed musicianship had depended for centuries on the presence of great cathedrals with their attendant schools to which the musically gifted could be sent in childhood for a long, exacting apprenticeship under masters of the art. The twenty years of Puritan rule between the beginning of the Long Parliament in 1640 and the restoration of the monarchy in 1660, accompanied as they were by the closing of the cathedral choir schools, had so impoverished musical life that when the great choirs once again began to function no boy could be found in the kingdom capable of singing the counter part properly until he had undergone at least a year's training. So in 1660 reports Henry Cooke, newly appointed master of the Children of the Chapel Royal. He adds that for about a year he had to use "men's feigned voices" and cornets for the "superior parts" in his choir.[30]

The very fact that scores of music-loving Massachusetts clergymen in the early eighteenth century, following the example set by English Independent clergymen and musicians during the first decade of the century, began a vigorous campaign to improve congregational singing, and that many people flocked to their standard, speaks for the continuing interest of New Englanders in music. Indeed, the acrimony with which some church members resisted the new "regular" singing (singing by note what was written in the tunebooks) and held out for the older singing by ear ("rote") testifies to the importance of music as a part of New England colonial life. The Reverend Cotton Mather revealed in a letter to Thomas Hollis written in 1723 the beginning of big-city complacency—now that Boston possessed 12,000 souls and 11 churches—when he commented that although the "polite City of Boston" had accepted the "regular" singing taught by the new singing schools, "in the Countrey, where they have more of the Rustick," some of the older and angry people decried the innovation as the "bringing in of Popery."[31] If they equated singing by note with praying by formula, such "rustics" also cherished the spontaneous improvisation of turns, passing notes, and other ornaments with which they had learned, during the era of the "lining out" of psalms, to give life and variety to tunes whose tempos had apparently grown slower decade by decade.[32]

From the beginning of the "regular singing" controversy about 1720, singing schools grew and flourished throughout the eighteenth century and well into the nineteenth. It was these singing schools, often conducted by singing masters who devoted more and more of their time to music, that provided the musical climate in which New England's first composers found breathing and elbow room. It requires a leap of the imagination to turn from the use of tunes that people have "always" sung to the making of tunes of one's own. Yet a gifted musician who is conducting a singing school and finds no tune available that the three tenors can sing is given a powerful nudge in the direction of writing a tune that they can sing. If, at the very time when the need for the tune arises, the air is full of new and distinctively home-grown literary efforts such as *Ponteach*, Robert Rogers's play of white man-Indian conflict, and new and distinctively home-grown political declarations such as Ethan Allen's "Surrender in the name of the great Jehovah and the Continental Congress!"—if such creativity is everywhere apparent, why not try one's hand at writing a tune?

Before the Revolution had added its own powerful impetus to the production of distinctively "American" products, material and immaterial, William Billings, Boston tanner and musician, had published one of his six books of music—all of which are devoted largely to his own compositions—and had gained some measure of recognition throughout New England and beyond. The stage was set. Between 1770 and 1800 twenty-six tunebooks devoted exclusively to music by American composers were published,[33] and dozens of the 111 tunebooks (running to 272 editions) published before 1800 included works by Americans.[34] When Justin Morgan, Jeremiah Ingalls, and Elisha West migrated to Vermont around 1790, any Vermonter would have taken the writing of music by an American for granted.

4

Two beliefs less widespread than the notion that the New England frontier of colonial days was a backwoods wilderness remain to be mentioned. One such belief, held by a number of historians writing before recent scholarly studies gave detailed accounts of the lives of Billings, Law, and other early American musicians, stems from the tendency to read the record of the past in terms of one's own time and place. Noting that most eighteenth-century singing masters were men of slender means, some of them dying in poverty, and noting also that they plied such trades as those of tanner, housewright, and cooper, the historians concluded that the singing masters were of that class referred to by Victorian novelists as "the Poor"—or, worse, "the Deserving Poor." Their poverty, these commentators imply, must have entailed impoverished educations and impoverished lives. Until quite recently William Billings, whose prose style is a delight, was described as "illiterate."

The historian who so classifies the singing masters is thinking of the slums and other elements of modern life that tend to hold entire families in an underprivileged status not only for a lifetime, but for generations. What is forgotten about colonial New England is its agrarian nature, the relatively small number of families that peopled the entire area, and how many children there were in each family. As the ten, twelve, fifteen, or even twenty children grew up, the home farm could not sustain more than two or three of the next generation. Therefore, everyone pitched in to help the most bookish boy get to college, from which he emerged to "read law," become a lawyer, and perhaps end as judge, congressman, or senator. So long as there was still open land in New England, perhaps two or three other sons moved to the new towns and worked for someone else until they could buy their own land and develop their own farms. Some of the family were apprenticed in various trades. A boy who had been apprenticed as a blacksmith might find, as the nineteenth century dawned, that the increasing demand for iron implements was turning his small blacksmith shop into a large factory. If one member of the family had chosen the role of singing master as his principal means of support, he might never know financial success or even security—but he was nevertheless still brother to the prosperous farmer, senator, and iron manufacturer.

Justin Morgan and several of his fellow Vermont singing masters came from substantial families that had cultivated the land in Massachusetts and Connecticut for four or five generations before any of their number ventured into Vermont. Members of their families had held various town offices, had become deacons in the churches, had served in the wars. The psalmodists had attended the same churches and schools, turned out for the same training days, helped to cultivate the same fields on the home farm as had their brothers. Direct and collateral descendants of the psalmodists played their part in the expanding life of the United States. One finds numbered among the sons and daughters, grandsons and granddaughters of the singing masters doctors, lawyers, preachers, teachers, businessmen, holders of political office—and very often singers who in their turn took their places as leaders in church choirs and other musical organizations. The singing masters sprang from the families that built New England and they passed on to their descendants a goodly heritage.

5

Finally, there is, if not a misconception, at least a difference of opinion on the extent to which the music written by the singing masters was sacred, as distinguished from secular. Some musicologists, noting what a large part the singing schools played in the social life of the villages and how the psalm tunes were sung by people at work and at play, as well as by worshippers in churches, have decided that the tunes were simply the popular music of the day in New England and that they cannot be classified as sacred music in the strict sense of that term. It is probable that the composers themselves differed one from another in this regard, some drawing their inspiration from their religious experiences, some finding the sources of their musical ideas in other human activities. It seems to this observer that, despite the number of Vermonters in the post-Revolutionary period who, like Ethan Allen, were skeptical regarding orthodox Calvinism, the average Vermont village fitted its many secular concerns inside a religious frame of reference, just as Chaucer's pilgrims fitted their often wordly interests inside a religious pilgrimage. Daily prayers were said in most households morning and evening; and if the college boy who came home for the holidays breathing religious doubts got most of the public attention, that fact stems from the natural tendency to talk about the odd-man-out—especially if he seems faintly scandalous. The Vermont singing masters apparently were sincere when they named their tunebooks *The Christian Harmony* or *The Sacred Musician*. Two at least wrote on the title-pages of their books the words of the psalmist, "Sing unto the Lord a New Song, and his Praise in the congregation of saints." If people sang their songs in the fields as well as in the churches, would any true believer have denied that God was present everywhere?

Bibliographical Note

In the following chapters no attempt has been made to document individually each public record from which facts about Morgan's life have been drawn. The system of record-keeping is fairly uniform throughout New England: vital records may be consulted in town clerks' offices, and also, in microfilm form, in such centralized locations as the Vermont Public Records Office in Montpelier or the state library of Connecticut. The early "town book" in each town clerk's office gives details of town elections, often of taxes assessed on the "Grand List," and of a variety of other town concerns. Land records are sometimes in town clerks' offices, sometimes in the offices of clerks of county courts, sometimes (in Massachusetts) in the Registry of Deeds within a given district of a county. Court records are of course maintained by the clerks of the various courts involved. So long as the Vermont Supreme Court was a circuit court, its records were kept in the various county courthouses in which it met, and they are still to be found in the custody of the clerks of the county courts. Probate records are maintained by the various probate districts in each state. Those in Vermont are also available in microfilm form in the Public Record Office at Montpelier.

The most extensive file of Vermont newspapers is in the Vermont State Library in Montpelier. A number of early newspapers from all parts of the United States are now available in the microcard series, *Early American Newspapers, 1704-1820* (New York: Readex Microprint Corp., various dates).

Notes

1. Seth Hubbell, *A Narrative of the Sufferings of Seth Hubbell and Family, in His Beginning a Settlement in The Town of Wolcott, in The State of Vermont* (Danville, Vt.: E. and W. Eaton, 1826), p. 8.

2. U.S., Bureau of the Census, *Heads of Families at the First Census of the United States. Taken in The Year 1790 . . .*, p. 9.

3. The tunebooks of "psalmody" compiled and edited by Vermonters before 1810 are:

Thomas H. Atwill, *The New York and Vermont Collection of Sacred Harmony* (Lansingburgh, N.Y.: first edition entitled *The New York Collection of Sacred Harmony*, the author, 1795; subsequent editions through 1805 entitled *The New York and Vermont Collection of Sacred Harmony*, Albany, N.Y., by "the proprietor," or by R. Buckley, or by Backus and Whiting).

Ebenezer Child, *The Sacred Musician and Young Gentlemen's and Ladies' Practical Guide to Musick* (Boston: Manning and Loring, 1804).

Eliakim Doolittle, *The Psalm Singer's Companion* (New Haven, Conn., 1806).

Joel Harmon, Jr., *The Columbian Sacred Minstrel* (Northampton, Mass.: Andrew Wright, 1809).

Uri K. Hill, *The Vermont Harmony* (Northampton, Mass.: Andrew Wright, 1801).

Jeremiah Ingalls, *The Christian Harmony* (Exeter, N.H.: Henry Ranlet, 1805).

Hezekiah Moors, *The Province Harmony* (Boston: J. T. Buckingham, 1809).

Elisha West, *The Musical Concert* (Northampton, Mass.: by Andrew Wright for Elisha West and John Billings, Jr., 1802; second edition by Andrew Wright for the compiler, 1807).

4. Irving Lowens, *Music and Musicians in Early America* (New York: Norton, 1964), pp. 177 and 280.

5. These words are from "Welcome Song," an English tune at least as old as 1700 that was known and loved in New England. Oliver Brownson incorporated the song in his *Select Harmony* (New Haven, Conn.: Thomas and Samuel Green, 1783), and it was included in many later tunebooks. It has been recorded by the Old Sturbridge Singers (*The New England Harmony*, Folkways No. FA 2377).

6. Marcus A. McCorison, *Vermont Imprints, 1778-1820* (Worcester, Mass.: American Antiquarian Society, 1963), p. 25.

7. Frederick P. Wells, *History of Newbury, Vermont . . .* (St. Johnsbury, Vt.: Caledonian Company, 1902); Hiel Hollister, *Pawlet for One Hundred Years* (Albany, N.Y.: J. Munsell, 1867); Henry Swan Dana, *History of Woodstock, Vt.* (Boston and New York: Houghton Mifflin Co., 1887 and 1889 editions).

8. Lucy Lockwood Hazard, *The Frontier in American Literature* (1927, Privately printed, n.p.), p. 26.

9. Lowens, *Music and Musicians in Early America*, p. 17.

10. Henry Nash Smith, *Virgin Land* (1950; reprinted; New York: Vintage, 1957), p. 155.

11. Thomas Jefferson Wertenbaker, *The Puritan Oligarchy* (1947; reprinted; New York: Grosset and Dunlap, n.d.). See especially chapter 2. Wertenbaker's analysis was anticipated by almost a century when Josiah Gilbert Holland described the typical pattern of the New England village and its effect upon New England culture. See Josiah Gilbert Holland's *History of Western Massachusetts* (Springfield, Mass.: Samuel Bowles and Company, 1855), 1: 62-64.

12. Wertenbaker points out (p. 46), citing William Cothren's *History of Ancient Woodbury, Conn.*, p. 65, that a home lot with a frontage of 198 feet might be a mile deep. Some settlers farmed their home lots for several years before bothering to begin cultivation of their farm lands.

13. Wertenbaker, *The Puritan Oligarchy*, p. 44.

14. Jacob Abbott, *New England and Her Institutions* (Hartford, Conn.: S. Andrus and Son, 1847), p. 25.

15. Nathan Perkins, *A Narrative of a Tour Through the State of Vermont* (1789, reprinted; Rutland, Vt.: Tuttle, 1964), p. 31.

16. Grant Powers, *Historical Sketches of the Discovery, Settlement, and Progress of Events in the Coos Country and Vicinity, Principally Included between the Years 1754 and 1785* (Haverhill, N.H.: J. F. C. Hayes, 1841), pp. 147-51.

17. As an old lady, Mary Palmer Tyler, widow of Royall Tyler, chief judge of the Vermont Supreme Court from 1807 to 1813, recalled that when she was a bride and her new husband decided in 1791 to go to Vermont from Boston, she thought of how many people considered Vermont "the outskirts of creation . . . where all the rogues and runaways congregated, and for that reason considered a good place for lawyers" (*Grandmother Tyler's Book*, ed. Frederick Tupper and Helen Tyler Brown. New York and London: Putnam's, 1925], p. 151).

18. John Andrew Graham, *A Descriptive Sketch of The Present State of Vermont* . . . (London: Henry Fry, 1797).

19. Washington Irving's unforgettable word-portrait of Ichabod Crane as singing master and choir director seems to owe more to Brother Jonathan, that prototype of the rustic but shrewd Yankee countryman who outsmarts the city slickers, in Royall Tyler's comedy of 1787, *The Contrast*, than it does to the actual singing masters who traveled and taught throughout New England. Remember that when Ichabod sang he created such sounds that "peculiar quavers" are still heard in the church in Sleepy Hollow—quavers that "are said to be legitimately descended from the nose of Ichabod Crane." The Ichabod Crane version of the country singing master, like the country schoolmaster, by the mid-nineteenth century took its place alongside the Yankee trader, the backwoodsman, and the plantation Negro as a popular type-character in skits, plays, and stories. As Constance Rourke has ably demonstrated in *American Humor* (1931; reprinted; New York: Doubleday & Co., 1953), p. 25 and passim, these brightly painted little portraits, depending for their effect upon comic exaggeration, came into being as writers and others puzzled over what manner of man that new creature, an American, might be.

20. Hazard, *The Frontier in American Literature*, p. 10. The Reverend Mr. Powers, in his *Historical Sketches*, pp. 96-98, tells of how Colonel Thomas Johnston, one of the first settlers in the Newbury, Vt.-Haverhill, N.H., area, encouraged his homesick wife by describing to her "the future village which they should ere long witness in that place. 'On such a line would be the main street; on

such a spot the court-house would stand; the academy would occupy such a site, and the meeting-house stand *there.*'" The young wife, after brightening up for a moment, grew sober again and said, "Mr. Johnson . . . it never will be in this world." Both husband and wife lived to see the prophecy fulfilled, "almost to a jot and tittle."

21. Geoffrey Chaucer, *The House of Fame*, lines 631-33.

22. Constance Rourke, *The Roots of American Culture* (1942; reprint ed., Port Washington, N.Y.: Kennikat Press, 1965), p. 57.

While many historians assumed that Puritanism was an enemy to the arts, others saw in America's alleged materialism and her love of the practical a force that they assumed must have worked against artistic development—not simply in Puritan New England but throughout the colonies and the early republic. These writers drew support, as Miss Rourke points out (pp. 3-11), from the remarks of Washington, Jefferson, and other eighteenth-century leaders that arts like engineering must, in a new country, precede arts like music. Miss Rourke adds that the Founding Fathers, while hoping for rapid developments in the fine arts and assuming that such developments would have to wait until European artists could show the way, were overlooking "the arts belonging to the common life of the time" (p. 11). Allen H. Eaton, writing in 1949 on *Handicrafts of New England*, hopes that "we of the West accept the philosophy of the East which holds that 'the artist is not a special kind of man, but every man is a special kind of artist'" (p. 348). There is evidence that colonial Americans, whether making a fish net or a psalm tune, held some such belief.

23. Rourke, *Roots of American Culture*, p. 109.

24. Another candidate for that frequently-awarded title might be one of the fifty or more treaties with the Indians that were of sufficient interest to be printed, and which Miss Rourke labels "in truth our first American plays" (*Roots of American Culture*, pp. 63-64) The Indians, with their strong sense of the dramatic and of the ceremonial, insisted on concluding every treaty in a public show.

The play about the conflict between white man and Indian, *Ponteach*, said to have been written in 1776 by Robert Rogers, who had won renown as leader of Rogers's Rangers in the New Hampshire Grants during the French and Indian Wars, antedated by more than ten years Royall Tyler's *The Contrast*, another "first" among American plays. In *The Contrast* Tyler dramatized the comic conflict between the colonial Englishman and the evolving American—and in the process created the stage Yankee, Brother Jonathan.

25. Robert Stevenson, *Protestant Church Music in America* (New York: W. W. Norton & Co., 1966), ch. 2.

26. *The Whole Booke of Psalmes, Collected into English Meetre* by Thomas Sternhold, John Hopkins, and others, had been published in many editions after its first printing in 1562.

27. Stevenson, *Protestant Church Music*, p. 7, n. 11.

28. Henry Wilder Foote, *Three Centuries of American Hymnody* (1940; reprint ed., New York: Anchor Books, 1968), p. 45 and n. 8.

29. J. Spencer Curwen, *Studies in Worship Music*, 1st ser., 3d ed. (London: J. Cunnen and Son, n.d.), p. 2.

30. Cooke reported his findings in *The Present Practice of Music Vindicated*, quoted by Ralph T. Daniel in *The Anthem in New England Before 1800*, Pi Kappa Lambda Studies in American Music (Evanston, Ill.: Northwestern University Press, 1966), p. 21.

31. Quoted in Stevenson, *Protestant Church Music*, p. 23.

32. Gilbert Chase in *America's Music, from the Pilgrims to the Present* (New York: McGraw-Hill Book Co., 1955), p. 31, suggests that as the deacon's "lining

Introduction 39

out," or reading of each line before it was sung, became standard practice in the late seventeenth century, the embellishment, or "gracing," of the tune by the people was a form of impromptu composition, each singer creating his own response to the words and idea suggested by the deacon's reading.

33. Allen Perdue Britton, *Theoretical Introductions in American Tune-books to 1800* (Ann Arbor, Mich.: University Microfilms, 1949), p. 163.

34. Ibid., p. 127.

Sing
the Lord's Song
in a Strange Land

─ 1 ─

Prelude

JUSTIN MORGAN, as the world of horse-lovers knows, had a horse.[1] Justin Morgan, as fewer people know, wrote the anthem that may have been the most popular of all anthems sung in New England churches during the 1790s. A peculiar difficulty arises when an attempt is made to tell the story of Justin Morgan's life. Numbers of men have become legends during their lives, or shortly after they died. Justin Morgan is the only man, it seems, who is plagued by having been the owner of a horse that turned into a legend.

Figure, known even in his master's lifetime as "the Justin Morgan horse," had the virtues that the American frontier of the eighteenth century needed in a horse. As Dorothy Canfield Fisher has said, Morgans "had excellent teeth and good digestions, ate what there was to eat and got the good of their food."[2] The hardy, adaptable, and likable Morgan could and did do all the jobs that the new America needed to have done by a horse—pulling a plow, rooting out a stump, drawing a wagon or cart, carrying a rider. Therefore the Morgan horse became an indispensable part of American life in the last decade of the eighteenth and the first decades of the nineteenth centuries—and therefore he became a legend. He must be, as English and American heroes have tended to be from the time of Dick Whittington and earlier, a little fellow who could accomplish miracles—tough and resilient and never-

UVM Flash, Morgan stallion bred and owned by the University of Vermont Morgan Horse Farm at Weybridge, Vt., poses in front of the statue of his great progenitor, Figure, or "Justin Morgan." The heroic-sized statue, given to the Morgan Horse Farm by the American Morgan Horse Association in 1921, was sculptured by Frederick Roth, whose "Roman Chariot" was featured at the Pan-American Exposition in 1904, and some of whose works are in the Metropolitan Museum of Art. *Photo by Paul Quinn, reproduced by courtesy of the University of Vermont Morgan Horse Farm.*

say-die. The original Morgan horse, Figure, is invariably called "little," although a 1796 advertisement of him at stud describes him as being fifteen hands three inches tall.[3] He must also be, in the best American legendary tradition, something of a loner, accomplishing his great feats of outrunning and out-walking and out-pulling other horses without benefit of any important stable or combination of trainers to give him support. He must have sprung from rather obscure origins that in the end turn out to have a hint of princely blood in them—as the heroes of popular English fables have done since the Middle Ages.[4]

Since the horse must have all these characteristics, so must his master. He must be a loner, bringing his horse to frontier country, and overcoming, even as his horse overcame, formidable odds. It is not necessary, especially if he is to be a schoolmaster, for him to chant, as folk-hero wrestlers of early-nineteenth-century song and story did, "down you go, w'ar you a buffalo!"[5]—but it is necessary for him to be a better judge and trainer of horses than are bigger, wealthier men on whom fortune has smiled.

A factor that probably entered into the development of the image of Justin Morgan as a frail schoolmaster was the inability of mid-nineteenth century American chroniclers to imagine that a working farmer could also be a singing master and a composer—a combination of activities that it is hoped that this study will prove was quite normal when Morgan was alive, some fifty years before people began to write his story. In 1857 Daniel Chipman Linsley in his *Morgan Horses: A Premium Essay*, the first authoritative history of the Morgan breed,[6] said of the man Morgan,

> He was naturally quick and intelligent, and by application obtained a thorough knowledge of the primary English branches, was an excellent penman, and a fine singer. Physically he was tall, slim and of feeble health, being inclined to consumption. In fact, he was unable to perform any manual labor of importance after he was twenty years

old, and supported himself almost entirely by teaching
singing, writing, and common district schools. As a teacher, he seems to have been successful, and was very much
liked wherever he went, on account of his urbane manners
and upright character. [P. 105]

Linsley adds,

It must be remembered that [Morgan] was not a farmer, or a
breeder of horses, and he had not brought his horse to
Vermont to improve the breed of horses there; but he kept
him to ride from school to school. [P. 128]

Even before Linsley published his book, *The Cultivator*
(Albany, N. Y.) in its autumn 1845 issue carried a story
quoting Maylon Cottrell of Montpelier as saying that Morgan, "a singing master," used his prize colt, when grown, to
carry him about "on his singing circuit."[7] In a later source
the story had grown to the point at which "the old time stage
driver from Royalton to Montpelier in those days, long time
well known at the old Pavilion, in Montpelier, used to say
that he had often met Mr. Morgan going to his singing
schools on the *par excellence* namesake of his race a hundred
years ago in Randolph."[8] The "old time stage driver" turns
out to be Maylon Cottrell, who was born in 1797, one year
before Morgan died.

Given this type of thinking about Morgan by the men who
first wrote about him, it is not surprising that when Morgan
enters into fiction he becomes a kind of western pioneer,
molded into the saddle like "The Virginian" and riding out
of staid Massachusetts to bring to the American frontier,
which in 1790 included the New England frontier, or Vermont, the only breed of horses named after a man.

This version of Morgan history has great charm and has
given rise to many good stories.[9] These anecdotes, however,
tend to blur the actual story of Justin Morgan's life, and in
doing so obscure his importance as a musician—particularly

RANDOLPH
Home of Justin Morgan

In 1791 Schoolmaster Justin Morgan brought into Vermont the colt that was to bear his name and to make them both famous. This Morgan Horse which Justin Morgan took as payment of a debt became the ancestor of one of the greatest breeds of horses ever established in America.

One of several historic markers that describe the first Morgan horse and his owner is this sign located in Randolph Center, Vermont, not far from where Justin Morgan made his home when he arrived in Vermont in 1788. Like other Morgan markers, this one includes what may well be errors in fact. The horse Figure, which had already been used at stud in Connecticut, and was therefore an adult horse, was probably brought to Vermont by Morgan in 1792. *Photo by Wesley Herwig.*

as a composer of significant, early, distinctively American music. How a man of slender means lived through the difficult years just after the American Revolution in that part of Massachusetts hardest hit by the post-war depression, how he scraped a living for himself and his family even while he was attempting to establish a home in Randolph on the Vermont frontier, and how, despite illness, he managed to summon up the energy required to compose music—all these make a story of great interest to anyone attempting to comprehend the power and persistence of artistic creativity, or the actual as opposed to the legendary life of America at the close of the eighteenth century. It is this story that will be told here.

It is risky, perhaps, to write the biography of a man who is himself silent. Man, the speaking animal, defines himself by his words. The only statements made by Morgan that can be accurately documented are the advertisements he placed in various newspapers offering his horse for stud service. One that appeared in the *Rutland Herald* of May 1795 (dated Williston, Vt., April 30), reads: "Figure will cover this season at the stable of Samuel Allen in Williston, and at the stable in Hinesburgh, formerly owned by Mr. Munson. Figure sprang from a curious horse owned by Col. DeLancey of New York, but the greatest recommendation I can give him is, that he is exceedingly sure, and gets curious colts."

What can one learn from this advertisement? First, that Justin Morgan stuck to the facts. There are comparable advertisements in the newspapers of the era that claim for stallions (which are serving mares at the lordly price of one dollar "the single leap") ancestries that seem to date back to the original Bucephalus, or perhaps even to the winged Pegasus.[10] For Morgan, the truth seemed sufficient. Second, one learns that Justin Morgan was apparently trained to use words carefully. In western Massachusetts, where Justin grew up, older usage would have persisted while new words came into fashion in Boston. Therefore Morgan uses *curious* in its old sense of "exquisite, choice, excellent, fine." The *Oxford*

English Dictionary relates that this meaning was retained in New England, at least among "the common farmers," until well into the nineteenth century.

The greatest deprivation that a would-be biographer suffers if he has no writings by his subject is utter lack of evidence as to whether his man had a sense of humor, and, if so, what kind. Insofar as a sense of humor is perhaps the mainstay that makes it possible for most of us to live through adversities, and inasmuch as a humane sense of humor is one of the characteristics that most quickly draw others to a given man or woman, it is particularly unfortunate that there is no evidence whatever about this attribute, or lack of it, in Justin Morgan. The solemn memoirs of Justin's daughter, Emily Egerton, have no place for humor.[11] The small number of anecdotes that have come down to us from grandsons of men who knew Morgan speak of him as an "old school gentleman," and include none of the joking that marks stories about some of his fellow psalmodists.[12] Perhaps there was less room for joking in Morgan's life than there was in the lives of some of his fellow Vermont composers.

Even without diaries, letters, or similar first-hand evidence, one can derive from the public records and from much circumstantial evidence a surprisingly full, often three-dimensional picture of Morgan's life.

Notes

1. Marguerite Henry's story, *Justin Morgan Had a Horse* (New York: Rand McNally & Co., 1954), has popularized this expression wherever children and older children read about Morgan horses.

2. Dorothy Canfield Fisher, *Vermont Tradition* (Boston: Little, Brown & Co., 1953), p. 214.

3. *The Burlington Mercury*, published in Burlington, Vt., advertised Figure on 1 April 1796 and weekly thereafter until early August. See Betty Bandel, "End of an Argument," *The Morgan Horse* 28 (April 1968): 41 and 71, for an analysis of the contents of the advertisement and its implications.

4. See Alfred Harbage, *Conceptions of Shakespeare* (Cambridge, Mass.: Harvard University Press, 1967), ch. 6, "Shakespeare as Culture Hero," for an amusing and

convincing analysis of this tendency at work among those who would attribute the plays of Shakespeare to some nobleman.

5. Constance Rourke, *American Humor* (1931; reprint ed., New York: Doubleday-Anchor, 1953), p. 40.

6. Daniel Chipman Linsley, *Morgan Horses: A Premium Essay* (New York: C. M. Saxton and Co., 1857).

7. *Cultivator*, Autumn 1845, p. 352.

8. Nickerson and Cox, comps., *The Illustrated Historical Souvenir of Randolph, Vermont* (Randolph, 1895), p. 11.

9. Perhaps best known today of the various Morgan stories presented as fiction is Marguerite Henry's *Justin Morgan Had a Horse;* but the story that first pictured Morgan as a "frail schoolmaster" is *Justin Morgan, Founder of his Race,* a tale for young people written by Eleanor Waring Burnham and published in 1911 by the Shakespeare Press of New York. Mrs. Burnham, whose father, George Houstoun Waring, is credited with introducing the Morgan horse into Georgia, was apparently knowledgeable about horses. She turned to the most authoritative book available in her day on the Morgan Horse—Joseph Battell's *The Morgan Horse and Register,* 3 vol. (Middlebury, Vt.: Register Printing Company, 1894-1915)—and from it drew much excellent information on the horse and some information, both excellent and less than excellent, on the man. Battell quoted Linsley as to Morgan's inability to do hard farm work after he was twenty and his turning to the work of a schoolmaster in his adult years. Mrs. Burnham emphasized this idea and wove into her story a romance in which a southern girl who occasionally visited New England recognized the worth of the Morgan horse and was allowed by the frail schoolmaster to become fast friends with his spl endid animal. Mrs. Burnham did not denude Justin Morgan of his fairly large family. When Marguerite Henry wrote her version of the story in 1954 she deprived Morgan of wife and children in order to emphasize the fine boy-horse relationship that she developed. Joel, a young lad who rides with Justin Morgan to collect the "colt" in Connecticut and bring him back to Vermont, steals the limelight from Justin Morgan the man, assumed to be a bachelor-schoolteacher who boarded with Joel's family. Miss Henry managed to catch something of the flavor of the New England frontier, even if she did endow the Randolph of the 1790s with schoolhouses equipped with harpsichords.

The Walt Disney film of recent vintage on Morgan and his horse uses the stereotype of a town dominated by one wealthy landowner—a stereotype that bears little if any relation to the Vermont experience, no matter how accurate it may be in depicting some settlements west of the Hudson. Jeanne Mellin's *The Morgan Horse* (Brattleboro, Vt.: Stephen Greene Press, 1961), an excellent study of the development of the Morgan breed of horses, emphasizes the presumed smallness of Figure and repeats the statement made by a number of earlier writers that Justin Morgan died in Woodstock and that Figure immediately thereafter passed into the hands of William Rice, then of Woodstock. Records indicate that Morgan died in Randolph. The question of when and where Figure went after he parted from Morgan will be dealt with later in this account.

10. In an advertisement in the *Vermont Journal* (Windsor) dated 26 April 1797, Thomas W. Pitkin of Hartford, Vt., makes fun of these extravagant claims by remarking, "as titles of nobility are not approved of, it is sure that no gentleman will search the *Herald* to find the pedigree of a horse."

11. Rufus Nutting, *Memoirs of Mrs. Emily Egerton, an Authentic Narrative* (Boston: Perkins and Marvin, 1832). See below, p. 130.

12. See, for instance, the note by Moses Ela Cheney, well-known Vermont singing master of the middle years of the nineteenth century, in Simeon Pease Cheney's

American Singing Book (Boston: White, Smith & Co., 1879), p. 171. As early as 1842 the *Cultivator* (Albany, N.Y.) carried an article based on information furnished by John Morgan of Lima, N.Y., a cousin of Justin's, that says of Justin Morgan, "As a teacher he seems to have been successful, and was greatly liked wherever he went, on account of his urbane manner and upright character" (quoted in Linsley, *Morgan Horses*, p. 105).

____ 2 ____

A Library Speaks

IF one does not have the words that a man has spoken or written, the next best source of his intellectual history is the words that he has read and cherished. One's library is perhaps more revealing than any other furnishing in one's home. Much has been made of the fact that when Morgan died in March of 1798 the inventory of his estate was meager.[1] Yet his estate included fifteen books—while the estates of some of his affluent neighbors, whose broad acres were valued at several thousand dollars, possessed, by way of library, only a Bible and that (New) "testament," which was often printed with a metrical version of the psalms for light reading when the entire Bible grew too heavy.

Morgan's fifteen books tell a great deal more than do the advertisements of Figure. There can be no doubt, for instance, that, as tradition has insisted, Morgan taught music, writing, and what would today be called grade school subjects. It is rare to find the names of teachers of common schools even in a "town book" that records the granting of so many shillings, payable in good wheat or other farm produce, to hire a master "to keep a school in the town for eight weeks this winter."

Although there is some evidence of Morgan's activities as a singing master, diligent search has thus far failed to uncover any specific mention, in town or church records, newspaper accounts, diaries, or other documents written during Morgan's lifetime of his activities as a teacher of common schools. Yet in the inventory of Morgan's estate are listed: "Salmons Geography, Perry's Dictionary, Scotts Lessons, Golden Treasury Book, Dilworths Arithmetick, 2nd part Grammatical Institute, Art of Writing & Copper plates"—as well as "Benhams singing book."

"Benhams singing book," which may be the most important item on the list, and which was valued by the appraisers at eight cents as compared to eighty-three cents for "Salmons Geography," is Asahel Benham's *Federal Harmony, Containing, in a Familiar Manner, The Rudiments of Psalmody, Together with A Collection of Church Music (Most of which are entirely new)*. This tunebook, printed by A. Morse in 1790 in New Haven, Connecticut, introduced Morgan's music to the world. Eight of the nine Morgan pieces that have survived appear in all editions of this book, including the sixth and final edition of 1796.

"Art of Writing & Copper plates" (valued at fifty cents) plainly indicates that the late owner taught writing schools—those eighteenth-century private schools, or classes, intended to teach fine writing, a useful clerical hand, and frequently accounting, navigation, engineering, and other practical applications of mathematics not taught in most public schools of the day. Certainly if the "Art of Writing" that Morgan used was the popular book by John Jenkins, writing master, *The Art of Writing Reduced to a Plain and Easy System on a Plan Entirely New* (Book 1 issued in 1791 by Thomas and Andrews in Boston), the little thirty-two-page book with its three "copper plates" was eminently practical.[2] Jenkins reduced the motions made in writing the alphabet to a few strokes and hammered at practicing those strokes until it became easy to reproduce them in any needed combination as one formed the various letters. One of his suggestions might have been of particular value in Randolph, Vermont, in the 1790s:

For the help of such youth as are accustomed to labour, and thereby have their fingers stiffened and rendered insensible of the weight of the pen, I have practiced the following method. A round piece of lead, an inch and a half in length, with one end sharpened, may be pushed up the barrel of the quill into the pith; this weight will at once be perceivable by the learner, and enable him more readily to acquire the command of the pen.[3]

Like singing schools, the writing schools were often conducted by masters who offered brief courses in the late afternoon or evening hours two or three times a week, first in one town and then in another close to the master's place of residence, or farther afield if he were a true itinerant master.[4] Morgan's smooth, clerkly signature as town clerk of Randolph during the early 1790s attests to his training as a writing master. Apparently he had good use for the "one lead inkstand" (value twelve cents) that was in his inventory.

The rest of the textbooks cover the entire curriculum usually followed by older students in the common schools of the late eighteenth century. These older students, needed in the spring and summer months for work on the family farm, generally attended the "winter schools" that were conducted by men teachers for two or three months during the season when no work could be done on the land. Presumably Morgan's teaching of common schools would have been done during such winter seasons.

Valued at the highest price (eighty-three cents) among his textbooks was "Salmons Geography," which is the one British book, apparently never reprinted in America, included in Morgan's library. From 1749, when Thomas Salmon, a copious writer on history and geography, brought out *A New Geographical and Historical Grammar . . . with A Set of 22 Maps* (London), edition followed edition of this popular work until in 1785 the thirteenth was issued under the title, *Salmon's Geographical and Astronomical Grammar, including the Ancient and Present State of the World*, thirteenth edition, with corrections and additions. By this time Jedediah Morse, known as "the father of American Geography" as well as of Samuel F. B. Morse, had published his *Geography Made Easy* (1784). Whereas the Salmon text ran to 605 pages in its tenth edition (1766), the Morse book contented itself with 214 pages, and had only two plates (a map of the United States and a map of the world). The style of the Morse book is direct, clear, and should have been easily comprehended by the "young gentlemen and ladies throughout the United States" to whom Morse dedicated the book. Salmon's dedication was to "His Majesty King George the Third, And to the British Princes and Princesses, His Royal Brothers and Sisters." Presumably this dedication did not discourage a schoolmaster in budding America who found the ample proportions, clear type, and beautifully engraved maps of the English book attractive. Also in this book he could find a paragraph devoted even to "Danish America" (the islands of St. Thomas and St. Croix in "the Caribbees").[5]

"Perry's Dictionary" is *The Royal Standard English Dictionary* by William Perry of Kelso, Scotland, the first American edition of which was printed by Isaiah Thomas in Worcester, Massachusetts, in 1788. Its 596 pages, revised from the fourth British edition, include a dedication to the American Academy of Arts and Sciences in which Isaiah Thomas declares that the book is "intended to fix a standard" of pronunciation conformable to "present practice of polite speakers in Great Britain and the United States." The British editions had stressed pronunciation "approved in London." The book includes a grammar and a list of scriptural and geographical names with their pronunciations. On the Vermont frontier Justin Morgan carried in the presumably capacious pocket of his tail-coat the newest thing in dictionaries—a bulky guide intended to help axe- and hoe-wielding youth to learn the best that was pronounced in the world. All this wealth was assessed for probate purposes at sixty-seven cents.

"Scotts Lessons" is *Scott's Lessons in Elocution,* by William Scott, teacher, Edinburgh, first American edition published by W. Young in Philadelphia in 1786, 396 pages. The full title reads *Lessons in Elocution, or, A Selection of Pieces in Prose and Verse for the Improvement of Youth in Reading and Speaking, as well as for the Perusal of Persons of Taste, with an Appendix Containing Examples of the Principal Figures of Speech and Emotions of the Mind,* by William Scott, teacher of English reading, first American from fourth British edition, "greatly altered and improved." Locked within this treasure house were such items as "Dodsley's Fables"; selections from Sallust, the *Spectator* and the *Tatler;* bits of Chesterfield, Gibbon, and Sterne; poems by Pope and Gray, Milton and Dryden; parts of such plays as Shakespeare's *Julius Caesar, Henry the Eighth,* and the *First* and *Second Parts of King Henry the Fourth*—these alongside such "modern" favorites as John Home's romantic tragedy *Douglas.* If Vermont youths of 1790, aged presumably under twelve, could properly "read and speak" all that Scott presented to them, a teacher of their descendants in the 1970s may perhaps be permitted to observe that they could more than hold their own in a contest with the said descendants.

"Golden Treasury Book" is *Golden Treasury* by Karl Heinrich von Bogatzky (1690-1754), "abridged . . . for the use of the children of God, whose treasure is in Heaven, consisting of select texts from the Bible, with practical observations in prose and verse, for every day of the year, with some alterations and improvements by various hands, together with a few Forms of Prayer," the whole printed by Henry Willis in Philadelphia in 1793. Once again, as with his dictionary and his book on literature and elocution, Morgan was staying abreast of the latest publications for the edification of youth. On January first youth was to be uplifted by the thought:

> And now, my soul, another year
> Of thy short life is past;
> I cannot long continue here,
> And this may be my last.

And so the year ground drearily on, the eyes of young and old presumably fixed upon eternity for at least ten minutes every day before one ran outside to laugh and shout, drink rum at a barn-raising or cider at an apple-paring.

"Dilworths Arithmetick" concentrated on the here, not the hereafter. Its proper title was *The Schoolmasters Assistant, being a Compendium of Arithmetic, both practical and theoretical,* which had reached its twenty-second edition by the time that Hugh Gaine published it in New York in 1784. Opposite the title page is an engraving of Thomas Dilworth, looking alert enough to turn out even more of the school-books on many subjects that poured from his pen during a good part of the eighteenth century. Dilworth dedicated his book to "the Reverend and worthy schoolmasters of Great Britain and Ireland," and not until 1799, after Morgan's death, did an American edition of the book come out that dealt in dollars and cents and in problems familiar to young citizens of the young United States. Morgan's students had not only to deal in pounds, shillings, and pence (which were of course still used in figuring debts in the United States up to 1800, and even a little later), but also to learn that England occasionally used such coins as moidores, guineas, and crowns. Furthermore, they might learn, if they wished, that England formerly dealt in jacobuses, caroluses, angels, and the like. What did the small boy or girl in Randolph make of "a London woolen-draper buys sixteen yards of drugget at 7/0 per yard?" If he were lucky, he made of it £ 5/12/0. But what did he do when he arrived at page seventy and found, "Being obliged by Bond bearing date August 19, 1776, to pay next *Midsummer* (which is Leap Year) 326 £, what must I pay down, if they allow Discount after the rate of 8 per cent?"

Surely one in a thousand must have guessed the answer: 305 £, 16 s., 6 d. 1/4. How many forgot the farthing?

"2nd Part Grammatical Institute" is, as any schoolboy would have known in 1790, Noah Webster's *A Grammatical Institute*, the first edition of which was published by Thomas and Andrews in Boston in 1790.[9] *Part Second* contained "a plain and comprehensive grammar," whereas *Part One* was the *American Spelling Book*, and *Part Three* an American selection of lessons in reading and speaking. In his brilliant introduction to *Part Second* the great maker of the American dictionary declares, "It is the business of grammar to inform the student, not how a language might have been originally constructed, but how it is constructed. . . . The Latin division of tenses, which is commonly followed, appears to me very arbitrary in our language, and rather calculated to mislead the learner, than to give him clear ideas of our verbs. . . . Grammar is the art of communicating thoughts by words with propriety and dispatch." And so Justin Morgan, riding on the coattails of another singing master,[7] brought to his students the very latest and best thought of his era on how language is constructed and how it can be mastered by the person who would use his native tongue effectively.

The alert reader and arithmetician will have noticed that not all of Morgan's fifteen books have been described when one has accounted for the tools of his teaching trades. There were, of course, the inevitable Bible and testament (worth twenty-five cents, coin of the realm, in 1798). But there were also "Lyric Poems," "Popes Essay on Man," and "Traders Companion." The *Trader's Companion*, listed at ten cents, was presumably Morgan's tool when he traded horses, or sold wheat or other produce, or dealt in liquor, or hired a team to make deliveries of farm produce here and there. One assumes that it delved into such mysteries as "How many board feet are in a log of twelve-inch diameter that is ten feet long?" At least all nineteenth-century books of this stamp explored such mysteries. There were scores of tables down which an inquiring forefinger could drift to find the proper total, rate, percentage, etc. And if one got fleeced after consulting this book, it was his own fault for getting a forefinger on the wrong column.

Now "Lyric Poems" and "Pope's Essay on Man" are different matters from the schoolbooks and the ready-reckoner. Throughout the eighteenth century, Alexander Pope's poem, "An Essay on Man," was a prime favorite with American readers.[8] Morgan's special use of a few lines from Pope will be discussed later. "Lyric Poems" is Isaac Watts's *Horae Lyricae,* or *Lyric Poems,* a work first published in England in 1706 and reproduced many times in the Colonies and States before Morgan came to Vermont in 1788. It is this work that was at least the partial inspiration of Morgan's "Judgment Anthem" that was, as has been said, perhaps the most popular of all anthems in the churches of New England during the 1790s.

There are two books left on the list. One is "Second vol. Lathrops Sermons," which translates as *Sermons on Various Subjects* by the Reverend Joseph Lathrop, D.D., pastor of the First Church of West Springfield, Massachusetts, two volumes, published by Isaiah Thomas in Worcester, Massachusetts, in 1796. Thus two years or less before his death, Justin Morgan, truly a man of "slender means," either bought or had given to him the latest publication by his old pastor, the man who in 1756, when Morgan was nine years old, accepted a call to the West Springfield parish and thereafter set the intellectual tone in the town where Morgan grew up, received his education, married, and spent most of his life. By the 1790s Lathrop, who was to live to the age of eighty-nine (dying on the last day of 1820 after having completed the sixty-second year of his ministry in 1818), was one of the best known clergymen in New England. A middle-of-the-road man, he wrote voluminously, as he preached voluminously, in an attempt to bridge the gap between old-line Calvinists and various splinter groups that leaned toward the new emotionalism that led to frequent revivals, or toward belief in Universal Salvation, or even toward opposition to infant baptism—although on this last point he had much to say in its support. In the Woodstock (Vermont) Historical Society's Collections there is a manuscript letter of 21 April 1807 from Lucy Gay Swan of Woodstock to her brother, William Gay of Suffield, Connecticut, in which Lucy writes that "our candidate [for the ministry in Woodstock] Mr. Porter leaves us next week." She adds that the only way to get agreement on a "settled minister" will be to find a man "of tallent of great warmth and zeal in religion—a Calvinist but not over distinguishing in doctrinal points, one who mixes up matters just as Doctor Lathrop does (to use Mr. Porters phrase) . . . ."[9]

Earnest young people usually find middle-of-the-road men hard to bear. In West Springfield, however, where Lathrop himself declared that he "avoided unprofitable controversy" and was careful "not to awaken disputes, which were quietly asleep, not to waste my own and my hearers' time by reproving imaginary faults,"[10] children preened themselves when the great Doctor, on his walks, singled them out for a personal greeting.[12] It seems probable that Justin Morgan, who gives every evidence of having been a middle-of-the-road man himself on controversial matters, was proud to announce to the church in Randolph that he and his wife had been of Parson Lathrop's flock in West Springfield.[12] In any event, when Morgan died he owned Lathrop's latest book.

The fifteenth and last book on the inventory bears so general a title, "Miscellaneous Pieces," that one's first impulse is to assume that it will defy identification, especially when it develops that Evans's bibliography of books printed in America before 1800 does not list it.[13] Evans does, however, list *A Miscellaneous Collection of Original Pieces: Political, Moral, and Entertaining,* printed by John Russell at Springfield, Massachusetts, in 1786. The flyleaf that precedes the title page carries the words, "Miscellaneous Papers"; and

when it is learned that the work, although published anony-
mously, was written by the Reverend Joseph Lathrop, little
doubt can remain that this is the volume that Morgan owned.
The industrious Mr. Lathrop, of whom it was said that
"Parson Lathrop has preached on everything under the sun
except a Conn. river fog,"[14] includes essays on industry,
frugality, and similar virtues; on profanity and similar vices;
on government and similar vexed and important problems.
His poetry includes odes to the New Year and to the various
seasons. His "Imitation of the XXIII Psalm" begins:

> God is my Shepherd, by whose care
> I'm safely kept, when danger's near;
> He, with unweary'd goodness, grants,
> Constant supplies to all my wants.

The first item in this book prepared by a quite orthodox
clergyman seems to take into consideration post-Revolutionary skepticism in matters religious and refutes such skepticism with arguments that Deists as well as the orthodox could
have approved. The poem, entitled "The Existence of a
Deity," begins:

> When I lift up my wond'ring eyes,
> And view the grand and spacious skies,
> 'There is a GOD!' my thoughts exclaim,
> Who built this vast, stupendous frame.[15]

Truly a middle-of-the-road man was the industrious, generous, popular Parson Lathrop.

If the books that Morgan owned when he died tell much
about his life, perhaps more mundane items listed in that
inventory of his estate will also be revealing. True, Morgan
owned only one straitbodied coat and one old "do." (ditto)—
but he did possess velvet breeches, a stock buckle and a pair of
knee buckles, two boot buckles and one broach, one pair of
silver sleeve buttons and one pair of brass shoebuckles. He no

longer possessed a horse, but he did have a saddle and bridle, saddle bags and a horse whip, a pair of spurs and a horse brush and meal bag. Whatever he rode out on during those last two or three years, he apparently saw to it that the buckle on his stock was properly arranged, the broach in place, and his velvet breeches tucked properly into the one pair of boots that remained to him. Then of course there was the one-third of Pew No. 38 on the lower floor of the Randolph Meeting House that was still in his possession, and that was appraised at twenty-five dollars. There were also one hundred acres of land in Moretown, near Randolph, valued at fifty dollars—but of this land, more later. There was also a half-ounce of opium—and of this, too, more later.

Notes

1. Orange County, Vermont, *Probate Records*, Randolph District, 1: 1792-1802, 93ff. A microfilm of these records, the originals of which are in the Orange County Courthouse in Chelsea, Vermont, is in the Vermont Public Records Office in Montpelier.

2. The book may, however, have been the older, still popular English book, *Art of Writing*, by Ambrose Serle (London, 1776). It also boasted copperplate engravings.

3. John Jenkins, *The Art of Writing Reduced to a Plain and Easy System . . .* (Boston, Thomas & Andrews: 1791) Bk. 1, p. 32.

4. For a full discussion of the writing schools and of the important part they played in teaching such useful subjects as accounting and navigation when the public schools offered no instruction in these disciplines, see Ray Nash's *American Writing Masters and Copybooks* (Boston: Colonial Society of Massachusetts, 1959) and Robert Francis Seybolt's *The Private Schools of Colonial Boston* (Cambridge, Mass.: Harvard University Press, 1935).

5. One of the fascinations of this book is a note on the final page: "Directions to the Binder for placing the Maps. I. The World, Page 14. . . . N.B. The Binder is desired to beat the Book before he places the Maps." Each of these maps folds out to double or triple the width of the book. In the copy that I examined in the University of Vermont's Bailey Library, either the original binder or perhaps a later repairer of the book got the world map in upside down.

6. It is interesting to notice that Webster is the first American writer of books for standard common school subjects to find his way into Morgan's library. Presumably men like Morgan, themselves trained on English books before the works of such writers as Morse, Webster, and Emma Willard were published, would have relied heavily, when they came to teach, on the books with which they were familiar. As Constance Rourke has pointed out in *American Humor*, her classic study of the development of the American character and of American literature, a political

A Library Speaks 63

revolution does not make one instantly feel like a new kind of person. (Cf. above, p. 37, note 19.) Culturally, citizens of the United States remained colonial Englishmen for some time after the Revolution; and, as Rourke suggests in the concluding paragraph of her book, it required a generation or more before people were sufficiently at home with human beings of the American breed to write novels that took as their starting point the American experience. The fact that Morgan adopted Webster, alone among the new American textbooks, speaks for the impact that Webster's writings were having upon teachers, students, and the public at large.

7. Noah Webster's achievements as a lexicographer and author have so overshadowed his achievements as a musician that few people know that in his early years Webster was, at least briefly, a singing master. Even *Webster's Biographical Dictionary*, first edition, p. 1553, issued by the company (G. & C. Merriam Co.) that in 1843 bought the rights to Noah Webster's *American Dictionary of the English Language*, is so busy listing Webster's achievements as a soldier, teacher of language, lawyer, journalist, author of the famed spelling book and dictionary, champion of the Federalist political cause, president of Amherst Academy and a founder of Amherst College, that it finds no space for the singing school that Webster conducted in Baltimore, Md., in 1785. Yet Webster's diary for that year, much of which is reproduced in Emily Ellsworth Fowler Ford's *Notes on the Life of Noah Webster*, 2 vol. (New York: Privately printed, 1912), is full of comments on singing in Baltimore, Charleston, and elsewhere, and on his own teaching of singing.

On 29 May 1785 Webster, in Baltimore, attended "Mr. West's church" and found "horrible singing." In Charleston by 26 June, he found that he did not like "the modern taste in singing" at St. Michael's Church and went in the afternoon to another church to "hear a little New England singing." Three days later he heard "Mr. Rodger's" school and was much pleased "at seeing the New England method adopted here." His own school was opened 25 July in Baltimore, at "Dr. Allison's" church, and by 4 September he was able to "astonish all Baltimore with ten scholars." His school immediately had "great additions," but by 4 October he recorded "a miff between Mr. Hall—a singer and myself—People in Baltimore have not been accustomed to my rigid discipline." (A wise and apparently long-suffering clergyman has described the choir as "the war department of the church.")

Webster, eleven years Morgan's junior, was thirty-two when he conducted his singing school in Baltimore. His interests so broadened and developed in the many years that lay between 1785 and 1843, the year of his death, that Webster apparently left the teaching of music to others as he wrestled with the great problems of language and politics. For a discussion of Webster's friendship and business relations with the renowned Connecticut singing master, Andrew Law, during the 1780s, see Richard A. Crawford's *Andrew Law, American Psalmodist*, Pi Kappa Lambda Studies in American Music (Evanston, Ill.: Northwestern University Press, 1968), pp. 48-51.

8. See Agnes Marie Sibley, *Alexander Pope's Prestige in America, 1736-1846* (New York: King's Crown Press, 1949).

9. Woodstock (Vermont) Historical Society manuscript collection, letter quoted by permission of the Society.

10. Joseph Lathrop, "Memoir," in *Sermons by the Late Rev. Joseph Lathrop, D.D., Pastor of the First Church of West Springfield*, n.s. (Springfield, Mass.: A. C. Tannatt, 1821), p. xix.

11. Comment by Deacon Thomas Taylor of Pittsfield, in *Account of the Centennial Celebration of the Town of West Springfield, Mass.*, comp. J. N. Bagg (West Springfield, Mass.: Published by the town, 1874), p. 32. Deacon Taylor remarked,

"Dr. Lathrop was very venerable in appearance, and the children were wont to form in lines on either side of the road as he passed, to do him reverence. With his hat turned up on three sides, he would bow in recognition, and after he had passed, those were the happiest who could say 'he bowed to me.'"

12. First Congregational Church in Randolph, Vt., Records, book 2, MS in Randolph Historical Society library. The 1794 entries of members list Justin and Martha Morgan as having transferred from West Springfield in 1789.

13. Charles Evans, *American Bibliography, 1639-1829*, 14 vols. (Chicago: Privately printed, 1903-55).

14. First Congregational Church of West Springfield, *History of the First Parish and the First Congregational Church of West Springfield, Mass.* (West Springfield, Mass.: Printed for the church, n.d.), p. 12.

15. The nature of Parson Lathrop's sturdy faith is nowhere more clearly indicated than in an anecdote that he relates in his "Memoir," p. xviii: As a young man just beginning his ministry he was returning from a pastoral visit late one night when his horse stumbled and threw him. Lathrop's left foot caught in the stirrup, and the frightened horse began to run, dragging his master after him. "My situation forbade the hope of human aid," Lathrop writes. "I committed myself to Providence." The horse made several turns, almost trampling Lathrop and dragging him over the "rough and frozen ground." Finally Lathrop's foot became disengaged, and he arose to consider the cause of his preservation. He writes, "I had, on the preceding day, exchanged my shoes, and put on a pair in a state of decay, which I had not worn for a length of time. . . . The horse, in plunging, pressed my foot so far forward, that the stirrup came over my shoe-buckle, and there hung. The leather being old and tender, gave way, and the strap which held the buckle was torn off. . . . Had the leather been firm, my foot probably would not have been released." Providence, in the shape of his decayed shoe, had saved Parson Lathrop for sixty-two years of labor in the Lord's vineyard: "A life preserved by God's interposing providence, ought to be devoted to the kind preserver," concludes the parson.

____ 3 ____

The Stage Is Set

IT is time to turn from the end of Morgan's life to the beginning. Like all stories worth telling, the story of Morgan's life begins before the beginning. It may have begun in the thirteenth century, when Thomas of Celano wrote the great hymn, *Dies Irae* ("Day of Wrath" or "Day of Judgment"), which inspired literally hundreds of later hymns on this subject so fascinating to orthodox Christians. It may have begun in Wales, from which Justin's ancestors are said to have come—and from which, if that should be the case, one would be inclined to trace the aptitude for music that many Morgans, including Justin, displayed.[1] It certainly began when Miles Morgan, yeoman, set foot in the town of Springfield in that part of Massachusetts that lies along New England's great western waterway, the Connecticut River. To that river, which stretches from the Canadian border 360 miles southward to Long Island Sound, providing a border between present-day Vermont and New Hampshire and a fine opportunity for traveling, establishing farms, and providing power for many miles—to that river had been attracted William Pynchon, Esq., of Springfield, Essex County, England, and seven associates, who in 1636 received a grant from the General Court of the Massachusetts Bay Colony to establish a plantation at "Agawam," or Springfield as it was re-christened in 1640. Only Windsor and

Hartford, in Connecticut, had been established before Springfield in the fertile Connecticut valley. The original Springfield was an area almost twenty-five miles square, embracing what are now a dozen towns (Northampton and Holyoke, for example) lying along the Connecticut River.[2] The statue erected to Miles Morgan on "Court Square" in Springfield speaks of him as an early settler of Springfield;[3] it appears that he probably came to the area about 1643, only some seven years after the Pynchon band arrived.[4] In any event, from the time of his arrival until his death in 1699 at the age of eighty-four, Morgan was one of the sturdy supports of that outpost of the Massachusetts Bay Colony—an outpost especially endangered during the Indian wars of the 1670s.

According to family tradition, Miles Morgan sailed from Bristol, England, with two older brothers, arriving in Boston in 1636. John Morgan went to Virginia, James to Connecticut, Miles to western Massachusetts. Miles married Prudence Gilbert, said to have come over from England on the same ship that carried Miles, and they proceeded to have eight children before Prudence died in 1660. Miles thereafter, in 1669, married Elizabeth Bliss, and by her had one son, Nathaniel, born in 1671 (twenty-six years younger than his oldest half-sister). It is from Nathaniel that Justin Morgan descends, as the son of Nathaniel's son Isaac.

What is important in the story of Justin Morgan is that Miles and his descendants were substantial yeoman farmers who played a large part in cultivating the farmlands of the Connecticut Valley, in protecting the towns, and in developing the culture that brought churches, schools, libraries, and other civilized and civilizing forces to western Massachusetts even in the days when it was still "frontier." Miles himself never held high political offices (he made his mark when called upon to sign documents).[5] As early as 1645 Miles Morgan and George Colton were appointed by the town "to doe theyre best to get a smith for ye towne."[6] If William Pynchon's son Major John Pynchon, the Holyokes, and the

Chapins held such offices as those of judge or representative to the General Court, still, "whenever a strong arm or a steady nerve was wanted," as Henry Morris notes in his account of Miles Morgan's life,[7] Morgan "was on hand. If Major Pynchon desired a load of beaver or moose skins, or of corn carried to Hartford for shipment to Boston, or a cargo of merchandise for his store brought up to his warehouse at the Point, or to his store at Springfield, . . . Miles Morgan was one who was ready to brave the dangers of the Enfield Falls and make the voyage, or if more convenient, to cart the loading with a team on land." In Major Pynchon's account books are such items as: 1652—"To credit of Miles Morgan, Reced by carriage corne down ye falls . . . 11/1/8." The item of 24 February 1656—"by killing 4 cattle 0/9/6"—indicates that among Miles's various activities there was some participation in the livestock business that throughout the colonial period figured prominently in the economic life of western Massachusetts. The mark for Miles Morgan's cattle was "two slits in ye neere eare straite downe, one of ym on one side of ye tip of ye eare, & ye other slit on ye other side of ye tip of ye Same eare."[8]

In that important matter, the "seating" of the meeting house, Miles Morgan in 1659—and again in 1662—was placed in the third seat of the ten principal seats on the main floor; and that he was a man not only of importance but of decision is indicated by the Selectmen's ruling of 1669 that "Miles Morgan and Jonath Burt are ordered to sit up in ye Gallery to give a check to disorders in youth & young men in tyme of Gods worship."[9]

When the train-band was organized and men were obliged to train eight days a year or be fined five shillings for any absence, there was Sergeant Miles Morgan to back up Captain John Pynchon and Lieutenant Elizur Holyoke. The year 1675 saw the eruption of that worst of New England's Indian Wars, King Philip's War, in which the son of Massasoit, who like his father had long kept the peace with Englishmen, took

up arms when it seemed to him and his fellow Wampanoags
that all their hunting grounds were being swallowed up by
English farms. During the savage warfare Springfield was
attacked in October, while forty-five of its garrison soldiers
were away on duty in Hadley. The Indians burned about
thirty-two houses, leaving only fifteen standing in Springfield. Presumably Miles Morgan's house was among those
burned. Family tradition has it that people sheltered in
Morgan's house, but Henry Morris believes it more likely that
Morgan saw service in defending one of the two fortified
houses in the south of town, that of Major Pynchon, a brick
house known as the "old fort." Morgan's son-in-law Edmund Pringridays was one of three men killed in the attack,
and Morgan's own son Pelatiah was killed the following
spring during an Indian raid on the west side of the river.
Shortly thereafter the Indian forces were scattered, King
Philip was killed, and the ability of Indians to make
organized war against the well-established towns of southern
New England was at an end.

People rebuilt their houses. There was much to be done in
the houses, on the land, in the towns, throughout the colony.
Miles Morgan had lived nearly forty years in Springfield.
Already his grandsons, together with other young men of the
second generation of English colonials to be born on American soil, were establishing their own farms, taking their
places as constables and tything-men and even as selectmen
in the towns. For this third generation of New Englanders the
feats of the immigrants of 1620 and 1630 may have seemed as
distant as do the feats of the soldiers at Chateau-Thierry to
American college students of the 1970s. Still, Miles's grandsons knew that great things had been done in the New
England as well as in the Old, since the troubled times of
Charles the First and the coming so long ago of Englishmen
to Plymouth and to Salem, to Charlestown and to Boston, to
Mystic and Watertown, Roxbury and Dorchester.[10]

Miles himself might best have remembered the time in 1664

when, with a king safely back on the throne of England, the king's commissioners had seen to it that all men "of competent estates" (not simply church members) could be counted as freemen and therefore could vote for representatives to the General Court. Perhaps he also remembered the time in 1686 when clergymen were first allowed to perform marriage ceremonies in a Puritan society that had insisted that there could be only two sacraments, baptism and the Lord's Supper.[11] Whatever he remembered best, and whatever his sons and grandsons had heard or read about, one could not afford to rest on past accomplishments.

In the Colony great changes were imminent. Agents of the Crown were reporting that Massachusetts was putting English citizens (Quakers) to death for their religious views and that freemen of the Colony were refusing to take the oath of allegiance to the new king. Massachusetts was buying out the heirs of Sir Ferdinando Gorges and thus in 1677 was placing Maine under her jurisdiction. Also, a royal commission was separating New Hampshire from Massachusetts. Finally in 1684 the blow—occasioned by Puritan opposition to Charles II and his Catholic brother James—fell: England's Court by Chancery annulled the Bay Colony's cherished charter. By 1686 Sir Edmund Andros arrived to become royal governor of nearly all of New England. His most unpopular decree with men like Miles Morgan was probably his demand that land titles be reexamined and that those who wished to retain their lands pay a quitrent.[12]

Long before the arrival of Andros, Miles Morgan had become a substantial landowner. As Springfield had grown and as families had begun to move out across the broad Connecticut River, Miles Morgan had taken up land on the west side, even while retaining his holdings in the old town. As early as 1669 he had conveyed to his daughter Mary and her husband Edmund Pringridays six acres on the west side of the "Great River." Grants to other children followed: in 1696 Miles gave to his youngest son, Nathaniel, two pieces of land, one in "Chicopee field" and the other at Agawam, both on the west side of the river, with the understanding that Nathaniel would pay to his father six pounds a year during Miles's life.

Quitrent indeed! Miles and his sons must have breathed a sigh of relief when Andros was sent packing, Protestant William and Mary were safely on the throne of England, and one could continue to buy land and put more and more acres under cultivation as numerous children were born to numerous children. By 1696, when the West Parish of Springfield was established (a parish that could not manage to get itself incorporated as the separate town of West Springfield until 1774), Nathaniel and various of his brothers were principal citizens of the parish. Their father Miles died in 1699, bowing out with the century, and leaving the next century to the care of his sons. Nathaniel, born in 1671, had married Hannah Bird in 1691; by 1707 he was listed as one of the inhabitants of the West Parish to whom land was to be allotted as the new settlement began to apportion home lots, meadow, and wood lots. The town made it perfectly clear, by a vote of the seventh of April of that year, that every male in his twenty-first year should be accounted an "inhabitant" of the town and therefore have a right to own land—without regard to church membership and other considerations that had plagued some earlier settlements in the Massachusetts Bay Colony.[13]

A year later, in 1708, Nathaniel's son Isaac was born. Shortly thereafter, in 1711, and not far from the Morgan house, a girl, Thankfull, was born to a neighbor, Ebenezer Day, and his wife, Mary (Hitchcock) Day. Ebenezer and Mary already had a son, Luke, born 1706, who would later figure in the Morgan story, just as Thankfull was to do.

Events moved forward both inside and outside the Morgan household. There was, of course, Queen Anne's War following on the heels of King William's War, and all that business of Indian raids on towns in Maine, and New Englanders serving in the forces that captured Port Royal, Acadia (Nova

Scotia), in 1704. With the exception of the destruction of Deerfield in 1704, however, that war was remote from western Massachusetts. Perhaps even the fact that in 1713 France ceded to Great Britain Newfoundland, Acadia, and Hudson Bay was of far greater interest to fisherfolk in the coastal towns than it was to farmers in the west—although doubtless Major Pynchon, who dealt heavily in furs, would have been alert to Hudson Bay developments.

Far closer to home than the fighting in Acadia was the arrival in the West Parish in 1720 of Samuel Hopkins as second pastor of the parish. When the church had been formally organized in 1698, it had called twenty-year-old John Woodbridge of Connecticut to be the town's first settled minister. The following year John had married Jemima Eliot, granddaughter of the "Indian apostle," John Eliot, and the pair had produced a thriving family before John died in 1717, at the age of forty. The young minister had apparently served his people well and faithfully.[14] The town was equally fortunate in its second choice. Reverend Samuel Hopkins served as pastor of the "West Parish" thirty-five years, and when he died in 1755 his people carved on his tombstone, ". . . Rev'd Mr. Samuel Hopkins, in whom, Sound Judgment, Solid Learning, Candour, Piety, Sincerity, Constancy and universal Benevolence combined. . . ." Eleven years later, in 1766, Samuel Hopkins's "relict," Esther, was buried under a stone that reads, ". . . a superior understanding, uncommon Improvements in Knowledge, exemplary Piety and exalted Virtue combined to form a distinguished female character."[15] It may be that Esther Hopkins's unusual powers were partly a matter of inheritance. She was a sister of the famed Jonathan Edwards who for so long dominated religious and intellectual life in Northampton, just north of Springfield.

Thirteen years passed after Parson Hopkins was installed in office before, in 1733, he performed the ceremony that united Isaac Morgan and Thankfull Day in marriage. The

next year, 1734, the parish purchased a church bell—to re-
place the drum with which John Ely had for many years
summoned the people to worship. The meeting house, which
had been occupied in 1702, was forty-two feet square by
ninety-two feet high—"well calculated to cause a shudder in
all lovers of elegant, architectural proportions," according to
the Reverend Thomas E. Vermilye.[16]

By 1737 the parish was forty-one years old, the meeting
house was thirty-five, and Isaac Morgan was twenty-nine. In
March of that year Isaac received from his father Nathaniel,
"in consideration of the natural love good will and affection I
have and do bear towards my loving son Isaac . . ." one parcel
of land "being my home lot in Chickopee containing three
acres" and a lot on the hill of ten acres, plus three acres in
Chickopee Field and three acres more in the said field. . . ."
All this done in the tenth year of the Reign of George the
Second, King of Great Britain.[17]

Isaac proceeded, in May of 1737, to buy from Nathan Sikes,
trader, an additional twenty acres.[18]

New troubles arose to worry land owners. Money was
scarce and the Province seemed to need a good part of what
little there was. Under such conditions it is not surprising to
find hard-working men in financial straits. David and Benjamin Morgan of Springfield, husbandmen, were forced to
mortgage two pieces of land to raise thirty pounds "in good
and lawful bills of credit" when, in 1717, the General Court
passed a law "for the making and emitting the sum of one
hundred thousand pounds in bills of credit on this province."
It is pleasant to discover that the two Morgans paid off their
mortgage in 1727.[19] In 1741 the General Court, taking under
advisement the unfortunate inflation that was plaguing the
New World, established "New Tenor" money, six shillings
ninepence of which suddenly equaled twenty-seven shillings
of "Old Tenor" money.

There was also, if not trouble, at least a stirring in the
church. An event that was to have a profound effect upon

Justin Morgan and his contemporaries must have seemed, at first, a matter of little importance. This was the move to improve singing in the churches, a reform which, as has been said, was begun by certain Massachusetts clergymen in the early years of the eighteenth century.[20] In January of 1721 Samuel Gerrish, Bookseller, advertised in the *Boston News-Letter* the publication of the first book on music issued in the Colonies.[21] Gerrish listed the book simply as "A Small Book containing 20 Psalm Tunes, with Directions how to Sing them, contrived in the most easy Method ever yet Invented, for the ease of Learners, whereby even Children, or People of the meanest Capacities, may come to Sing them by Rule ...."[22] Subsequent advertisements indicate that the book was written by the Reverend John Tufts, pastor of the second parish church in Newbury, Massachusetts. On the title page of the fifth edition of 1726, the first that has survived today, is the title, *An Introduction to The Singing of Psalm-Tunes, In a plain & easy Method.* Tufts's "plain and easy method" was simply to write the first letter of the syllable that was to be sung (*F* for *fa*, *S* for *sol*, and so on) upon the proper line of the staff, rather than to draw in the perhaps unfamiliar notes. That this aid to learning was needed by colonials now three or four generations away from the age of Morley and Dowland will not be doubted when one remembers that expert musicianship had been maintained and fostered in England largely by the great cathedral schools.[23] By 1700 or thereabouts country parsons in England were also calling for improvements in that part of the worship service devoted to music, and a new breed of worker—the itinerant singing master—was already appearing in England and would shortly appear in New England. As Irving Lowens has pointed out, Tufts's little book began that "remarkable new social institution, the New England singing-school, which was to control the destinies of native American music for well over a hundred years."[24] He adds that it was the singing-school, conducted by teacher-composers, that gave rise to the "tremendous upsurge of musical creativity" that Morgan and the other psalmodists manifested in the last quarter of the eighteenth century.

"Rule" is the word to concentrate upon in reading the title of Tufts's manual. No war ever fought, between the High Heels and the Low Heels of Swift's *Gulliver's Travels,* or the Long Curls and Cropped Heads of Oliver Cromwell's or Richard Nixon's times, was ever waged more acrimoniously than was the battle between those who would sing by Rule and those who would sing by Rote in eighteenth-century America.[25] As men and women had tired of singing the ever-diminishing number of familiar tunes that were repeated, Sabbath after Sabbath, to twenty or thirty stanzas of a metrical psalm (once the deacon had "lined out" each phrase), they had, as has been suggested, begun to create their own music by improvising variations and embellishments of the tune as they went along.[26] These embellishments, evidently sometimes wild and eerie, fell as anything but music upon the ears of the musically literate, such as the Reverend Mr. Tufts. He proposed that people learn once again to read music—and stick to what was written on the page. It is probable that this singing by Rule seemed to the improvisers an invasion of their sacred rights, possibly a shackling of their creativity, and certainly a wearisome nuisance.

The battle was promptly joined. In the letter that Cotton Mather wrote to Thomas Hollis in 1723, the renowned clergyman gave his view of the whole matter.[27] "A mighty Spirit," he declared, "came Lately upon abundance of our people, to Reform their singing which was degenerated in our Assemblies to an Irregularity, which made a Jar in the ears of the more curious and skilful singers. . . . Such Numbers of Good people (and Especially young people) became Regular Singers, that they could carry it in the Congregations." He then called attention to how some of the "rusticks . . . Elder and Angry people, bore zealous Testimonies against these wicked innovations, and this bringing in of Popery."[28] To sing by

Rule was next door to praying by Rule. Popery, without a doubt. Mather adds that the angry ones would "call the Singing of these Christians, a worshipping of the Devil." They would "run out of the Meeting-house at the Beginning of the Exercise. The Paroxysms have risen to that Heighth, as to necessitate the Convening of several Ecclesiastical Councils, for the Composing of the Differences and Animosities, arisen on this occasion."

Fifty, even seventy years later people were still at loggerheads. It has been pointed out that in 1786 the people of Tinmouth, Vermont, made psalm tunes a matter of legal action in the annual town meeting.[29] In Justin Morgan's neighbor town, Longmeadow, while it was still the third Parish of Springfield, the Reverend Stephen Williams wrote in his diary on the thirteenth of February in 1769, "This day I perceive some are uneasy upon the account of the new singing—what a strange thing—that some are displeased with that which is very pleasing to others—but why—do I say *tis stranger* had it not been so—"[30]

Not only the tunes sung, but also the manner of keeping on tune and in time was causing difficulties. Added to these troubles were the quarrels that sprang up when certain daring liberals urged the introduction of the metrical version of the psalms written by the learned Dr. Isaac Watts, the Independent English clergyman whose *The Psalms of David, Imitated in The Language of The New Testament, and Applied to The Christian State and Worship* had first been issued in England in 1719. Many a Puritan, nurtured on the *Bay Psalm Book*, which had of course been developed to provide as literal a translation of the psalms into metrical English as the ingenuity of Puritan divines could devise, found himself more than unhappy when he was confronted with a version of the 147th psalm that read not:

> Praise ye the Lord: for it is good to
> sing praises unto our God; . . .

The Lord doth build up Jerusalem:
he gathered together the outcasts of Israel . . .

but instead:

O Britain, praise thy mighty God,
And make his honours known abroad;
He did the ocean round thee flow;
Not bars of brass could guard thee so.[31]

What Watts was doing was breaking the hold of the metrical psalm upon the musical portion of the worship service, and making it possible for English Independents who came after him to write "hymns of human composure." It is not surprising that people with an ear for poetry could not resist versions of the psalms that began with lines like "Our God our help in ages past" and "Joy to the World." Not everyone, however, was convinced. As late as August of 1770 the Chocksett Church in Lancaster, Massachusetts, "met and voted that the use of the pitch pipe and taking the pitches, and keeping time by swinging the hand in public worship was not acceptable to them," and that "they were not willing to sing Dr. Watts' Hymns, together with the New England Version of the Psalms, part of the time." Eight months later, in March of 1771, the church remained adamant; they voted "that they were still of the same mind about the Pitch pipe and taking the pitches, and they were not willing the Chorister sh'd beat time according to discretion."[32]

No one who reads comments like those of the Chocksett fellowship in the records of church after church can doubt the importance of music to eighteenth-century congregations in New England.

Music was not the only aspect of church life that was undergoing profound changes shortly before Morgan's birth. There was the whole matter of the "Great Awakening." By 1730 New England was a long century away from the time when Puritans and Pilgrims had covenanted together and with God to form churches. If one believed that a church should be made up of those who covenant together, how were children to be brought into the church? Even the "gathered churches" of the early years had provided for the baptism of the children of church members; but suppose that such children, grown up, failed to have that miraculous experience known as conversion that was deemed essential to full church membership and therefore to participation in the sacrament of communion?[33] What, then, did one do with the children of these baptized non-members? What the churches did was to create the so-called Halfway Covenant (approved by a synod in 1662) by which such children could be baptized and enter into the same kind of half-membership that their parents enjoyed. This provision led to a gradual softening of the line between the "elect" and the rest of the population—a softening fostered by the secularism that was growing even in Massachusetts. The Reverend Solomon Stoddard, in Northampton, went so far as to admit to communion persons who had not experienced conversion, on the theory that the sacrament itself would hasten conversion. The philosophically inclined were beginning to discuss the new notion that the mind of man is a tablet to be written on by our sensations—a view about as far as one can get from the notion of an all-powerful, all-seeing, all-directing God.

There came the inevitable reaction. On the twenty-ninth of October in 1727 New England experienced what has been described as a great earthquake. At ten o'clock of a clear, moonlit night the shocks began, centering about Newbury, and throwing "cartloads of earth" out of the ground. But, say the old historians, "the most remarkable and important effect was the panic, which seized the public mind, and the general seriousness, which followed." We are told that "numbers were awakened, a reformation of morals was visible, family prayer was more generally attended, and great additions were made to many churches."[34] Just six years earlier there had been a particularly virulent outbreak of smallpox, especially

in and around Boston. In Boston alone almost 6,000 persons
had contracted the disease, and 844 had died of it.[35] More
lasting than the effect of either pestilence or earthquake was
that created by the appearance of a great religious thinker and
writer, Jonathan Edwards. The Reverend Mr. Edwards, aged
twenty-three, arrived in Northampton in 1726 to assist his
grandfather, the Reverend Mr. Stoddard, who was by that
time eighty-four years of age. For Mr. Stoddard's moderate
liberalism Edwards, who has been described as "soul-kin to
the great mystics,"[36] had little sympathy.[37] The earthquake
occurred at the right moment. Edwards could soon thereafter
rouse the most somnolent church-goer with

> What a mighty strength would it Require only to move one
> mountain how Great a strength then must that be that will
> shake the whole Globe to which the greatest Mountains are
> Less than molehills. . . . how will it amaze you if you are in
> a sinfull state when the whole Globe shall be as it were
> Rocked to pieces and you shall hear the foundations of the
> Earth Crack and shall see the mountains Overturned and
> the whole heaven at the same time filled with flashes of
> lightening and the air tortured with perpetual and Innu-
> merable Claps of Thunder far more Awfull than the most
> horrible that we hear in thunder storms, and all this at the
> visible Presence of the Almighty and an angry God.[38]

After the death of Stoddard in 1729, when Edwards became
Northampton's pastor, the great preacher concentrated his
powers on setting forth what has been called a "neo-
orthodoxy" with emotional overtones.[39] Central in his beliefs
was a sense of the sovereignty of an all-powerful God; and in
preaching of that sovereignty he dwelt upon "the sweetness
of communion with God," the necessity to recognize the
brevity of life and to prepare for the hereafter, "the sinfulness
of sin."[40]

In New England, Edwards's was the most powerful voice
calling for that first American series of revivals, beginning

about 1730 and lasting twenty years or more, to which the name "The Great Awakening" has been given. Although he avoided the excesses of the extreme revivalists and was primarily a parish pastor and a New Englander whose fine mind brought close reasoning to the service of his preaching, still his insistence upon the importance of what has been called "heart religion" moved his hearers as no appeal to reason alone could have done. Of Northampton in the early years of his preaching it has been said, "The town was reborn, the old church could not hold the people and grew to more than six hundred members."[41] He spoke out against what a biographer Ola Elizabeth Winslow has called "the Seven Deadlies in village dress"—irreverence in God's house, disregard of the Sabbath, neglect of family prayer, disobedience to parents, quarreling, greediness, sensuality, hatred of one's neighbor.[42] If in the end his congregation dismissed him largely because of his insistence that the Halfway Covenant was not good enough—that only those who had experienced genuine religious conversion should partake of Christian communion—still he had stirred up smoldering religious embers that were to blaze brightly when twenty-six-year-old George Whitefield, the Anglican who became "the first great footloose Protestant evangelist,"[43] reached American shores in 1739 and began to preach the "whosoever will, shall be saved" doctrine. This doctrine, with its emphasis upon individualism and the power of the individual to guide his own destiny, was, as Ola Elizabeth Winslow says, "a step toward 1776."[44]

It was into a world stirred by religious and attendant musical questions; free for the moment from warfare; busy with the growth of farms and towns, manufacture and commerce; vexed and challenged by political questions swirling particularly thickly around the question of royal governors and their prerogatives—It was into this world that Justin Morgan was born.

Notes

1. The range of Morgan's voice is unknown, but many a singing master of the eighteenth century seems to have had a tenor voice. Perhaps the fact that, in church music of the day, the melody was written for the tenor made good tenors natural leaders when psalms were sung, and thus encouraged some of them to become singing masters. Timothy Swan, a well-known singing master of the period, is described by his daughter, Emily C. Swan, as having had a fine bass voice. She adds, however, that he seldom sang because he could not reach the upper register (much used in the music of the day) to suit himself. This information is in a letter written by Emily C. Swan from Northfield, Mass., dated 12 August 1842, to the Reverend George Hood, author of *A History of Music in New England* (Boston: Wilkins, Carter & Co., 1846). The letter is in the George Hood scrapbook, Boston Public Library, and is cited by courtesy of the trustees of the Boston Public Library.

Justin's son, Justin Morgan, Jr., is said to have been "an excellent tenor singer" (note by Moses E. Cheney in Simeon Pease Cheney, *The American Singing Book* [Boston: White, Smith & Co., 1879], p. 171.) Should it be the case that Morgan himself was also a tenor, one would be inclined to suspect inheritance from some fine Welsh tenor of an earlier day.

2. See Esther M. Swift's *West Springfield, Massachusetts* (West Springfield, Mass.: West Springfield Heritage Association for the Town of West Springfield, 1969) for an account of the Springfield area's early history, and especially of that section which in 1774 became West Springfield.

3. The inscription reads, "Miles Morgan, an early settler of Springfield, died 1699 aged 84. Erected in 1882 by one of his descendants of the fifth generation."

4. Henry Morris, "Miles Morgan," *Papers and Proceedings of the Connecticut Valley Historical Society, 1876-1881* (1881): 250-262.

5. Hampshire County, Mass., Book AB for Recording Deeds, Hampshire County Courthouse, Northampton, Mass., p. 67 and passim.

6. Springfield, Mass., Town Records, 1: 45, as quoted in Frank Farnsworth Starr, *The Miles Morgan Family of Springfield, Mass.* (Hartford, Conn., 1904), p. 5.

7. Morris, "Miles Morgan, p. 256. The remainder of this account of Miles Morgan's life is drawn from the Morris essay and from Starr's *The Miles Morgan Family*.

8. Starr, *The Miles Morgan Family*, p. 10.

9. Ibid., pp. 12-13.

10. Samuel Eliot Morison's *The Intellectual Life of Colonial New England*, 2 ed. (1956; reprint ed., Ithaca, N.Y.: Cornell University Press, 1965) ably demonstrates that Charles Francis Adams's term for the seventeenth century in New England, "the glacial period," is misleading in the extreme. Morison declares that English Puritans "transmitted European civilization to the New World" (p. 272), and he shows how they developed that civilization even while they adapted it to new conditions that in the end were to produce a distinctively American culture. Morison points out that throughout the seventeenth century there was vigorous forward movement in education, printing, the founding of libraries, the cultivation of some forms of literature, and even the encouragement of scientific inquiry. All this activity went on not only in Massachusetts but also in the other settlements that for twenty years in mid-century were known as the "United Colonies of New England." Just as Massachusetts pushed forward in government to commonwealth status in 1652, and Connecticut to her faintly democratic "Fundamental Orders" of 1639; just as New Englanders evolved in the Cambridge Platform of 1648 a new form of church

organization that was adopted by English Independents as well as by Congregationalists of New England; just as the Colonies founded their great fishing and trading industries as well as their farms—so in the seventeenth century they fostered and made habitual the Puritan "habit of considering values other than material" (p. 274). By this means, says Morison, were New Englanders of the eighteenth century "as well prepared as any people in the world to be quickened by new ideas, and to play their part in the coming drama of the Rights of Man" (p. 274). If Morison underplays seventeenth-century New England's interest in music and in the visual arts, so do most other historians writing before the last score of years.

11. In the *Commonwealth History of Massachusetts,* ed. Albert Bushnell Hart (New York: States History Company, 1927-28), 1: 117, Governor Winthrop is quoted as declaring that "to make a law that marriages shall not be solemnized by ministers is repugnant to the laws of England; but to bring it to a custom for a magistrate to perform it is no law made repugnant. . . ." Thus within ten years of the beginning of the Massachusetts adventure it became the ironclad custom for marriages to be performed by civil magistrates. Not until a half century had passed did Puritan attitudes relax sufficiently to permit marriages once again to become ceremonies performed in churches, with clergymen as the presiding officials (*Commonwealth History of Massachusetts,* 1: 279). The law of 1686 that permitted clergymen to perform marriages was confirmed by the laws of the Province of Massachusetts in 1692.

12. Only the Glorious Revolution of 1689, bringing William and Mary to the throne in place of James II, gave New England the upper hand over Andros and returned to her some measure of self-government. Still, from 1691—when a royal charter formally incorporated Maine and Plymouth within Massachusetts—until the American Revolution, Massachusetts the province, rather than the colony, was under the rule of a governor appointed by the crown. She managed throughout her years as a province, however, to salvage many of her old rights and to operate largely by the laws drawn up under her ancient charter of 1629.

13. Lyman H. Bagg, "Early Settlers of West Springfield," *New England Historical and Genealogical Register* 29 (1875): 283-89.

14. That the Reverend John Woodbridge made an indelible impression upon his community is indicated by the fact that descendants of his parishioners in 1852, 134 years after Woodbridge's death, placed a monument in his honor in the oldest West Springfield cemetery, today called the Cold Spring (Union Street) Cemetery. The inscription reads, "The Righteous will be held in everlasting remembrance" (Swift, *West Springfield,* p. 83).

15. J. N. Bagg, comp. *Account of the Centennial Celebration of the Town of West Springfield, Mass.* (West Springfield, Mass.: Published by the Town, 1874.) p. 139.

16. "Historical Address" in J. N. Bagg, p. 33.

17. Hampshire County, Mass., Book L for Recording Land Deeds, p. 253.

18. Hampshire County, Mass., Book K for Recording Land Deeds, p. 547.

19. Hampshire County, Mass., Book C for Recording Land Deeds, p. 221.

20. See above, p. 30.

21. Irving Lowens in *Music and Musicians in Early America* (New York: W. W. Norton & Co., 1964), p. 41, points out that there is debate about when Tufts's *Introduction* was first issued, but that the first specific evidence of its existence is the advertisement of 1721. Lowens also calls attention to the fact that both the 1698 edition of the *Bay Psalm Book* and the 1713 Boston reprint of the Tate and Brady *New Version of the Psalms of David* included a small number of tunes (p. 39). The primary concern of both these books was, of course, the text of the psalms presented in metrical form, rather than the tunes.

22. Quoted by Lowens, *Music and Musicians in Early America*, p. 41.

23. See above, p. 30.

24. Lowens, *Music and Musicians in Early America*, p. 24.

25. See above, p. 30.

26. Gilbert Chase, *America's Music, from the Pilgrims to the Present* (New York: McGraw-Hill Book Company, 1955), p. 31.

27. See above, p. 31.

28. Cotton Mather, *The Diary of Cotton Mather* (New York: Frederick Ungar Publishing Co., [1957]), 2: 693, letter dated 5 November 1723.

29. See above, p. 16.

30. Diary, TS, p. 139, in the Richard Salter Storrs Library of Longmeadow, Mass., quoted by permission of the library and of the First Congregational Church of Longmeadow, owner of the original manuscript diary.

31. Psalm 147, quoted by Arthur Paul Davis, *Isaac Watts, His Life and Works* (New York: Dryden Press, 1943), p. 199.

32. Lancaster, Mass., *The Birth, Marriage, and Death Register, Church Records, and Epitaphs of Lancaster, Massachusetts*, ed. Henry S. Nourse (Lancaster, Mass.: Clinton, 1890), p. 377.

33. Gaius Glenn Atkins and Frederick L. Fagley, *History of American Congregationalism* (Boston and Chicago: Pilgrim Press, 1942), pp. 92 and 269.

34. Jedediah Morse and Elijah Parish, *A Compendious History of New-England*, 3d ed. (Charleston, Mass.: S. Etheridge, 1820), p. 269.

35. Ibid., p. 268.

36. Atkins and Fagley, *American Congregationalism*, p. 107.

37. When, some nine years after Edwards came to Northampton, the town of Springfield attempted to install the Reverend Robert Breck, aged twenty-two, as pastor of Springfield's First Parish, Jonathan Edwards was among those who opposed ordaining young Breck. Opposition apparently stemmed from a sermon that Breck had preached in New London in which he had gone so far as to venture the hope that "God, in his boundless benevolence, will find out a way whereby those heathen, who act up to the light they have, may be saved." The controversy is described by Mason A. Green, "The Breck Controversy in the First Parish in Springfield in 1735," *Papers and Proceedings of the Connecticut Valley Historical Society, 1876-1881* 1 (1881): 8.

38. An undated sermon quoted by Ola Elizabeth Winslow in *Jonathan Edwards, 1703-1758* (New York: Macmillan Co., 1940), p. 143. Winslow speculates that the sermon, in "early handwriting," may have been composed shortly after the earthquake.

39. Atkins and Fagley, *American Congregationalism*, p. 108.

40. Ibid. Also, in Winslow, *Jonathan Edwards*, p. 329. Winslow, remarking that Edwards's insistence upon the sovereignty of God is akin to modern hope for "a world order that can be trusted," declares that Edwards's beliefs were "the beliefs of the great religionists of all ages. He believed that man's life is of eternal consequence. He believed that the imperfect world we see cannot be all. He believed that reality is of the spirit. He believed that there is a pathway to present peace in spite of the frustrations of life, and that man can find it, but not of himself" (p. 329).

41. Ibid., p. 109.

42. Winslow, *Jonathan Edwards*, p. 162.

43. Atkins and Fagley, *American Congregationalism*, p. 109.

44. Winslow, *Jonathan Edwards*, p. 176. Winslow points out that long after Edwards's death, when the Revolution had given impetus to the separation of church and state and ministers were no longer obliged to devise systems that would

allow all inhabitants of a town to be considered church members in order to exercise a full franchise, Edwards's insistence that a church must be made up of believers prevailed: the various sects with their divergent views that were to grow and flourish during the nineteenth century were established or expanded (p. 296).

___ 4 ___

Enter Justin Morgan

WE have arrived, by a route as circuitous as that which Tristram Shandy took to arrive at his beginning, at February and March of 1747 (1746, Old Style), and the date of Justin Morgan's birth. The eighth of Isaac and Thankfull Morgan's eleven children, Justin was baptized on the twenty-ninth of March, a date that is frequently given as Morgan's birth date. The vital records of Springfield, Massachusetts (2:80), however, give Justin's birth date as the twenty-eighth of February, 1747 (or 1746 as the date was actually written, since the old system of beginning the new year on March 25 prevailed until 1752). It is doubtful indeed if anyone outside the immediate family circle, or perhaps beyond the midwife's circuit, noticed this event. Almost any family in West Spring-field could boast at least eight children, and some could count up to twenty. The birth of an eighth child could scarcely have been called an innovation. Perhaps, if all went well, it was hardly considered an event—except by the mother and baby. Possibly one should in charity include the father and the midwife.

From February of 1747, when Justin Morgan was born, until 21 March of 1761, when his grandfather Ebenezer Day made his will, there is no documentary evidence whatever regarding Justin. The grandfather's will reveals that Ebenezer Day remembered not only his four sons and seven daughters but also all the children of his daughter Thankfull, wife of Isaac Morgan: out of his small estate the sum of three pounds seven shillings was to be divided equally among Isaac, Jr., Caleb, Stephen, William, Justin, and the two girls, Thankfull (already the wife of Thomas Miller) and Eunice. Of Isaac's and Thankfull's brood, the only names not mentioned are the first Isaac, born in 1734, and the three children who followed Justin—Daniel, Hannah, and Nathaniel—all four of whom died in infancy. It may be that Ebenezer mentioned so carefully all the children of his daughter Thankfull because she, having borne eleven children between the first Isaac in 1734 and Nathaniel twenty-one years later in 1755, herself had died on the thirteenth of February in 1756—when she was forty-five and her son Justin was almost nine. In 1760 her widower Isaac, then fifty-two, provided Justin and his brothers and sisters with a stepmother in the person of Ruth Alvord. No children were born of this second union, however, and it is therefore clear that Grandfather Day made some provision for all the issue of both his daughter Thankfull and his son-in-law Isaac Morgan.

Grandfather Day died in 1763. History is silent as to how sixteen-year-old Justin spent his four-shilling inheritance— or whether, indeed, he got it, after debts were paid when the small estate was settled. How he had spent his first sixteen years must remain, so far as presently available evidence reveals, a matter of pure speculation. It is apparent from his later activities that Justin Morgan must by the time he was sixteen have absorbed a good bit of farming know-how and a good bit of book-learning. It is probable that he had already learned something about the art and mystery of music, although records of other highly gifted singing masters indicate that some of them acquired all their formal musical education in a three-month singing school that they attended when they were full-grown eighteen-year-olds.[1]

There is no indication that Justin Morgan attended grammar school or that he studied with Parson Lathrop in the hope of preparing for college. It is obvious that he must have attended common school, either the old school on the Common "on the west side of the river"[2] or some school closer to his family's farm on the northern borders of the town. In 1748 John "Wilistone" was paid eight pounds eleven shillings (Old Tenor money) to keep a school on the west side of the Great River "from Widow Parsons's to Samuel Morgan's."[3] It is hard to determine just where Justin Morgan went to school when one discovers that if a man lived too far from any school to send his children there, the town voted him two pounds "to school his children."[14] Wherever he attended, Justin Morgan encountered Dilworth's spelling book, the primer and the Bible[5]—and perhaps let the name *Dilworth* sink into his consciousness against the time when he himself would be choosing textbooks. It is probable that when he reached the upper grades Justin attended the school on the Common, where the upper room was reserved for the older scholars who were ready for such heady stuff as *Salmons Geography*.[6] One is told that as the Revolution approached, the quality of common school education diminished[7] but Justin Morgan was well out of school long before the first stirrings of the Revolutionary period were noticeable.

As to the great events that occurred during Morgan's youth, who can say how many of these he noticed? How many high school lads of today can tell you what office Henry Kissinger filled? During his babyhood Justin Morgan could not have known of the excitement attendant upon Jonathan Edwards's dismissal from his Northhampton church and his assumption of the role of missionary to the Indians in Stockbridge. During his childhood Justin probably knew little of the far-off fighting that began on the Ohio River and developed into the French and Indian War, but as a stripling he very likely heard his fellow townsmen who were returning to West Springfield from the battles at Crown Point, Quebec, and Montreal, speak of the open land that lay between Massachusetts and New France and that beckoned to men who yearned to own and develop their own farms. When the Treaty of Paris in 1763 turned New France into Canada, Englishmen from the Springfield area were among those from all parts of the older New England who flocked to the "New Hampshire Grants" that were soon to become Vermont. News of these pioneers and their adventures must have drifted back to West Springfield whenever someone returned through the forest, or down the river, to collect the family he had left at home while he made the first clearing and built the first cabin.

There were matters close at home to occupy an observant boy's attention. There was probably no reason for six-year-old Justin to pay much attention to the birth of a cousin Martha, to Justin's uncle Luke Day and his wife Jerusha (Skinner) Day, or to that cousin's baptism on the twenty-seventh of May in 1753; Justin would pay more attention to her later on. Cousins were, after all, being born more or less contantly in the Springfield area. For instance, the line of Justin's father's brother, Joseph Morgan, a prominent weaver, in 1766 produced Quartus (grandson of Joseph), who was to marry a Tuttle and late in the century establish himself in Bellows Falls, Vermont, as an innkeeper. Another grandson of Joseph's, the third Joseph in that line, was to marry a Spencer, produce a son named Junius Spencer Morgan, and a grandson, John Pierpont Morgan, not unknown to later history. Justin Morgan, it will be seen, took a different road from that traveled by Joseph and Junius and J. Pierpont— and that did make all the difference.

Any boy would very likely have been interested when his father bought and sold farm lands. When Justin was seven Isaac sold to his brother Ebenezer Morgan two pieces of land on the west side of the "Great River" in Chickopee Field, the six-acre piece lying beside Brother Samuel Morgan's land, the three-acre piece beside Brother Nathaniel Morgan's. The deal enriched Isaac's family coffers by twenty-four pounds. Just four days after making his sale on April 12, Isaac bought for eighty-four pounds from Josiah Farnam, cooper, "the houselot of the late Nathaniel Sikes" and Sikes's grant for a mill, the whole presumably lying beside the land that Morgan had bought from Sikes in 1737.[8] There is an interesting deed dated the thirtieth of March, 1759, by which Nathaniel Morgan, born in 1693, eldest of the brothers and unmarried, yielded his forty-three acres of land and "all movable and personal estate" to his brother Isaac, fourteen years his junior, who had "undertaken to support Nathaniel in sickness and health for life." Isaac's responsibility for Nathaniel continued for four years until the eleventh of February in 1763, when Nathaniel died at age seventy.

There were events in the 1750s that must have had a profound effect upon Justin. Mention has been made of the death of his mother in 1756. Just the year before, the Reverend Samuel Hopkins had died after thiry-five years as Springfield's pastor. That same year, young Mr. Lathrop began his ministry, which was to stretch out twenty years beyond Justin's death in 1798, to 1818. In 1754 a son, Asahel, was born to Samuel and Phebe Benham in New Hartford, Connecticut—a fact presumably quite unnoticed in West Springfield, but one that was to make all the difference for Justin Morgan the musician.[9]

In the sixties, after Isaac Morgan married Ruth Alvord, records tell of Isaac's being elected constable and of other Morgans holding other town offices, but it is not until 1771 that Justin Morgan himself figures in an important event, other than a musical one that will be discussed shortly.[10] On the twenty-sixth of May in 1771, when Justin was twenty-four, his father Isaac, yeoman, sold to Justin, husbandman, for thiry pounds, twenty-two acres on the west side to the Great River, "part of my homelot on which I dwell," bounded northerly by Israel Brooks's land, easterly by Israel Brooks and Thomas Bagg, southerly by Thomas Bagg, and westerly by "my own land." The sale included "one-third of my barn with the privilege of the yard as he has need of going in and out of my barn." The deed was executed in the eleventh year of His Majesty George the Third's reign, but was not recorded until 31 January 1786, when Justin was presumably thinking of selling his property. Isaac's father Nathaniel had given land to his sons, but apparently by Isaac's time customs had changed. In 1763 Isaac had sold to his eldest son, Isaac, Jr., cooper, seventy-four acres, the cost being five pounds.

It is important to note the term *husbandman*, which is applied to Justin Morgan. Nineteenth-century writers have commented that Justin was frail throughout his life, did little farming after he was twenty, and made his living largely as a teacher of singing and common schools.[11] The record, however, indicates that Justin thought of himself as a farmer throughout his life. He called himself a simple husbandman in this, his first land deed, and in all later transactions described himself as a yeoman—the term that placed him between the *husbandman* and the *gentleman* as one who tilled the soil for his livelihood and who owned land, but who did not hire others to do most of the manual labor, as a *gentleman* did.[12] Invariably in the deeds of the eighteenth century a man identified himself by his principal occupation; and if Justin Morgan had thought of himself as a singing master, he would have labeled himself as one. It seems evident that he viewed music as his "cash crop" (or "staple crop," as the seventeenth century would have said)—an activity to be practiced in the long winter months when one could not farm but when one could turn to other activities to piece out one's meager income.[13]

Throughout the seventies, when the new America was being born, Justin Morgan stuck close to his job and his family ties. On the twenty-fifth of February in 1774 West Springfield was finally incorporated as a separate town, but is seems likely that Justin paid less attention to that fact than he did to the fact that on the twenty-ninth of October, at the age of twenty-seven, he and his first cousin Martha Day, aged twenty-one, filed their intention to be married. They were married on the eighth of December. In 1775 the Battles of Lexington and Bunker Hill attracted a number of volunteers from the Springfield area, including some Morgans—but not Justin. In 1776, when Justin was twenty-nine, the Declaration of Independence was made public, but before that historic announcement was made, Martha Morgan, first child of Justin and Martha, was born on the thirteenth of May. In that same year Justin and Martha were formally admitted to memberhsip in the church. In 1777 William Morgan sold to his brother Justin seven acres bordering on the north on "our honored father Isaac Morgan's home lot" together with a third part of the barn standing on "our honored father's home lot with the privilege of going in and out of said barn."

In 1778 Justin Morgan, at thirty-one, made public the activity to which he was to devote much time—the maintenance of a stable at which mares could be bred to stallions cared for and managed by Morgan. How many horses he himself owned cannot be determined from existing records. On May 18 of 1778 an advertisement appeared in the *Connecticut Courant* (Hartford) stating that "Sportsman, the dapple grey horse, will cover this season at Justin Morgan's stable in West Springfield, Mass., at eight dollars the season, and four the single leap." The advertisement declared that the horse was unexcelled for "beauty, strength, saddle, harness, and the colts are so well known that there needs no further description." Finally the advertisement remarked that Sportsman was "the same horse that covered . . . last season by the wrong name of Young Ranger." The fee for Sportsman's services, in that time of inflation, was higher than the fees that Morgan later asked for the services of other stallions, including his prized Figure.

Thereafter Justin advertised other stallions. On the thirteenth of May in 1783, the *Massachusetts Gazette* (Springfield) announced that "at the stable of Mr. Justin Morgan in West Springfield the horse called Diamond, who sprang from a good mare, and from the horse formerly owned by Mr.

Church of Springfield, will cover." Diamond is of special
interest because he is thought by those who have devoted
lifetimes to tracing the ancestry of the Morgan breed of horses
to have been the sire of Figure's dam—"Figure" having been
the actual name of the stallion owned by Morgan in the 1790s,
called finally after his master's name, and credited with being
the progenitor of the Morgan breed.[14] Two years later, 3 May
1785, Morgan advertised Beautiful Bay in the *Hampshire
Herald* (Springfield). In 1788 John Morgan, Jr., of Springfield, cousin of Justin, advertised in the *Hampshire Chronicle* (Springfield), "the famous, full-blooded English horse,
called True Britain or Beautiful Bay, said to be the surest and
finest horse for colts in New-England," who "will cover this
season at the stable of the subscriber at the very low rate of
eighteen shillings the season (cash, grain, wood, or flax)."
Morgan added: "N.B. It is the same horse that was kept three
seasons ago by Mr. Justin Morgan at West-Springfield, and
got so many fine colts in that, this, and the neighboring
towns." Apparently this stallion was the sire of Figure.

Another of Justin Morgan's various activities began in
1781, when for the first time he was licensed to sell retail
liquors from his house. It has been said that Justin ran a
tavern, but the province of Massachusetts made a sharp
distinction between "innholders" and "retailers of liquor."
In the records for 1781 of the Court of General Sessions of the
Peace for Hampshire County (at Northhampton) there is a
license for John Morgan to keep an inn at Springfield, but
Justin Morgan is licensed only to be a "retailer" in West
Springfield. He, Jesse Rogers, and Simeon Smith paid ten
pounds as "sureties for each other," and thus obtained licenses to sell liquor from their several houses. At least ten
other "retailers" seem to have been operating in West Springfield that year, of whom only four had inns. The thirst of
West Springfield, which ten years later numbered just 2,367
souls, must surely have been slaked. In 1782 Justin Morgan
and Jesse Rogers were again licensed

Although no portrait exists of Justin Morgan, this charcoal portrait drawing of his son, Justin Morgan Jr., suggests much of the contemplative nature that one associates with the senior Justin Morgan. The drawing, by an unknown artist, was probably executed in the 1840s, when Justin Morgan Jr. was a member of the Vermont state senate. *Collection of the Vermont Historical Society.*

to sell spiritous liquors by retail out of their respective houses there to be spent out of doors only for one year next ensuing, and they recognize to the Commonwealth as Principals in the sum of fifty pounds each and as sureties in twenty-five pounds each for each other, with the condition presented for Innholders and Retailers respectively, and that they severally do keep and render the accounts and pay the duties required by Statutes in such cases made and provided.

The statutes were made and provided to see that all liquor sold in the Commonwealth was taxed—and that is why sellers had to be licensed, and why one learns what Justin Morgan was doing to gain a part of his livelihood. His license was renewed in 1783, 1784, and 1785.

Justin's livelihood was also the livelihood of a growing family. After Martha came Emily, born on the Fourth of July in 1779, who died when she was four years old, 25 January 1784. Then came Nancy, born in 1781, who died, at five, 17 May 1786. Next was Emily the Second, named, as was the custom, after her older sister who had died, and born 16 February 1784, shortly after the first Emily died. Finally a boy, Justin Junior, arrived 15 March 1786. The last two of the seven children—the second Nancy and Polly—were not to be born until the family had moved to Vermont in 1788. Nancy the Second was born 3 September 1788, and Polly 10 March 1791—fifteen years after the birth of her eldest sister, Martha.

Notes

1. In *American Writers and Compilers of Sacred Music* (New York and Cincinnati, Ohio: Abingdon Press, 1925), Frank J. Metcalf says that the well-known singing master Timothy Swan at the age of sixteen "obtained his musical education by attending singing school for three weeks" (p. 104).

2. Springfield, Mass., Town Records, Book 5, entry of 14 November 1748 and passim.

3. Ibid., 14 November 1748.

4. Ibid. The money was voted to Samuel Brooks.

5. Warner B. Sturtevant, "Colonial Education in Western Massachusetts," TS

dated 20 April 1932 in Springfield Public Library, p. 7; cited by permission of the Springfield Public Library. J. N. Bagg comp. *Account of the Contennial Celebration of the Town of West Springfield, Mass.* (West Springfield, Mass.: Published by the town, 1874.)

6. Bagg, 128-29.
7. Sturtevant, Colonial Education," passim.
8. See above, p. 72.
9. See below, pp. 142-43.
10. See below, ch. 5.
11. See above, p. 45.
12. The term *gentleman* is a particularly slippery one in the America of the eighteenth century. Contemporary English law and custom describe a gentleman as one who bears a coat of arms or whose ancestors have been freemen. The term *yeoman* is defined as "a freeholder under the rank of gentleman." In England *yeoman* came to be confined to those whose lands yielded incomes of forty shillings or more annually. The term was used in America, so says Henry Campbell Black's *Law Dictionary*, 4th ed. (St. Paul, Minn.: West Publishing Co., 1951), "without any definite meaning." Yet it seems apparent from a study of the deeds of the eighteenth century that Americans were quite sure of what they meant when they wrote *gentleman, yeoman,* and *husbandman.* All three worked the land; the gentleman often had hired help and always had freemen among his forebears; the yeoman owned land (was a "freeholder"); the husbandman generally worked for someone other than himself or had a small holding of his own. Apparently the colonists still remembered the English legal distinction between the yeoman, a "freeholder" (one who held his land in "fee simple"), and the husbandman, a "copyholder" (one who held his land as a tenant on a manor, on whose rolls his name had been copied). Any "gentleman" who made his living by means other than farming (e.g., as a physician) invariably used his calling as the descriptive term to add to his name in land deeds and other public records. When one comes across "John Doe, Gentleman" in an eighteenth-century deed, he may be sure that he is dealing with a farmer—just as he would be if he encountered Richard Roe, yeoman, or Silas Poe, husbandman. The term *farmer* was in the eighteenth century used to designate tenants who cultivated leased land.
13. Some men made potash to gain the bit of money that was needed to piece out the subsistence farming that provided the essentials of life; some men did a little blacksmithing or shoemaking; always the women wove and spun, and sold or traded the cloth that was surplus to their families' needs; some men and women taught common schools or singing schools or writing schools. In November, 1780, the Town of West Springfield voted forty shillings to Miss Tryphena White for keeping a school.

An examination of the eighteenth-century records of the Morgans and allied families reveals to what extent women were partners with their husbands in providing the necessities of life before the Industrial Revolution removed industry from the home. The will of Isaac Morgan's brother, Ebenezer the Second, made 9 May 1770, indicates clearly that what a man left to his wife was not simply land or money but an active enterprise: Ebenezer leaves to "Lidia" the use of what household movables she needs, one-third of his real estate (her dower right), the use of one cow, as much of his provisions as she will need "till the new crop comes in," the use of one room in the dwelling house with room to store her part of the provisions yearly "as also room in the barn for her part of the stores and other things her part produces that want housing." She is also to get "all of the household moveables she brought with her and the liberty to my said wife to cut her firewood on any of my lands during her natural life." As was customary, the four sons inherited the buildings and the land other than the widow's third.

14. See especially Joseph Battell, *American Stallion Register* (Middlebury, Vt.: American Publishing Company, 1911), 2:395 ff.

____ 5 ____

Controversy over Singing

AT no time during these years does Morgan seem to have advertised his singing schools.[1] One would be inclined to doubt that he was in fact a singing master were it not for a detailed account of his activity, when he was in his early twenties, as a teacher of singing in Wilbraham, which ceased to be a parish of Springfield and became a separate town in 1763. In *An Historical Address Delivered at the Centennial Celebration of the Incorporation of the Town of Wilbraham, June 15, 1863*,[2] the Reverend Rufus P. Stebbins told of the war that developed in the Wilbraham church over what to sing and how to sing it, and of "Mr. Morgan's" part in that war. There seems no doubt that the "Mr. Morgan" involved was Justin, since comments made by contemporaries identify only one Morgan as a composer and singing master in late eighteenth-century New England, and since there seems no doubt that Justin Morgan was, among other things, a singing master. Mr. Stebbins places the controversy in 1770, when Morgan was twenty-three. A more recent authority suggests the date 1780,[3] but the fervor with which Morgan upheld his position in the argument seems more in keeping with a man of twenty-three than with one of thirty-three. According to Stebbins, at a town meeting held on the twenty-fourth of September in 1770 Wilbraham chose a committee of ten men "to take into consideration the Broken state of this Town with regard to Singing in the Publick Assembly on Sabbath Days, and to consult together and agree upon some Plan or Method whereby to encourage & promote regular and Universal Singing in said assembly." At the same meeting the town was to vote on whether it was willing "to sing four Times in the Publick worship on the Sabbath." One learns, that "Mr. Stickney" had recently given singing instruction to the young people of the town, and that old Deacon Nathaniel Warriner, who had "raised the pitch" and thus led the singing for twenty years, was unhappy over the results of this instruction. The committee reported to a town meeting on the twenty-second of October.

From the report one learns not only how vital a part singing played in the life of a New England town in the late eighteenth century but also exactly why the "new singing" being promoted by the singing masters was causing a furor. Wilbraham's is almost a classic case: complicated, ornate tunes were being taught—frequently "fuging tunes" in which one part chased another after the manner of a round— which were fun to sing if you had considerable aptitude for and training in singing, but which many in the congregation could not sing. Yet, as Deacon Warriner doubtless pointed out, it was a solemn obligation of "all" to sing praises to the Lord. Furthermore, these tunes seemed to many parishioners far too brisk and gay to have a part in religious worship. Furthermore again, as one part chased another it was difficult if not impossible to follow the words and therefore to employ the song as a true means of worship. Add to these difficulties the fact that the newly trained singers wanted to sit together so as to hear the various parts as they made music; what then happened to the ancient custom of "seating" the meetinghouse according to the dignity of members, and sometimes also dividing the men from the women?

According to the committee's report, the new singers both won and lost. The report recommended that "all who Assist in Singing Shall be at their pleasure either to Stand or Sit when Singing without giving Offence to any; that the singers lately instructed by Mr. Stickney who are seated in the Gallery ... are at their Liberty to make a decent and orderly Exchange of Seats as They shall agree among themselves." The leader "shall be at Liberty to Use the Motion of his hand while singing for the Space of Three Months." Deacon Warriner is to lead the singing in the forenoon, and "one of the Young Men lately Instructed by Mr. Stickney" in the afternoon, "excepting when Mr. Morgan is present, then it is expected he will carry the singing."

The new singers thus won Round One. Round Two goes to the Deacon and his sympathizers. The committee chooses twenty-three tunes—all old and familiar psalm tunes such as "Low Dutch," "Windsor," "Old 100d"—which are to be placed in a list "to be transmitted to Mr. Morgan (now singing-master in this town) in order that he may Teach or Instruct his scholars to Sing them according to Rule." The scholars are to learn to sing by Rule—but they are to stick to the tunes that the whole congregation knows and can sing.[4]

The report urges that, "as the Beating with the hand in the Congregation when singing is offensive to some it be laid aside as quick as may be and confine the same to the school only." The committee recommends further "that all in the Town whose voices will admit of it speedily use proper means to get themselves acquainted with the art of Singing Ruleably & Well" and that in the meantime "both old and Young ... Join in Singing in the Worshiping assembly and ... sing as well as they can." Finally, "we cannot but recommend to ourselves & others to studdy the Things which make for peace, and the things whereby we may Edify one another."

This statesmanlike report was accepted by the town, but from a less impersonal source than a town report came word that things did not work out according to plan. In 1931 Frances Grace Smith, having discovered a letter written to her ancestor, Moses Stebbins of the South Parish in Wilbraham, wrote an article, "The American Revolution Hits Church Music," which indicates what did in fact happen.[5] Miss Smith quotes extensively from a letter written by Ezra Barker, clerk of town and parish in Wilbraham, and schoolmaster in the northern part of the town, to his friend and fellow schoolmaster, Moses Stebbins. The letter is said to be dated 31 August 1780, but it clearly deals with the controversy described in the Rufus Stebbins account; presumably the confusion in date is caused by the difficulty of reading eighteenth-century handwriting, perhaps in faded ink.

Master Barker writes,

> When our singing wanted to be revived, We got Mr. Stickney and lastly Mr. Morgan among us for that Purpose. I was one who cast in my Mite to encourage the Singing. But they so Suddenly exchanged old Tunes for New ones and introduced them into the Publick Worship and the old ones being neglected it was but a few that could bear a part in the delightful part of Divine Worship. . . .The Town took the Matter in hand and at a Legal Meeting selected out a number of Tunes, injoining the School to practice upon them only until further orders. The Clerk was ordered to Serve the Master of the School with a Copy, I think he paid no regard to it, Saving one Night. . . . Some Tunes were introduced soon which by Some were thought not fit to be Used in So Solemn Worship. Several have Showed their dislike by going out. . . .

Master Barker has dark thoughts as to the matter of the singers' seats: "Now Seats are Shifted, Some of the Males have stretched a Wing over upon the Female Side and have intruded upon their Right, and all with this Cloak, v.z. for the Convenience of Singing. Were our Antient Pious fore-Fathers permitted to arise from their Silent Graves and to take a view, perhaps they would blush at the Sight."

The "Merry Tunes" that are introduced are "so full of Cords or Discords that Another Set of good Singers are Shut out. . . ." Worst of all, when the minister names a psalm, the

"Tunester" names the Tune and "as if he were independent, cries out, Continue." Presumably the leader, whether Master Morgan or one of his scholars, is seeing to it that the song is sung without a break for the "lining out" (reading each line before singing it) that had been the custom in most New England churches for generations. Morgan's own church in West Springfield gave up the custom of lining out the hymns in 1781.

Barker complains that most of those who sing are "out of the Church" (non-members). The worshippers are obliged to "hang their Harps upon the Willows. We hear the Sound but know not the Matter Sung. . . . Doubtless our Animal Frame (or at least Some of us) is Charmed but our Souls, or Rational parts remain barren and wither away as the Fields, whereon it rained not."

The address by Rufus Stebbins tells of further acrimonious disagreement in Wilbraham's town meeting of 7 January 1771, until finally the minister, the Reverend Noah Mirick, is asked to call a meeting of the church Society "in order to come into some method of Reconciliation with regard to Singing in the Publick worship." The town meeting adjourns, and Mr. Stebbins says that no further reports have come to light that might reveal how the matter ended.

Of special interest in the controversy is the mention of "Mr. Stickney" as the first teacher of the "new singers." Presumably this teacher was John Stickney, who was born in Stoughton in 1744 and who attended one of the singing schools of the well known William Billings in that town.[6] Stickney, who had been apprenticed at the age of seven to shoemaker and butcher, Isaac Davenport of neighboring Milton, at fifteen returned to Stoughton and there learned from William Dunbar, a lawyer and justice of the peace, "the new style of music just being introduced by William Billings."[7] After his training by Dunbar and Billings, Stickney moved to South Hadley, where he and his wife (Elizabeth Howard) were members of the Congregational Church.

Aided by his wife, who was an accomplished singer, Stickney taught music in Connecticut Valley towns such as Northampton, Wethersfield, Hartford, and New Haven. Hadley is, of course, no farther from West Springfield than is Wilbraham, and like it was once part of Springfield. It seems quite possible that Morgan's musical training came from Stickney, whose own training had come partly from Billings—a highly inventive and original composer, the best known of America's first school of composers.

Stickney's life shows that same combination of musical activities with other endeavors that is characteristic of the life of Morgan. Stickney's home in South Hadley was a farm near the Connecticut River "where he cultivated the soil during the summer, while in winter he often accommodated the lumbermen and fishermen of that vicinity with board."[8] One learns that "his efforts to displace the old method of singing by rote met with considerable opposition, but he succeeded in teaching many in the towns which he visited to read and sing by note." He continued to conduct singing schools until he was about sixty-five (1809), and he played a part in the Revolutionary War, serving as a private in 1776 at Castleton, Vermont, and being present at the surrender of Burgoyne at Saratoga in October of 1777. It is interesting to notice that his second marriage (in 1813) was to Lucy N., widow of Azariah Alvord. It will be remembered that Morgan's stepmother was an Alvord.

Stickney's tunebook, *The Gentleman and Lady's Musical Companion*, published in 1774,[9] enjoyed considerable success. In his introduction to that book Stickney clearly indicates that, whatever the old guard thought in Wilbraham, he was very conscious of the need to keep church music an act of genuine worship. He writes: "Singing is an act of religious worship; while persons are learning the art, indeed, they can scarce be considered in a devout exercise. If, therefore, they choose to sing in the words of a psalm, it is most proper to choose those that are not peculiarly devotional." In Scotland at this time the psalms were considered so sacred that persons practicing singing outside the church were required to substitute "practice verses" of a secular nature, sometimes with hilarious results.[10] Stickney goes on to urge upon the singer in church "the utmost care . . . not only to avoid all levities and indecencies of carriage, which are intolerable, but to adopt no expressions which we cannot conscientiously use, to enter thoroughly into the sentiments of the psalm . . . thus singing with the understanding and the affections, we make melody in our hearts unto the Lord; but if otherwise, whatever harmony our voices may make, we affront and provoke Almighty God."

Notes

1. The fact that Morgan did not advertise his singing schools at any time during his life is fairly clear evidence that he did not classify himself primarily as a singing master. The itinerant singing masters whose principal business in life was to teach singing tended to gravitate, at least fairly part of the time, toward fairly big centers of population and there advertise in the newspapers their intention to open a school and their willingness, not to say eagerness, to have people come from outlying districts to attend the school. Men like Morgan and most of the other Vermont psalmodists of his period seem simply to have ridden over to a neighboring town, gone to church on a Sunday, and let people know, perhaps during the noon period between services, that they would be glad to conduct a class for the next month or so if enough people wanted to join. When Morgan's business—providing a stallion at stud service—required people to come to him, he advertised; when his business—providing musical training—required him to go where the people were, he apparently saw no need to advertise.

2. Rufus P. Stebbins, *An Historical Address Delivered at the Centennial Celebration of the Incorporation of the Town of Wilbraham* (Boston: George C. Rand and Avery, 1864), pp. 85-90.

3. See below, p. 99.

4. The entire list includes: Low Dutch, Windsor, Old 100d, New 100d, Stroudwater, Meer, Buckland, Broomsgrove, Bangor, St. Martin's, Warwick, St. Hellens, All-Saints, Little Marlborough, Cambridge, Portsmouth, Southwell, Quercy, Worksop, Wantage, Standish, New York, and 149 Psalm Tune.

5. The essay was published in *The New England Quarterly* 4 (1931): 783-88.

6. Details of Stickney's life are taken from Frank J. Metcalf, *American Writers and Compilers of Sacred Music* (New York and Cincinnati, Ohio: Abingdon Press, 1925), pp. 41-45. Metcalf says that he derived his information from an article on Stickney that was first printed in *The Choir Herald.*

7. Ibid., p. 42.

8. Ibid.

9. Printed by Daniel Bayley in Newburyport, Mass.

10. Millar Patrick in his fine study of Scottish church music, *Four Centuries of Scottish Psalmody* (London: Geoffrey Cumberlege, Oxford University Press, 1949) tells of one John McQuisten of Greenock who loved the old Scottish ballads and often sang them on a Saturday night to tune up in preparation for Sunday's service, at which he led the singing. One Saturday he fixed on "Sir Patrick Spens" for practice, and the next morning when the preacher gave out Psalm 107, John, in the precentor's place below the pulpit, arrived at Verse 23 ("They that go down to the sea in ships"), and by the time he reached Verse 25 ("For he commandeth and raiseth the stormy wind . . .") was shunted off into "Sir Patrick Spens" ("O laith, laith were oor guid Scots lords/ To weet their cork-heel'd shoon . . ."). The congregation meekly followed John's resounding bass voice right through the ballad, while the scandalized preacher in the high pulpit was powerless to change the course of events. The town never let John forget that day, and on many a Sunday thereafter the minister would say before the service, "Gi'e us nane o' your ballants the day, na, John" (pp. 167-69).

____ 6 ____

From Husbandman to Yeoman

THROUGHOUT the decades when Morgan was breeding horses, selling liquor, and conducting singing and writing and presumably common schools, he was engaged in farming, as was many another jack-of-all-eighteenth-century-trades. He began, as has been said, as a husbandman. The buying of that piece of land, however, made him a freeholder and therefore a yeoman. This was a status that he never lost, no matter how much his land shrank and his fortune changed, as the fortunes of the emerging country ebbed and flowed about him. His buying and selling of land indicate a gradual reduction of his holdings to a small area around his house and barn, possibly out of necessity, possibly to permit him to concentrate upon his liquor trade and horse breeding.

He began in 1771 with twenty-two acres and the third of his father's barn, the whole bought from his father Isaac for thirty pounds; he added seven acres bought from his brother William, for another thirty pounds, in 1777; but in December of 1781 he and his father sold to Justin's brother Stephen fifty-five acres "together with all buildings," the sale bringing them 222 pounds "current silver money." To this deed Justin and Martha set their signatures, Isaac his signature, and Isaac's wife Ruth her mark. The following month, 1 January 1782, Justin bought of David and Anna Miller, now "of Marlborough, in Windham County, Vermont," five acres bounded conveniently on the west by "the highway." Justin paid 165 pounds for the property, but from the records of the Hampshire County Court of Common Pleas it appears that there was trouble between Justin and David over money.

In an action brought against Justin and Isaac Morgan, Jr., in the August 1784 term of the Hampshire County Court of Common Pleas,[1] David Miller of Marlborough, Vermont, claimed that on 1 January 1782 (the day of the land sale) Justin Morgan signed a note promising to pay Miller forty-two pounds and eight shillings, half in liquors and half in money (i.e., in wheat at four shillings a bushel, rye at three, Indian corn at two) by a date in the spring of that year. Miller claimed that Morgan had failed to make payment. Justin defaulted, although "called three times to the court," and judgment was given for the plaintiff. Through his attorney, Justin Ely, Esq., Morgan appealed the case to the Supreme Judicial Court at its September session in Springfield; and on October 18, 1784, finding Justin still absent, the court gave judgment for Miller, awarding him a total of one hundred pounds, nineteen shillings, eleven pence, when all court costs were included. Justin was some four pounds worse off than he would have been if he had accepted the decision of the lower court.[2]

Other land transactions are also tangled with court actions. On the thirtieth of December in 1783 Daniel and William Leonard sold to Justin Morgan, for one hundred and two pounds, a grist mill on Pocketuck (Paucatuck) Brook, it having been an original grant to John Bagg and others in 1713. Not a year later, 14 August 1784, Justin mortgaged his grist mill and seven acres back to the Leonards for 124 pounds, but the deed was to be void if Justin and Isaac Jr. paid back a bond, listed at 220 pounds, by the first of June next.[3] Once again the matter went to the Court of Common Pleas, and in the November term of 1784 the Leonards sued Justin and Isaac Jr. for 220 pounds. The Morgans defaulted; and in the February 1785 court term judgment was given for the Leonards in the amount of 120 pounds nine shillings plus costs. The case was appealed to the Supreme Judicial Court sitting at Springfield in September of 1785; the Morgans again failed to appear; and judgment was rendered in favor of the Leonards, damages and costs now amounting to 112 pounds 12 shillings.

Justin Morgan did not lose all his court cases. An action brought against Caleb and Solomon Smith in that busy August court term of 1784 brought Morgan ten pounds seventeen shillings sixpence in damages. Another case tells us much about Morgan's way of making a living. On the twentieth of May in 1783, at the Court of Common Pleas at Springfield, Justin Morgan, yeoman, brought an action of "trespass" against Isaac Marsh, gentleman, of Stockbridge in the county of Berkshire, Massachusetts. It develops that on the tenth of August in 1782 Marsh gave a promissory note "for value received" to pay twenty-five pounds three shillings ten pence worth of good merchantable wheat flour at fifteen shillings the hundred-weight, to be delivered at Isaac's store in Stockbridge by the first of January 1783. Isaac "did not and would not" deliver the flour, although Justin hired two teams from West Springfield and drove over to Stockbridge to take the flour to Boston for sale. He paid six pounds for the teams. Justin asked forty pounds in damages, and the following September received thirty-seven pounds plus costs when the defendant failed to appear.

Be it noted that Morgan, described as "frail" by nineteenth-century historians, hired four horses, when he was nearing the age of thirty-six, drove them thirty-five miles in the dead of winter, and then was prepared to load over a ton and a half of flour on his sleigh or wagon and drive about 125 miles across Massachusetts in order to make a sale in Boston. Frailty, thy name was not Justin.

Perhaps the most interesting of Justin Morgan's court cases is the one that reveals his attitude toward and conduct during the Revolutionary War. On the tenth of June in 1782, when the war was wearing itself out but when Massachusetts was still under obligation to provide a certain number of three-year men for the Continental forces, a most fascinating case was brought against Morgan's cousin and brother-in-law, Luke Day, Gentleman, by about a platoon of West Springfield people, including Justin Morgan. The case had to do with how to raise an army in agrarian America in the 1770s and 1780s. Many men volunteered unhesitatingly for three months or six months of service, or for any sudden "alarm"—but three years? Three years away from one's farm? How would one survive? How would one's children survive?

West Springfield's "Town Book One" records on page 172 that on the third of January in 1781 the selectmen divided the town into twenty-five classes, each class to procure one man for the Continental Army for three years. This provision was made in compliance with a mandate from Massachusetts's General Court, which was under obligation to provide 4,240 men for the Continental Army.[4] At the March town meeting in 1782 the town voted three pounds twelve shillings to Captain Luke Day, who had already given distinguished service in the Continental Army, "for monies paid by him towards hiring three years, six and three months men to go into the service." The suit against Day suggests that his recruiting zeal got out of hand.

Forty people brought suit against Luke Day, Gentleman, in the Court of Common Pleas held at Northampton, first in June and later in November 1782, for having nefariously done them out of the man who was to fill their quota for the Continental Army. The names of the plaintiffs include some of the best known West Springfield families, many of which contributed volunteers for the alarm at Lexington, or the Battle of Bunker Hill, or other short-term emergencies. There were Morgans, as well as Baggs and Ashleys and Elys and Millers, who volunteered for all these engagements, generally as militiamen. But when it came to sending a man for three endless years into military service, the same names showed great enthusiasm for sending somebody else. Among the plaintiffs in this suit are Nathan Morgan, Gentleman; Justin Morgan, yeoman; Justin's brother Stephen; Justin's cousins Miles (with his sons Ezekiel and Enos), and Samuel and Timothy. There are also Baggs and Alvords and Smiths and the David Miller with whom Morgan later crossed swords in court. Most interesting of all is Elizabeth Dwight, gentlewoman, of Springfield. Most of the plaintiffs were members of a class expected to provide one three-year "volunteer" for the army. At first blush it seems that Elizabeth Dwight must have gotten in by mistake, unless a Revolutionary WAC Corps existed of which no one has any knowledge; but elsewhere there is reference to Elizabeth Buckminster Dwight, wife of Colonel Josiah Dwight, as "one of nature's noble women," and it may be simply that she was moved to aid either one of the plaintiffs, or Prince Freeman, the black who is featured in this case and who was willing to go to war if by doing so he could obtain his freedom.[5]

It develops that when the class of which Justin Morgan was a part was faced with providing one soldier for the Continental Army, "a certain conversation was moved and had" between the plaintiffs and Luke Day in which Day told of "a certain Negro man named Prince Freeman, who was supposed to have run away from his master" in New York State, and who was now confined in the Springfield jail. Luke averred that Prince Freeman was willing to enlist, provided his former master could be satisfied. Luke volunteered to go to New York State to try to "hire or purchase said Negro servant," if the plaintiffs would bear his expenses, and so on. The plaintiffs put up twenty-seven pounds, and Luke "purchased" Prince Freeman. Upon his return, Luke discovered that he could get forty dollars more than the total amount that the plaintiffs were to pay him if he presented Prince Freeman for enlistment in a neighboring town. He therefore "subtilly and craftily" informed the plaintiffs that the Negro was reluctant to enlist and demanded fifty dollars more than had been agreed upon. Now Prince Freeman knew nothing of all this, but Luke Day "did then and there let sell and assign the said Negro man . . . to one Seth Bannister, a captain in said service" who was then stationed in Springfield to muster recruits. Seth gave forty-five pounds for Prince; the said Seth was "wholly ignorant of the promises to and for the use and benefit of another class and in another of our towns. . . ." The said Negro was then and there readily enlisted into said Service without being paid any sum to his own use, or receiving any gratuity or reward whatever.

Naturally, somebody found out about all this and brought suit against Luke. The plaintiffs say, among other things, that they cannot find another recruit, and that they are "liable and exposed to pay the whole penalty of the Law." They ask damages of one hundred pounds, and the Court of Common Pleas awards them fifteen. Even this amount is appealed by Luke Day, but the Supreme Judicial Court finds for the plaintiffs, and in September of 1783 Luke Day is commanded to pay twenty-three pounds lawful money damage and costs of nine pounds fifteen shillings.[6]

One is, of course, eager to learn what happened to Prince Freeman. The archives of the United States reveal four Prince Freemans in the Revolutionary War, but none of them quite matches the Prince Freeman of the Justin Morgan case. A Prince Freeman, age twenty-one, height five feet six, enlisted in the Ninth Massachusetts Regiment in June of 1780 and deserted on July 20. The list that includes his name was drawn up at West Point August 17, 1782. It would be tempting to assume that the clerk had gotten the wrong year for Prince Freeman, and that he was indeed the man who in 1782 was enlisted by Captain Seth Bannister, an officer in the Fourth Massachusetts Regiment. The other Prince Freemans served in two Connecticut regiments and in the Vermont militia. There is apparently no way of telling what happened to the particular Prince Freeman who took the place—even if only briefly—of Justin Morgan, et al., in the wars.[7]

The war was almost over by 1782, and Justin found himself caught up in that period of post-war hard times that drove an "enormous" number of Massachusetts residents into debt, and that sparked the popular uprising that was known as Shays's Rebellion.[8] He did manage to buy from his brother Stephen, on the fifth of November in 1782—just at the time the Prince Freeman trial was going on—three acres in the fertile bottomland that was known as Chicopee Field, and that lay close to the west bank of the Great River toward the north end of town, where the various Morgan home farms, or house lots, were located. The land cost twenty-five pounds. Two weeks later, on the eighteenth of November, Justin bought for eighty-one pounds from Stephen and his wife Mary two pieces of land totaling less than four acres. These were apparently adjacent to the three acres just purchased. One of the pieces, containing a house and barn, had been the home lot of Warham Bagg. Possibly it was at this time that Stephen was settling his affairs with a view to moving to Vermont.[9] These purchases represent the end of Morgan's attempts to expand his holdings, except for the ill-fated short ownership of the grist mill bought from the Leonards in the following year. In 1785 there is an interesting exchange between Warham Bagg and Justin Morgan: On the first of April Warham, for sixty-one pounds ten shillings, sells to Justin one acre with house and barn on the west side of the country road. Warham's wife Sarah for one shilling relinquishes her dower right to one-third of the property. On the same day Justin Morgan, for 117 pounds ten shillings, sells to Warham three and a half acres, with house, barn, and "shop" on the east side of the country road—the property having been formerly the "house lot" of that David Miller who went off to Marlborough, Vermont and sold Justin five acres in January of 1782. The previous April Justin and Martha had sold to Noadiah Loomis one and a half acres in Chicopee. It therefore seems that with what looks like an exchange of properties as Justin Morgan and Warham Bagg crossed the

country road and took each other's houses, Morgan gave up
the last of his Miller acres and gained some cash by reducing
his land from three and a half acres to one. Evidently Justin
and Martha gained further cash by selling for thirty-eight
pounds four acres in Chicopee Field. This sale, to Daniel
White, was made on the seventeenth of December 1785. It may
have been part of the land that Justin bought from his brother
Stephen in 1782. There were no more land sales until 1787, a
short time before Justin and Martha moved to Vermont.

It is easy to understand the attraction that Vermont held for
stuggling Massachusetts farmers in the 1780s. In addition to
having much virgin land to be claimed and developed, Vermont also had the great advantage of not owing money to the
emerging United States. She had not been one of the thirteen
colonies, all of which had been heavily taxed during the war
for support of the war effort, and were to be even more heavily
taxed after the war to pay off funds promised to the new
federal government during the war and not yet paid. Since the
taxes had to be paid in cash, the farmers of western Massachusetts, who dealt almost entirely in farm produce, were
particularly hard pressed. To add to all the other miseries,
paper money issued by the shaky new federal government
came to be "not worth a continental," until in 1780 men were
demanding fifty Continental dollars for one dollar in specie.[10] "The depression of 1785 occurred," according to one
historian, "because a country just finishing an exhausting
seven years of war was not in a condition to pay for large
importations no matter how much they were needed in order
to restore the pre-war standards of living."[11]

The Havenots noted with rising anger that the very justices
of the peace who sat as judges in the Courts of Common Pleas
and the General Sessions of the Peace were also the law-
makers in the Massachusetts General Court who insisted that
taxes must be paid in specie and who set exorbitant court fees
that lined the pockets of justices and lawyers alike. Witness
the fact that when Luke Day finally lost his case before the

Supreme Judicial Court in the matter of Prince Freeman he had to pay twenty-three pounds "lawful money" in damages—and nine pounds fifteen shillings in court costs.[12]

Many a man began to say in one form or another the immortal line of the rebel Dick the Butcher in Shakespeare's *Henry the Sixth* plays, "First thing we do, let's kill all the lawyers."[13]

On the twenty-first of April in 1780 the Town of West Springfield recorded its objection to the proposed new constitution for Massachusetts, stating that justices of the peace and ministers of the Gospel should be excluded from the General Court. On 15 January 1782 the town protested to the governor that the excise tax on distilled spirits "from the produce of our own orchards" was double the duty on New England rum. Such heavy excise taxes "bear down on the poor," the town declared. In March of 1782 a committee representing the town recommended a general impost on imported articles in place of excise taxes. It also recommended that each town be allowed to record its own land deeds, and that a number of probate districts be set up, pointing out that the cost of travel to the county seat in order to record deeds or probate wills was burdensome.

Western Massachusetts towns more hot-headed than West Springfield, which numbered a good many conservatives among its leaders,[14] began to call for direct and if need be violent action to reform the courts or close them, and to provide some relief from taxes. Disgruntled ex-soldiers, unable to hold on to their army notes until they matured and aware that speculators had bought up the notes at low cost and would cash them at face value, were in the forefront of the force that finally brought the commonwealth to the brink of civil war.[15] Leader of the group was a former captain in the Revolutionary army, Daniel Shays of Pelham, who commanded a group that was successful in preventing the sitting of many Courts of Common Pleas (which had jurisdiction over actions regarding debts) and in the end, in 1787, the

sitting of the Supreme Judicial Court itself, both at Springfield and elsewhere along its circuit in western Massachusetts.
Although Shays was considered the leader of the protesting
group, and although his name is attached to the rebellion,
historians agree that his number two man—Captain Luke
Day of West Springfield, he of the Prince Freeman case,
cousin and brother-in-law of Justin Morgan—was as active
in the uprising as was Shays.[16] Luke turned his men out on
the Common, drilled them, and placed in their hats the sprig
of green hemlock that was the badge of the insurgents.[17] Pro-
government men wore a bit of white paper in their hatbands,
and it is recorded that prudent men carried both badges in
their pockets.[18]

West Springfield, despite its basic conservatism, showed a
genuinely divided mind about the rebellion. The town seems
always to have sympathized with its inhabitants who were
caught in the toils of the money crisis. At the March meeting
in 1785 the town voted "a grant for James Phillip's rates for
which he is now confined in prison"—the grant being the
large sum of forty pounds. On the twenty-first of June in 1787
the town voted "to liberate Captain John Williston from
gaol"—he whose name headed the list of plaintiffs in the case
of John Williston, et al., vs. Luke Day, Gent., in the matter of
Prince Freeman. When West Springfield came to assess the
entire grim situation, it stated in its town record of 8 January
1787, "Civil war with all its horrors stares us in the face." It
pleaded with the General Court to repeal grants to Congress
of impost and supplementary aid, to abolish Courts of Common Pleas, to lessen government expense, and above all to
repeal its recent suspension of the sacred right of Habeas
Corpus.[19]

In the midst of all this pother, on 23 March 1784, the town
saw fit to elect Justin Morgan collector of taxes. Rather, it
acquiesced when Caleb Bliss and Warham Bagg, elected as
collectors, were excused "by hiring said Morgan to serve in
that capacity for them."[20] The harried commonwealth of

Massachusetts had provided a law by which constables and other tax collectors who could not raise the money they were expected to collect could have their own estates attached and if necessary sold at auction in order to raise the required money.[21] Furthermore, the Commonwealth had provided that a person chosen as a constable and not exempted because he had served as constable or collector of taxes within seven years or because he was currently holding some other office, must serve. Should he refuse to do so, he would be fined five pounds.[22] Still furthermore, "if a collector abscond or secrete himself for the space of a month," the selectmen may "file a declaration against his agent . . . for recovery of his rates, as other creditors have for recovery of their debts."[23] It will be seen that there could scarcely have been a rush to apply for the office of tax collector, even though the said collector was to receive two and a half percent of all that he collected for the commonwealth, county, and town.[24]

Morgans were constables and tax collectors at various times from 1776, when Ebenezer Morgan was elected constable, Joseph Morgan assessor, and Joseph's son Lieutenant Joseph selectman and a member of the town's Committee of Correspondence—on which Captain John Morgan also served. In 1778 Titus Morgan was constable. In 1782 Jesse Morgan was both constable and tax collector. Finally in 1784 it became Justin Morgan's turn. In November of that year the town awarded three pounds to Justin "in consideration of his collecting the taxes in the north part of the town." The following year, 1785, Justin was not elected a collector, but Ezekiel Morgan became constable. In May of that year Abner Morgan became a collector of taxes and promptly hired Deacon Pelatiah Bliss to serve in his place. The north part of the first parish had been divided into two districts, and Oliver Bagg, saddled with the job of tax collecting in the other district, also hired Deacon Bliss to take his place. In March 1786 the town voted "to inquire after absconding collectors" and to try to collect from them.

In 1787 Justin was again tax collector, and in December of that year the town voted to raise the sum of eighteen pounds eleven shillings and three-quarters of a penny, "out of which Justin Morgan is to be paid his collecting fees when they are due." The town then proceeded to grant to Justin Morgan "in discharge of Joseph Young's state tax, to pass to said Morgan's account with the treasurer, for overplus money on his state assessment committed to him," the sum of fifteen pounds three shillings threepence. Anyone who can deduce the meaning of the foregoing sentence will know precisely how Morgan and the town were handling the tax problem, and will doubtless also understand why varying amounts were granted "to do [ditto] in discharge of" Josiah Ward's, David Powers's, Gideon Jones's, Justin Morgan's, and Bushman Negro's taxes. In 1773 the town had voted "to indemnify and save harmless any constable who shall pay their province rates into the town treasury." It would seem that the town was attempting to help its tax collectors by setting up a fund into which the collector could place what he received, and out of which could be paid the amounts due state, county, and town.[25] In any case, Justin was apparently expected to collect from six people, including himself. We read that on the third of January in 1788 the town "voted Lt. Benjamin Ashley a collector to collect the arrears of Justin Morgans collection in the North Parish."

Nothing in the record indicates whether Justin was too soft-hearted or too inefficient to make the required collections. The state of affairs in Massachusetts in 1787 suggests that with the best will in the world many a man was simply unable to pay his taxes. On the twenty-fifth of July in that year Justin sold sixty-five rods, "the southerly part of my home lot," to Ebenezer Day. He received eight pounds two shillings for the land. One wonders if he needed the money to pay his—and perhaps other people's—taxes.

During most of 1787 it is probable that when West Springfield people were not thinking about taxes they were thinking about Shays's Rebellion and their fellow townsman Luke Day, who had helped to bring the war about their ears. He it was who gathered 400 insurgents at West Springfield, and he it was who failed to rendezvous with Shays in the crucial fight of the rebellion. When the rebellion had been broken and the government in June of 1788 went about the business of granting pardons, it stipulated that pardoned enlisted men might not, for the space of three years, be schoolmasters, innkeepers, or retailers of spirituous liquor. Now Justin Morgan was identified with two of these three callings, yet it is obvious from the fact that he was a tax collector in 1787 that he took no more part in his brother-in-law's war than he had in the Colonies'. However much he felt the pinch of hard times, he seems to have been a man of peace.

When the rebellion was quelled in Massachusetts, a number of its ringleaders fled to Vermont, New York, and New Hampshire. Others who had taken little if any part in the rebellion but who were in financial straits also flocked to the northern frontier country. It is probable that Vermont owes a debt of gratitude to Shays's Rebellion and the depression of 1785 for some of its most interesting pioneers—among them, perhaps, Justin Morgan.

The poor men who already lived in Vermont were sympathetic with the poor men who arrived in the late 1780s. Both Shays and Day spent some time in Vermont, but the people somehow seemed unable to point out to pursuing Massachusetts officers where the ringleaders of the rebellion were.[26] In November of 1786 Vermont had had its own taste of near-violence when a mob had gathered at Windsor and attempted to prevent the Court of Common Pleas from sitting. The crowd had dispersed after the Riot Act had been read; but sturdy farmer-governor Thomas Chittenden showed awareness of the problems of both the Haves and the Havenots when he declared, "In the time of the war we were obliged to follow the example of Joshua of old, who commanded the sun to stand still while he fought his battle; we commanded our creditors to stand still while we fought our enemies."[27] The creditors, he implied, could not be expected to stand still forever; yet on the other hand he recommended that "a small bank of money" be issued to relieve the debtors, who both in Massachusetts and in Vermont had been clamoring for more "paper money" that would, they felt, somehow pay their debts.

Mary Palmer Tyler, wife of Royall Tyler, who was soon to be Vermont's chief justice, said that in the 1790s Vermont was considered "the outskirts of creation by many, and where all the rogues and runaways congregated."[28] The rogues and runaways—and the simple poor folk who could not pay their debts—prevailed. In 1787 both Vermont and Massachusetts passed "specific tender" acts that allowed men to pay their creditors in certain farm commodities such as neat cattle and wheat, in lieu of cash.[29] Vermont had already passed a law, in 1785, which did much to help men of limited means. The law, proposed by Governor Chittenden and revised in a form that made it acceptable to the lawyers by Nathaniel Chipman, a member of the legislature who was later to become a chief justice of Vermont and a United States senator, provided that settlers who were evicted from farms on which the titles were not clear should receive the full value of their improvements and half the "rise of the land."[30]

Justin Morgan, yeoman and singing master, came to Vermont on the tide of settlement that rolled northward as men sought a second chance.

Notes

1. Hampshire County, Mass., Records of the Court of Common Pleas, Book 17, p. 73. These records are maintained by the Clerk of the Superior Court of Hampshire County in the county courthouse in Northampton.

2. It seems to have been a general practice to appeal the judgments of the Court of Common Pleas, both as a delaying tactic and as a means of questioning the validity of the courts' judgments. See Robert J. Taylor, *Western Massachusetts in the Revolution* (Providence, R.I.: Brown University Press, 1954), p. 29.

3. Since the payments that were to be made, under the provisions of the deed, were seventy-three pounds plus interest by 15 December and forty pounds fifteen shillings plus interest by the first of June, it seems evident that the intention was to pay back the 124 pounds named as the amount of the "sale," with interest. See Hampshire County, Land Records, Box 24, p. 176.

4. Henry A. Booth, "Springfield during the Revolution," *Papers and Proceedings of the Connecticut Valley Historical Society* 2 (1904):306.

5. Apparently a number of Springfield people of Elizabeth Dwight's time felt sympathy for blacks caught in the toils of slavery. A score of years after the Prince Freeman case was tried, a subscription was raised to free a Negro woman, Jenny, alias Dinah, who had been seized in her home in Springfield and returned to her master in the state of New York. Among the subscribers was another "Mrs. Dwight," presumably the wife of one of Elizabeth Dwight's sons. She gave five dollars—a large sum in that day (Henry Morris, "Slavery in the Connecticut Valley," *Papers and Proceedings of the Connecticut Valley Historical Society* 1 (1881):214.

6. Williston et al. vs. L. Day, Records of [Massachusetts] Supreme Judicial Court, II, 222, on file in Clerk's Office, County of Suffolk, Commonwealth of Massachusetts, Boston. The sitting was held in Springfield for Hampshire County the fourth Tuesday of September, 1783.

7. The writer is indebted to the National Archives and Records Service of the General Services Administration, Washington, D.C., for supplying copies of records regarding the several Prince Freemans.

8. Taylor, *Western Massachusetts*, p. 104.

9. Stephen Morgan and his wife, the former Mary Bagg, were in Randolph at least by 6 June 1787, when their daughter Lucretia was born in that Vermont town.

10. Margaret E. Martin, *Merchants and Traders of the Connecticut River Valley, 1750-1820*, Smith College Studies in History, 24, Nos. 1-4 (Northampton, Mass.: Smith College Department of History, 1938-39), p. 37.

11. Ibid., p. 42.

12. See above, p. 109.

13. William Shakespeare, *The Second Part of King Henry the Sixth*, act 4 sc. 2, line 84.

14. West Springfield had no powerful "river gods"—no great landowner, merchant, or holder of high political or military office such as John Stoddard of Northampton or Israel Williams of Hatfield or John Worthington of Springfield—to side with what has been called the "prerogative party" (Taylor, *Western Massachusetts, p. 11*). It did, however, have substantial merchants, land owners, and farmers who, with property to protect, tended to support the status quo. Typical of these leading citizens was Justin Ely, Esq., a merchant who speculated widely in land in Vermont and elsewhere, who was selectman in 1775 and West Springfield's representative in the General Court from 1780 to 1785 and again from 1790 to 1797. It was not until soaring inflation and other financial woes began to threaten even sizeable farms because men could not raise the money to pay their taxes that some of West Springfield's citizens—especially those who did not have the resources of a Justin Ely—moved toward the position of the Shaysites.

15. Taylor, *Western Massachusetts*, p. 147.

16. Ibid., p. 157.

17. Bagg, *Account of the Centennial Celebration of the Town of West Springfield, Mass.*, p. 126.

18. William L. Smith, "Springfield in the Insurrection of 1786 (Shays's Rebellion)," *Papers and Proceedings of the Connecticut Valley Historical Society* 1 (1881): 79.

19. West Springfield, book 1 for Recording Town Acts, p. 341.

20. Ibid., p. 267.

21. Law of 1786, described in Samuel Freeman, *The Town Officer* (Boston: Thomas and Andrews, 1808), pp. 137-38.

22. Ibid., p. 151.

23. Ibid., p. 159.

24. West Springfield, book 1 for Recording Town Acts, 8 March 1780, p. 136.

25. The writer is indebted to Professor Andrew Nuquist of the political science department, University of Vermont, for suggesting that this fairly common eighteenth-century procedure was being followed in Justin Morgan's West Springfield.

26. Royall Tyler, on orders from Major General Benjamin Lincoln to apprehend the fleeing ringleaders, wrote from Bennington, Vt., 22 February 1787, "Luke Day was yesterday half an hour in this town and I couldn't with the assistance of the first characters here prevail upon the sheriff or constable to apprehend him . . . whilst we disputed he moved off" (Letters, 1787-1882, Royall Tyler Collection, Vermont Historical Society, Montpelier, Vt., quoted by permission of the Society). The letter seems to have been addressed either to General Lincoln or to Massachusetts's Governor James Bowdoin.

27. *Vermont Gazette*, 28 August 1786, and *Vermont Journal*, 4 September 1786, as quoted in E. P. Walton, ed., *Records of the Council of Safety and Governor and Council of the State of Vermont* (Montpelier, Vt.: J. and J. M. Poland, 1873), 1:358.

28. See above, p. 37, n. 17.

29. Walton, ed., *Records of the Council of Safety*, 1:375. George Richards Minot, in *The History of the Insurrections in Massachusetts in the Year 1786 and the Rebellion Consequent Thereon*, 2d ed. (Boston, James W. Burditt & Co., 1810), explains that Massachusetts passed a "tender act" in 1782 that permitted people to pay their private debts in neat cattle and other named commodities but required them to continue to pay their public debts (taxes) in specie. In October of 1787 the General Court passed an act that allowed for the payment of taxes in specific articles at fixed prices (Minot, pp. 14 and 59).

30. Daniel Chipman, *The Life of Hon. Nathaniel Chipman, LL.D.* (Boston: Charles C. Little and James Brown, 1846), p. 64. The lawyers objected that the bill compelled the legal owner "to pay a man a bounty for trespass"; but Chipman's revision of this "quieting bill" answered the legal objections, and the law was so popular in Vermont that some "sister states" adopted a similar system.

Something of the vision of Vermont pioneers, even while they struggled to clear land and then to establish a legal claim to that land, is indicated by Chipman's reasons for advocating that Vermont enter the new United States. His brother Daniel reports (p. 87) that in a speech made at a convention in Bennington in January 1791—a convention called to determine whether Vermont should "accede to the union"—Nathaniel Chipman declared that entry into the union would promote "learning and liberal science." He explained,

> Confined to the narrow bounds of Vermont, genius, for want of great occasions and great objects to expand the powers of the mind, will languish in obscurity. The spirit of learning, from which states and kingdoms derive more solid glory than from all heroic achievements, and by which individuals, raised above the common lot of humanity, are enabled to contribute to the happiness of millions in distant parts of the globe, will be contracted, and busy itself only in small scenes. . . . In proportion as the views are more confined, more limited, and more local, the more is the mind contracted by local prejudices. But, received into the bosom of the union, we become bretheren and fellow-citizens with more than three millions of people. . . . Genius will soar to the heights of science. . . .

——— 7 ———

A Decade in Vermont

JUSTIN MORGAN, caught like many another man in the jaws of the post-Revolutionary depression and unrest, moved to Vermont. On the twelfth of March in 1788 Justin and Martha Morgan sold to Abner Morgan, the son of Justin's first cousin Lieutenant Nathan Morgan (who was married to Mary Day, first cousin of Martha), their remaining two-thirds of an acre, with their house and barn. The property was bounded on the east by the highway, on the north by Joseph Ashley's home lot, on the west by Warham Bagg, on the south by Ebenezer Day. The Morgans were leaving their cousins and lifelong friends—but they were to find Morgans and Days and Baggs scattered here and there in Vermont. The sale brought Justin and Martha thirty-three pounds seventeen shillings. Or did some of that money go to clear up the taxes that Justin was supposed to collect, and a part of which Lieutenant Benjamin Ashley presumably did collect? If they were in fact allowed to keep the whole sum, then it is apparent that Justin began, when he was twenty-four, by paying sixty pounds for thirty acres of land, and ended, when he was forty-one, with about forty-one pounds (from the sale to Ebenezer Day in July of 1787 and the sale to Abner Morgan in March of 1788)—and no land. He had, of course, had the use of the land in the intervening years. The Morgans had lived, brought forth and nourished their children, bred horses and taught music and sold liquor, tried to run a grist mill, spun flax and wool, woven cloth, listened to Parson Lathrop's sermons. Did Morgan ever conduct the singing in the West Springfield church? No one knows. The record speaks of Deacon Pelatiah Bliss's leading of the singing for many years.[1] About Morgan, no one knows.

In the 1880s, when interest in Morgan horses had risen to high tide, the industrious Joseph Battell of Middlebury, owner of broad acres, breeder of Morgan horses, editor of *The Middlebury Register*, and subsequently author of the massive three-volume *The Morgan Horse and Register* (Middlebury, Vermont, 1894-1915), ran a series of columns in his newspaper on the probable ancestry of Morgan horses, and incidentally on the man Justin Morgan.[2] The letters and articles contributed to his newspaper by men who had themselves seen "the Morgan horse," or whose fathers had, give what seem to be some of the most authentic anecdotes about Morgan that now exist. Allen W. Thomson of Woodstock, in an article dated 2 October 1885, wrote that Morgan moved his family to Vermont "on an ox sled." When they arrived, according to another Thomson article (23 January 1885), the family settled "in a log house" near the northern border of Randolph where it touches the town of Brookfield. The spot, said Thomson, was "about forty rods from . . . where Judge Frederic Griswold lived." One knows that the Griswolds had Springfield connections; one knows also that the Reverend Joseph Lathrop had speculated, or invested, in land in Brookfield, just above that Randolph border—as had his sons, Seth and Joseph and Samuel. From whom Morgan rented his house, or how he perhaps "went shares" or worked for someone else in order to provide his family with a house, is not known. The records seem to indicate that during the remaining ten years of Morgan's life he owned no "home farm" in Randolph.

The Randolph of 1790, as has been said, was a very different place from the West Springfield of that date.[3] The Morgans had left the largest town in western Massachusetts—a place of 2,367 inhabitants—which for more than a century had been settling down into the life of an established, civilized community. Parson Lathrop's sermons were printed and published; when General Riedesel and his captured Hessians came through town en route to Cambridge, the general was entertained by Mr. Lathrop—and the two talked Latin together, since Lathrop knew no German and Riedesel no English.[4] In Randolph, things were different. There were 893 inhabitants by 1790, and a great broad street had been laid out through Randolph Center in the hope that a good-sized village would grow up around it.[5] But in a 1793 Vermont newspaper is the account of a woman, lost in the woods, who kept herself alive by milking her own breasts.[6] True, the event took place in mountainous and woody Sunderland in the southwest corner of the state and not in Randolph, which already possessed considerable rolling meadowland; but it did take place in Vermont. Surely no one in West Springfield had had to resort to such an emergency method of survival for a century or more.

It will be obvious that the Morgan who came to Vermont in 1788 was not the "loner" of popular American legend.[7] He was, in fact, the "land-hungry nester" who has been described as the typical pioneer who came from settled Massachusetts and Connecticut to the New England frontier.[8] He brought with him his wife and children, and possibly his widowed sister Eunice Miller and some or all of her children. Accounts of Morgan's coming to Vermont, and of his early widowerhood, stress the fact that he had a small son, Justin (born 15 March 1786), and a small daughter, Emily (born 16 February 1784), and that shortly after the Morgans arrived in Randolph another baby, Nancy, was born to them (3 September 1788).[9] The last child in the family, Polly, was born, also in Randolph, 10 March 1791. Most stories of Morgan picture him as surrounded by very young children when his wife Martha died in 1791 and fail to mention the fact that the oldest daughter in the family, Martha, born 13 May 1776, apparently accompanied her parents to Randolph and certainly married and had her own family in Vermont. A man who has a fifteen-year-old daughter to help him when his wife dies is quite a different matter from a widower whose oldest child is seven.[10]

As for Morgan's sister, Eunice Miller, news of her surfaces in a *Middlebury Register* article of 23 January 1885. The writer states that Morgan's widowed sister came with him to Randolph with her son and daughter. Eunice Morgan, born 1741, married Ebenezer Miller the third in West Springfield. The last of Ebenezer's seven children, a daughter Eunice, was born posthumously, arriving on the sixteenth of July in 1776, when her father had died on the twenty-eighth of May. It is apparent from the Randolph records that several of Eunice's children either came with her to Randolph or arrived later. We read of Heman, born 1763; Moses, born 1767; and Daniel, born 1773.[11]

The *Middlebury Register* article that mentions Morgan's sister also declares that "Mr. Morgan" had two brothers who lived in Randolph, "Calif and Stephen." "Calif" turns out to be Caleb (eight years older than his brother Justin), who first settled in Brattleboro at least before 21 May 1779, when a daughter, Tabitha, was born to Caleb and Ann (Brooks) Morgan in that town. The last child of Caleb and Ann to have been born in the old home, West Springfield, Massachusetts, was Catherine, born in 1777. Caleb and Ann lost six of their eight children in what must have been a dreadful epidemic of diphtheria, or some similar disease, in the fall of 1791. Only Tabitha, aged twelve, and Rufus, aged ten, survived. Tabitha grew up to marry Phinehas Smith, who moved from Brattleboro to Randolph in 1799, and land records reveal that in April of 1803 Phinehas sold his father-in-law Caleb Morgan, still listed as "of Brattleboro," fifty acres of land in Randolph. Caleb had sold his Brattleboro property a year earlier, in September of 1802. It is evident that he did not move to Randoph until some five years after his brother Justin died;

but his grave in the Randolph Center cemetery is very near to Justin's, and Caleb's surviving son Rufus, cousin to Justin's children, brought up a large family in Randolph. Justin's brother Stephen, as has been said, was already living in Randolph at some time before 1787.[12] The 1790 census does not list Stephen, but it does list Aaron Smith and his wife Jerusha (Day) Smith, the sister of Martha Morgan.

Justin Morgan came to Vermont not as a loner but as a member of a clan.

The public record of Morgan's life during his Vermont decade indicates that Justin Morgan, yeoman, kept on trying to farm and to breed horses, just as he had done in Massachusetts. There is some evidence that he also tried once more to become a "freeholder"—an owner of that most precious eighteenth-century commodity, land. In March of 1789, less than a year after he arrived in Vermont, Justin added a new activity to his repertoire—that of a town official of some importance. At the March town meeting in 1789 Randolph elected Justin Morgan, then forty-two years of age, a "lister" and grandjuryman. Evidently the town found Morgan's schoolmaster accomplishments—perhaps especially his clerkly handwriting —of value, since in the following year, in March 1790, they elected him town clerk and treasurer, positions that he held until 1793. Thus Morgan obtained the prized title of "Squire," reserved in the New England of his day for lawyers and public officials.[13]

Morgan's buying and selling of land present a far greater puzzle than does his clerkship. It has been suggested, since in some cases Morgan apparently held title to a piece of land for only a few days, that he was acting as the "straw man" of real estate deals in which members of a family, perhaps, wished to pass a piece of property through a third person's hands to insure the validity of the transaction.[14] Yet there is evidence that Morgan held some land for a considerable length of time and that most of the land was a part of "Lot Thirty-Three" in the original proprietors' division of the town, an area in the southeastern corner of town some miles distant from the area where Morgan presumably lived. In the fall of 1792 Morgan bought some 240 acres from Andrew McKinney of Elington, Connecticut, paying one hundred pounds for the land. Almost at once he sold eighty acres of this land to Joseph York, for twenty pounds. Records of the Orange County Court, sitting in Newbury 10 June 1793, disclose a suit brought by Justin Morgan against Joseph York, in which York defaulted and Morgan was awarded ten pounds eight shillings plus costs. It appears that York sold back to Morgan forty acres of "Lot 33" on the twentieth of September 1793—for ten pounds. Presumably York was satisfying the claim against him by this means.

Four days later Joel Smith of Sharon, Vermont, son of Martha Morgan's sister Jerusha Smith, sold to Morgan some forty acres for which Morgan paid a little over thiry-three pounds. Quite incredibly, Morgan two days thereafter sold the same piece of land to William Rice, storekeeper and sometime buyer and seller of real estate, for 110 pounds. The following July 5, 1794, Morgan sold to Rice his remaining two hundred acres for 120 pounds—and thereafter owned no land in Randolph. The deals with Rice are especially puzzling, particularly when the 23 January 1885 issue of the *Middlebury Register* states that William Rice "was a dishonest man, and it is believed he cheated Mr. Morgan out of what he had." The picture is further clouded when one turns to Justin Morgan's probate record and discovers that in the first inventory of Morgan's estate, made 2 October 1798, the appraisers listed as Morgan assets a "stock note against William Rice" valued at $25.00 and a "cash note against William Rice" valued at $94.24—but on 14 August 1799 the administrator, Ezra Egerton, "prayed allowance" for "one note vs. William Rice wrongly inventoryd 25.00, same, 94.24."[15]

Whatever Morgan was doing or trying to do with real estate, there is evidence that he was still trying to farm. In December of 1795 Morgan brought action, in an Orange

County court held at Newbury, against Ephraim Tucker of Moretown, for "trespass." It develops that on the first of December in 1792 Justin Morgan was "seized and possessed" of 207 shocks of good wheat valued at fifty pounds lawful money and eight shocks of good oats valued at four pounds lawful money. Morgan still possessed this grain on 2 April 1793, but on that day "out of his hands and possession" it was "casually lost"—and "by finding came into the hands and possession of the said Ephraim who well knew the same to belong to the Plaintiff." Even when one discovers that "casually" meant "accidentally" in the eighteenth century, the thought of someone accidentally losing 207 shocks of wheat is little short of staggering. How and where did Ephraim "find" it? In any case, Justin won twelve pounds three shillings eight pence (plus costs of twenty pounds, nineteen shillings, four pence) as a result of this trial. It is obvious that Justin was trying to farm, on somebody's land, somewhere.

During these years of the early 1790s Morgan was continuing to advertise a stallion at stud, as will be seen. He was also, presumably, continuing his activities as singing master and writing master, although of these interests there is no evidence other than the books that he owned when he died and the anecdotes that were told of him fifty or more years after his death.

Morgan's life as a member of the church continued, as is indicated by the statement in the Randolph church records of 1794 that Justin Morgan and his wife, Martha, were admitted to the church in 1789, having transferred their membership by letter from West Springfield, Massachusetts.[16] The church, which had been organized in 1786 and at first had occupied a log cabin, in 1791 determined to build "a meeting house which should be of such proportions that the Sunday worship should carry along with it the recollections of the pinnacle, belfry, pulpit, tripple galleries and high box pews and the broad aisles of the old Somers meeting house in Connecticut."[17] In November of 1791 the church held a

The church in which Morgan worshipped during the last ten years of his life was this first church erected in Randolph, Vt. The meeting house was begun in 1791 and was designed to "carry along with it the recollections of the pinnacle, belfry, pulpit, tripple galleries and high box pews and the broad aisles of the old Somers meeting house in Connecticut." The drawing by an unknown artist, which shows the nearby graveyard in which Justin Morgan is buried, and Killington peak looming in the background, forms the frontispiece of *Memoirs of Mrs. Emily Egerton* written by Rufus Nutting and published in 1832. In the drawing the funeral procession carries the bier of Emily Egerton, a daughter of Justin Morgan, from her house to the church. *Courtesy Vermont Historical Society.*

"vendue" of pews, selling some for as much as fifty pounds to so affluent a man as Captain Timothy Edson, who was charged with the actual building of the new meeting house. Justin Morgan's name does not appear among the buyers of the original pews—but when he died he possessed "One Third of Pew No. 38 on the lower floor in Meetg House."

The minister of the church throughout Morgan's years in Randolph was the Reverend Elijah Brainard, a Dartmouth graduate and Randolph's first "settled minister." The attitude of the church on doctrinal matters is suggested by a letter that Mr. Brainard sent to the moderator of the town meeting on 30 March 1795, when illness forced him to seek a substitute to fill his pulpit for a time.[18] The pastor offered to try to find a "candidate" to preach for him, saying that he would pay such a substitute one pound four shillings per Sabbath, the sum to be provided out of his own salary "next January." He would secure, Mr. Brainard declared, "a regular and sentimental preacher of the gospel." Since *sentimental* was defined, in the late eighteenth century, as "characterized by refined and elevated feelings," one may assume that the term was meant to be laudatory, and one may sense in it some of that approval of the expression of spontaneous feeling that was characteristic of the developing romanticism of the era. The term *regular* of course meant that the proposed substitute would adhere, as Mr. Brainard must have, to the basically Calvinistic tenets embodid in the Confession of Faith accepted by the church in 1786. In that Confession the church members, after affirming their belief in "one eternal only living triune God, Father, Son, and Holy Ghost," went on to state their belief that "all who believe in him are justified, and shall be kept, by the mighty power of God, through faith unto Salvation"—and that "at the last day Christ shall descend from Heaven and condemn all ungodly men to everlasting fire."[19] A woman who could not rid herself of her belief in universal salvation was excommunicated;[20] as late as 1802 Brother Andrew Steele was censured for believing in universal salvation, although he finally admitted to the error of his ways.[21]

Toward the end of the century, and toward the end of Morgan's life, Mr. Brainard and his parishioners parted company. His recurrent illnesses sometimes kept him from his duties, and apparently he and the town did not see eye to eye about his salary. The church records grew increasingly full of salary discussions, until on the twentieth of December in 1797 the church asked its pastor "to take dismission because he is sick and unable to officiate."[22] On the fourth of January 1798, less than three months before Justin Morgan died, Mr. Brainard was dismissed.[23] Two preachers, Mr. Lathrop of West Springfield and Mr. Brainard of Randolph, both orthodox but apparently far from narrow Congregationalists, had provided Justin Morgan with spiritual leadership throughout his lifetime.

There is no evidence as to Justin Morgan's possible role in the musical life of the church after he came to Vermont, although there is evidence of the church's interest in good music, both in Randolph and in neighboring communities. As early as 1793 Caty Doty, first schoolteacher in Randolph's neighbor-town of Brookfield, wrote to her parents in Montpelier that they must both "come and go to meeting; they have a fine minister and good singing."[24] Records of the Randolph Church did not mention music until 1802, four years after Morgan's death. In that year the church voted that "brothers Asahel Woodward, Moses Pearson, Oliver Egerton, and Samuel Steel be a committee to select tunes for singing in the church at communion." The four men were also enjoined to lead the singing and to furnish "such members of the church as may be able to sing with the tunes they may select."[25] In that same year, Randolph having acquired a newspaper in 1800, the *Weekly Wanderer* of 25 December called on "all those who are desirous of promoting that glorious part of public worship, SINGING, in Randolph" to meet at the house of Mr. Jonathan Smith, on Monday evening next.

Justin Morgan's family life underwent great changes dur-

ing his years in Vermont. His last two children, Nancy and
Polly, were born in Randolph—Nancy a short time after the
Morgans arrived in 1788 (September 3) and Polly on the tenth
of March in 1791. Ten days after the birth of Polly, Martha
Day Morgan, who had been baptized on the twenty-seventh of
May in 1753, died. The stone that marks Martha Morgan's
grave in the cemetery in Randolph Center reads "Martha
Morgan, Wife of Justin Morgan, Died 20 March 1791, About
the 40th year of her age." How does it happen that those who
marked the grave did not know the precise age of this woman
who, married at twenty-one, had spent almost seventeen loyal
years at the side of her husband? She had borne seven children, and she died before she reached her thirty-eighth birth-
day. What Morgan felt about her, and about her death, seems
to reveal itself best in his music.

There is another, more pedestrian account of how he faced
the loss of his wife—an account that does not ring true to one
who studies the uncompromising statements of what Morgan evidently viewed as religious truth: the texts he chose to
set to music. When in 1832 a memoir of the short life of
Morgan's daughter, Emily Egerton, was prepared by the
Reverend Rufus Nutting, the tone of the narrative is that of a
Sunday school tract. The narrator reports that the father,
Justin Morgan, said to seven-year-old Emily one day on her
return from school, "Come Emily, my dear, come quick with
your little brother and sisters. Your dear mamma is very sick;
perhaps she is going to heaven!" A deathbed scene follows
during which the mother reminds her children "of the love of
Jesus; of the faithfulness of Him who has promised—'When
thy father and thy mother forsake thee, then the Lord will
take thee up.'" The narrative described Morgan as "an excellent instructor of youth; and an engaged Christian." There is
no mention whatever of Morgan the farmer, Morgan the
breeder of horses, Morgan the town clerk, Morgan the composer and singing master.[26]

The memoir correctly states that Emily was the second of

five children; and since the memoir is indeed of Emily, perhaps there was no need to mention the fifteen-year-old daughter Martha, and what role, if any, she played in the care of the family at the time of her mother's death. It seems evident, however, that the narrative's emphasis upon seven-year-old Emily and her younger brother and sisters and its description of Morgan simply as "an instructor of youth" did much to create the popular image of Morgan the frail schoolmaster, surrounded, at the death of his wife, by a flock of small children.[27]

No gap in the history of Justin Morgan is wider than that which should be filled with the life story of his oldest daughter, Martha. Only if one happens on Evelyn Lovejoy's *History of Royalton, Vermont* does one find casual mention of "Mrs. Patty, daughter of Justin Morgan of Randolph and widow of Barzillai [?] Thacher of Tunbridge," who in 1814 married Jacob Cady of Royalton, and after Cady's death took as her third husband Captain Amasa Edson of Brookfield.[28] The third marriage took place in 1826, when Martha was fifty. By her first husband Martha had five children, and there are probably more descendants of Justin Morgan through this line than through that of any of his other children.

It develops that Martha's first husband was Bliss Thatcher (sometimes spelled *Thacher*), a resident of Norwich, Vermont (listed as the head of a family there in the census of 1790), and a member of a pioneer family in that town. He moved to the Randolph-Tunbridge border some time in the early 1790s, perhaps just after he acted as executor for the will of his father, Peter Thatcher, in 1791.[29] Bliss, listed as a yeoman "of Randolph," sold land in Norwich to his brother Peter in May 1794, and in 1796 and 1797 bought two pieces of land in Randolph. Both of these were sold by June 1799,[30] and there is evidence that Bliss and Martha Thatcher had moved from Randolph by the turn of the century, or shortly thereafter.[31]

Although the vital records of Vermont do not reveal either

the time or the place of Martha Morgan's marriage to Bliss Thatcher, and although the records are equally silent as to the time and place of the births of their children, Bliss's name appears in the probate records that deal with Justin Morgan's estate. At a court of probate held in Randolph 30 April 1798 Ezra Egerton, who by that date was foster father of Justin's daughter Nancy, was named administrator of the estate. He "accepted of said trust and with Bliss Thatcher of said Randolph became bound in the sum of six hundred dollars security" for the faithful administration of the trust.

Once again, the 1885 articles in the *Middlebury Register* seem to shed some light on the question of Martha Thatcher and of Justin Morgan's household affairs generally. Allen W. Thomson's article of 2 October declares that in 1793 Morgan "sold all of his real estate and broke up keeping house." The land records show that Morgan's last real estate transaction in Randolph occurred in July of 1794. If, however, he did break up housekeeping in 1793, it seems possible that he did so when his daughter Martha, by that time seventeen, married and left her father's house in order to establish her own home. One learns that at some time during these years Justin, in the words of the Emily Egerton memoir, "determined to place his children in the families of some of his judicious and pious friends."[32] Emily and her brother Justin went to the household of David and Elizabeth Carpenter, whose family of three children included a boy slightly younger than Justin and a girl slightly younger than Emily. Ezra and Anna Egerton welcomed Nancy Morgan, whom Ezra in his will, made 12 October 1801, described as "our adopted daughter given to me by Justin Morgan her natural parent."[33] It is not clear who looked after Polly, but since she married in Randolph, presumably she also was reared in that town. Perhaps her sister Martha cared for the youngest of the family. It is clear that the children remained in close contact, since one learns that after Martha and Bliss Thatcher left Randolph, their daughter Emily "made her home as a girl with her Uncle Asa Egerton in Randolph.''[34] Since Asa Egerton married Justin's daughter Emily in 1806, it appears that Emily had her niece and namesake in her household perhaps even before the birth in 1807 of her own first child, Albert Mirabeau Egerton.

It is interesting that no attempt was made, apparently, to place the Morgan children in the households of their various relatives, including the uncles and aunts who were living in Randolph and surrounding towns. Justin Morgan seems to have followed the English custom, which harked back to the Middle Ages, of placing his children in substantial households that could offer the best opportunities available for education and advancement. It appears that Justin, Jr. did not leave the Carpenter household until he was of age, presumably in 1807, when he felt free to go to Stockbridge and begin to make his own way there as a storekeeper.[35] Perhaps, as Emily's memoir suggests, similarity of religious attitude, as well as opportunity for sound education, was of special importance to Justin Morgan. The cemetery in Randolph Center bears evidence of the Egertons' deep religious convictions. Although many gravestones of the era simply list names with birth and death dates, Ezra Egerton's gravestone adds ''Blessed are the dead who die in the Lord''; and his wife Anne (listed also as second wife of Deacon Isaac Palmer) has on her headstone, ''I know that my redeemer liveth, that He will stand at the latter day upon the earth, whom I shall see for myself. . . .''

The tie among the Carpenters, the Egertons, and the Morgans must have been one of affection. One learns from Justin, Jr.'s son Charles Morgan that Justin Morgan died at the Carpenter farm, which was located about two miles south of the Meeting House in Randolph Center.[36] Nancy Morgan, who married Rufus Adams in 1815, named her children Ezra Egerton Adams, Anna Egerton Adams, Martha Maria Adams, Justin Morgan Adams, and Emily Adams. There is a ''Martha Elizabeth'' among Justin, Jr.'s children. Each of the four Justin Morgan children who had issue saw to it that one of his or her children carried on the name "Justin Morgan." Thus there is Justin Morgan Thatcher, son of Martha; Justin Egerton, who died in infancy, son of Emily; Justin Morgan III, son of Justin, Jr.; and Justin Morgan Adams, son of Nancy. Justin Morgan Thatcher in turn named his son Justin Morgan Thatcher, Jr.—and that son named his son Justin.[37]

Notes

1. J. N. Bagg, *Account of the Centennial Celebration of the Town of West Springfield, Mass.*, p. 89.

2. *The Middlebury Register and Addison County Journal*, January-October 1885.

3. See above, pp. 23-24.

4. First Congregational Church of West Springfield, *History of the First Parish and the First Congregational Church of West Springfield, Mass.*, undated pamphlet, p. 12.

5. See above, p. 21.

6. *Spooner's Vermont Journal* (Windsor), 6 May 1793.

7. See above, p. 45.

8. See above, p. 20.

9. Since an older Emily had been born in 1779, dying in 1784 just before the second Emily was born, and since an older Nancy had been born in 1781 and had died in 1786, it will be seen that the Morgans had seven children, of whom five grew to adulthood.

10. Although Daniel Chipman Linsley *(Morgan Horses: A Premium Essay* [New York: C.M. Saxton and Co., 1857]) correctly states that Morgan had five children, many later writers, including the editor of *Who Was Who,* credit him with only four.

11. The close tie between Justin and his sister Eunice is suggested by the fact that when Eunice's husban Ebenezer Miller 3d made his will on 27 May 1776 (Hampshire County Probate Records), he named his wife Eunice and her brothers Caleb and Justin as executors. The will was witnessed by another brother of Eunice, William Morgan, and by Ebenezer Miller's own cousin, Thomas Miller 2d—whose wife was Thankfull (Morgan) Miller, sister to Eunice, Justin, Caleb, and William. The *Middlebury Register* article of 1885 that mentions Justin's sister calls her "Eunice Williams," but all official vital records of Massachusetts and Vermont list her as Eunice Morgan, wife and widow of Ebenezer Miller 3d. The *Register* article states that Eunice's daughter married Jude Moulton, and the vital records of Vermont list Jude Moulton as marrying "Eunice Miller."

12. See above, p. 118. n. 9.

13. In the memoir of Morgan's daughter Emily Egerton, Morgan is called "Esq. Morgan" by Elizabeth (Mrs. David) Carpenter, who after the death of Morgan's wife Martha took young Emily and young Justin into her household (Rufus Nutting, *Memoirs of Mrs. Emily Egerton, an Authentic Narrative* [Boston: Perkins and Marvin, 1832], p. 7).

14. The writer is indebted to Mr. Wesley Herwig of Randolph, member of the

Randolph Historical Society, for suggesting this explanation of the appearance of Morgan's name as the fleeting owner of one and another piece of property in the Randolph of the 1790s.

15. It is interesting to discover that when Joseph Battell, editor of the *Middlebury Register*, came to use much of the Morgan material that had appeared in his newspaper as the basis for his extended treatment of the origin of "the Justin Morgan horse" in his *The Morgan Horse and Register* (Middlebury, Vt.: Register Printing Co., 1894-1915), he deleted the comment about Rice's alleged dishonesty. Battell states that the 23 January 1885 article in the *Register* was written by Allen W. Thomson of Woodstock, and had appeared earlier in an 1883 issue of *Turf, Field, and Farm*. Whatever the state of William Rice's honesty, his sense of humor certainly left much to be desired. Henry Swan Dana in his *History of Woodstock, Vt.* (Boston and New York: Houghton, Mifflin, 1889), p. 307, writes that Rice, who moved from Randolph to Woodstock in 1797, and who was for a time sheriff of Windsor County, was a "terrible joker." The evidence that Dana gives in support of this statement is an account of how Rice early one morning looked through a kitchen window in the house of a Mr. Richardson, and, seeing Richardson shaving himself, burst into the room and shouted that Richardson's son, who worked for Rice in a linseed oil mill, had just been crushed to death in the mill. The "joke" was the sight of the horrified Richardson running down the street, his shirt unbuttoned and his face half shaved—only to discover his son alive and well and working hard at the mill.

16. See above, p. 64, n. 12.

17. Nickerson and Cox, comps., *The Illustrated Historical Souvenir of Randolph, Vermont* (Randolph, 1895), p. 12.

18. File Folder No. 1, Miscellaneous Town Papers, Randolph town clerk's office.

19. First Congregational Church in Randolph, Records, book 1, hereafter cited as Church Records.

20. Church Records, bk. 2, p. 41, as quoted by Genieve Lamson, *The Heritage of Bethany Church* (Randolph, Vt., 1955), p. 6.

21. Church Records, bk. 1, p. 32.

22. Church Records, bk. 1, entry 20 December 1797.

23. Mr. Brainard later went to North Carolina, where he preached for some years. He died there in 1828.

24. Letter from Caty Doty to Capt. Barnabas Doty and Mrs. Catherine Doty, Montpelier, Vt., dated from Brookfield, Vt. 14 May 1793. The letter is No. 15 in a notebook of letters copied by Dr. Sarah Emery Youngman for the Vermont Historical Society from original manuscripts in the Hopkinton, N.H. Historical Society. The notebook is in the Vermont Historical Society manuscript collection, Misc. File No. 387.

25. Church Records, bk. 1, p. 32.

26. Nutting, *Memoirs of Mrs. Emily Egerton* p. 8.

27. The historical marker on the main street in Randolph Center reads in part: "Randolph, home of Justin Morgan. In 1791 schoolmaster Justin Morgan brought to Vermont the Colt that was to bear his name and to make them both famous. . . ." The evidence seems to indicate that Yeoman Justin Morgan—or by that time Squire Morgan—in the early summer of 1792 brought Figure, a young stallion which had already served at stud for one or possibly two seasons in Hartford, Conn., to Randolph. See below, pp. 166-67.

Another historical marker emphasizing the "schoolmaster" concept of Morgan is one in Woodstock, Vt. that marks the place where William Rice, one-time sheriff of Windsor County, lived. The marker reads: "On this site the progenitor of the famous

Morgan breed of horses was owned by Sheriff William Rice about 1800. Justin Morgan took his name from that of the singing schoolmaster who originally brought him to Vermont, but who lost possession of the later famous horse to Sheriff Rice in payment of a debt." See below, pp. 171-72, for this writer's view of how and to whom Morgan probably sold his horse.

28. Evelyn Lovejoy, *History of Royalton, Vermont* (Burlington, Vt.: Town of Royalton and the Royalton Woman's Club, 1911), p. 712. "Patty" seems to have been an almost universal nickname for "Martha" in the eighteenth century.

29. The will of Peter Thatcher, on record in the Hartford Probate District (1: 86-87) gives an interesting insight into the position of women in the 1790s. Peter Thatcher, husbandman, leaves to his beloved wife Lydia "the right to live in my house as her home" and "the privilege of a hors to ride to meeting and to perform other business which shall be necessary and comfortable . . . as long as she shall remain my widow with her industry when abel to labour to be recoverable out of my property." Four children receive five shillings each (in wheat), but Bliss receives all of his father's "goods, chattels, and lands."

30. Randolph Land Records, 2: 88; 2: 486; and 3: 57.

31. It appears that by 1803 Bliss and Martha Thatcher had joined the band that was beginning the country's westward march. They had gone to Chazy, a town just west of Lake Champlain in the northeastern corner of the state of New York—a town that was attracting a number of Vermonters. There Bliss was working on a new state road in 1803, and in 1805 his name appeared among the founding members of the Presbyterian-Congregational Church. Bliss Thatcher died in 1810 or 1811, and shortly thereafter his widow sold their Chazy property and returned to Vermont. Information on the Thatcher family's Chazy years is given in Nell Jane Barnett Sullivan and David Kendall Martin, *A History of the Town of Chazy, Clinton County, New York* (Burlington, Vt.: George Little Press, 1970), passim.

32. Nutting, *Memoirs of Mrs. Emily Egerton*, p. 7.

33. Records of Randolph Probate District, 1: 320.

34. Lovejoy, *History of Royalton, Vt.*, p. 712.

35. Harry H. Cooley, article on Justin Morgan printed in the *White River Valley Herald*, 15 September 1959. The Vermont law that provided that a child owed his earnings to his parents, guardian, or in the case of an apprentice to his master, until he was of age, in exchange for maintenance, education, and the training necessary to provide him with a livelihood was not finally repealed until the middle years of the twentieth century, although it had long been honored in the breach.

36. Interview with Charles Morgan of Rochester, Vt., printed in the *Middlebury Register*, 8 January 1886, as quoted by Battell, *The Morgan Horse and Register*, 1: 97.

37. Information about these children is scattered through Vermont vital records; Lovejoy's *History of Royalton;* other town and county histories; Carroll Andrew Edson, ed., *Edson Family History and Genealogy: Descendants of Samuel Edson of Salem and Bridgewater, Mass.* (Ann Arbor, Mich., n.d.); the *Boston Evening Transcript* genealogical column for 31 March 1930 (No. 9895); the Stockbridge, Vt. cemetery; and letters of the Justin Morgan III family now in the possession of his great granddaughters, Janet Morgan Mahony Wilson (Mrs. Robert Whitelaw Wilson) of Washington, D.C., and Mary Murray Mahony Brown (Mrs. Leland Scott Brown) of Bedford, N.Y.

——— 8 ———

Music-Maker

WHERE, amidst all the hurly-burly of horse-breeding, losing shocks of wheat, keeping town records, fighting court cases, presumably teaching singing and writing and perhaps common schools—where, among all the anxieties and sorrows of his personal life—where among all these insistent demands Justin Morgan found the leisure and the quietude necessary to make music, either to sing it, to conduct it, or above all to compose it, one can scarcely imagine. Yet the record is clear: Morgan took part in the performance of music and—most important for later generations—he composed music.

In a letter written 11 November 1791 the Reverend Andrew Law, then teaching music and peddling his tunebooks in and around Alexandria, Virginia, wrote to his brother William Law in Cheshire, Connecticut, "Mr. Spicer tells me he has done with Adgate, and shall return to his friends in Connecticut next Spring . . . he tells me that Morgan is teaching out of Adgates book and about 200 miles from this on Susquehannah River. . . ."[1] The story of Andrew Law of Connecticut, one of the most prominent singing masters of the late eighteenth century, a man whose voluminous publications did much to establish and change musical tastes and a man who was suspicious of any rival, is told in detail by Richard Crawford in his definitive biography, *Andrew Law, Amer-*

ican Psalmodist.[2] It is apparent from Crawford's account that one of Law's primary aims was to sell his many tunebooks and to see to it that singing masters throughout the country adopted those books. Therefore anyone who chose another book was looked upon with immediate suspicion. In early August, Law had written from near Winchester, Virginia, to his brother, "I have been within 40 miles of Carlisle [Pennsylvania], but can hear nothing of Mr. Morgan. Mr. Cook, who is near Baltimore, says he was not to return till fall, and that he was to let him know when he did return, and that he is sure he has not got back. . . . I am thinking he has been to see you upon the same plan that Benham did: to find out what we are about doing."[3]

Now it was Asahel Benham of Wallingford, Connecticut, who first published eight of Morgan's nine pieces that have survived, issuing them in the first edition of his *Federal Harmony* (New Haven, Conn.: Abel Morse, 1790) and continuing to include them in each of the six editions of his tunebook. This was the Benham "singing book" that was included in the inventory of Morgan's estate. It was Andrew Adgate of Philadelphia who, in a 1791 edition of a tunebook that changed its title with each new edition, published five of the Morgan tunes that had appeared in Benham and added "Despair," a Morgan tune not previously published. Adgate's book was actually two books—a short explanatory manual for musical beginners entitled *Rudiments of Music,* and a tunebook entitled *Philadelphia Harmony.* These two works were published, usually as one volume, in varying editions beginning in 1788, and it is in Part Two of the third edition of *Philadelphia Harmony,* which is bound with the fourth edition of the *Rudiments,* that Morgan's music first appears in this series. To be sure that bibliographers would remain on their toes, the publishers of this edition used the index of the 1790 edition, which in no way matches the contents of the book. Not until the 1796 edition of the work was published did the index match the contents and credit Morgan with his six tunes.

Early editions of the Adgate work state that the tunes were "selected by Adgate and Spicer"; and there are tunes by Spicer, including one called "Carlisle," in the 1789 edition. "Spicer" was Ishmael Spicer of Connecticut, a singing master whose success in Carlisle, Pennsylvania, Baltimore, Maryland, and points between aroused Law's jealousy.[4] "Adgate" was Andrew Adgate of Philadelphia, a manufacturer of "cards" (those currycomb-like objects essential in the smoothing out of good woolen fibers) and one of Philadelphia's finest musicians. He had assisted Andrew Law in the early 1790s and then had made the mistake of proving himself as able as his master.[5] Adgate not only published books of music, but he also organized fine concerts and even established a school, the "Uranian Academy," to which he boldly suggested that promising but indigent students should be admitted free, under the patronage of those who could afford to be patrons. He did more: he proposed, through his *Philadelphia Harmony,* that singers use the seven syllables (do, re, mi, fa, sol, la, si) familiar to modern students of music rather than the four repeated syllables (fa sol la fa sol la mi) that Law and other teachers were accustomed to using. As Crawford remarks, by the time that Adgate proposed this new way of identifying a particular syllable with a particular note, Adgate had become, to Law, "a touchstone of villainy."[6]

It is apparent from Andrew Law's letter of 11 November 1791 that although Spicer gave up the new Adgate system, Morgan did not. What is not apparent is how Morgan, busily running his affairs in Randolph, Vermont, could at the same time be someplace in Pennsylvania or across the Pennsylvanian border in New York. One has the feeling that he must be reading about two different people until he checks again and finds incontrovertible evidence that the Justin Morgan of Randolph was, indeed, the only Morgan "singing master" of New England in the 1790s. He then begins to check further and discovers that New Englanders of the period were far more peripatetic than a feebler and more recent breed might assume that one could have been, given the frozen or muddy forest trails of the 1790s. The life story of another of the Vermont psalmodists, Joel Harmon, Jr.,[7] suggests that it was almost routine for a busy farmer who was also a singing master to spend the long winter months traveling far afield to organize and conduct singing schools, and thus to piece out his farmer's livelihood.

In the case of Morgan, one is quite incredulous at the thought of his spending the fall of 1791 teaching singing someplace on the Susquehanna—until he checks the town records of Randolph and discovers that from the fourth of September to the sixth of December 1791, no deed is entered by the town clerk in the Randolph records. Then suddenly a number of deeds are recorded, some of them bearing dates as early as 26 May and jumping back and forth between 6 December and 1 August, as if a man had had a stack of papers piled up on his table, waiting to be recorded when he found the time to attend to that important business. One notes, further, that on 26 October 1791 Timothy Bayliss was clerk "pro tempore" at a Randolph town meeting.

In addition, an article by Margaret Gardiner on the pedigree of Morgan's horse reveals that in the fall of 1791 Justin Morgan paid Judge Griswold for the hire of a horse and saddle.[8] Miss Gardiner says that F. A. Wier, a Morgan horse enthusiast of the last century, made this discovery and speculated that Morgan used his hired horse to ride down to Springfield, Massachusetts, in order to collect the young stallion Figure; but evidence indicates that Morgan brought Figure to Vermont in the late spring of 1792.[9] It seems likely that Morgan hired the Griswold horse in 1791 for the long ride to the Susquehanna.

By laying a ruler along the map, one discovers that a spot 200 miles north of Alexandria, Virginia, on the Susquehanna River ends in the area of the Wyoming Valley—that part of Pennsylvania filled, thanks to the Susquehanna Company of

Connecticut, with so many New England settlers that for a few turbulent years (1776-82) the region was considered a Connecticut county. Not far to the north, across the border in New York but still along the Susquehanna River, there was even a town, Jericho (the present Bainbridge), most of whose land had been granted in 1786 to "the Vermont sufferers"— those Vermonters who had sided with New York in its long struggle with New Hampshire over which colony owned the area that later became Vermont. When Vermont declared itself an independent commonwealth in 1777, many of those who had sympathized with the "Yorkers" found themselves in trouble; during the 1780s dozens and scores of people went across into New York to found the new town of Jericho. On the list of early settlers there are Carpenters, Days, and Edgertons—names connected both with Springfield, Massachusetts, and with Randolph, Vermont, and names long familiar to Morgan.

There is, as usual, no newspaper advertisement to give proof, but Justin Morgan may have taught music in the New England communities along the Susquehanna in the fall of 1791—just as he may have avoided competing with better-known musicians in fashionable Philadelphia, farther to the south. Law's letters suggest that Morgan may have been at some time as far west as Carlisle, perhaps as far south as Baltimore. The Benham and Adgate tunebooks prove beyond a doubt that Morgan knew, perhaps by letter but probably personally, some well-known singing masters of his era.

If Morgan did in fact teach in Pennsylvania in the areas north and west of Philadelphia, it is quite likely that he met Spicer there, since Spicer seems to have been active throughout that region. The *Carlisle Gazette* of 27 May 1789 "assures the public" that Mr. Spicer and "as many of his scholars both from town and country as choose to attend, will sing many of the best pieces of church music, at the commencement" of the "Presbyterian College" (now Dickinson College) on Tuesday next. On August 5 of that year one reads of "the first meeting of the Carlisle Uranian Society," and presumes an Adgate influence in the naming of the society. A publication of that same year entitled *A Discourse on Psalmody* . . . by the Reverend Samuel Blair[10] describes a performance by Spicer and his students in the Presbyterian church in Neshaminy, that stronghold of Presbyterianism some twenty miles north of Philadelphia where the "Log College," predecessor of Princeton, was founded in 1727. The pamphlet states that the performers had been three months under Spicer's tutelage in separate schools in "several neighboring religious societies." They had not practiced together before the concert, yet their performance elicited from "a lady of judgment and taste in music," whose letter is printed in the booklet, the statement that the 250 singers, appearing before an audience of some 1,200 people, "surpassed my most sanguine expectations." She speaks of the "rural simplicity and elegance" of the handsome and well-dressed girls, and of "remarkably fine" voices. She declares that the parts were so well proportioned and the "time so accurately observed, that not a jar . . . offended the ear." When Spicer himself, who is described as "master in sacred music," addressed the congregation, he "could not omit mentioning . . . the obligations of society to Mr. Adgate, for his assiduity" in replacing "ill-measured dullness and harsh discord" with "well-ordered and commanding melody." Spicer urged churches to "institute proper choruses" so that entire congregations could follow them and unite heartily in the singing of sacred music. If Morgan was approved by men such as Spicer and Adgate, he was approved by able and well-known singing masters.

The connection of Morgan with Benham may have been based on long personal acquaintance as well as mutual interest in good music. Benham was born in New Hartford, Connecticut, in 1754, the son of Samuel and Phebe Benham, and spent most of his life in Wallingford, dying there in 1803. Both he and many other Benhams are mentioned frequently in the records of Wallingford and adjoining Cheshire, which was the stronghold of the Doolittles—and the Doolittles produced Eliakim, another of the psalmodists who taught singing schools in Vermont. One reads in the settling of the estate of Ambrose Doolittle, father of Eliakim, that heirs included two sisters of Eliakim—Eunice, "wife of Joseph Morgan," and Lois, "wife of Uri Benham."[11] Is it not likely that the musical Morgans and Benhams and Doolittles all knew each other? For Justin Morgan, there is a further link with Hartford, since two horses kept at stud at his stable in West Springfield were owned by Hartford men, and since any West Springfield man who took wagonloads of flour for sale to large centers of population would have been familiar with Hartford, the city downriver that had been an important shipping point for a century or more.

Andrew Law and his brother William took the same dim view of Benham that they did of Adgate and his followers. In a letter written from Cheshire in 1802, William declared to his brother Andrew in Philadelphia, "I am sorry to tell you that singing runs low in Cheshire nothing but the hideous cries of Benham and his party to be heard. . . ."[12] Daniel Read, another well-known composer and compiler of tunebooks and prominent citizen of New Haven, Connecticut, whose letter-books provide some of the most detailed information available regarding musical activities in the New England of 1790-1810,[13] also seems to suggest disapproval of Benham's business methods. Writing to Jacob French of Uxbridge, Massachusetts, on 10 June 1793, he said, "There has an anthem entitled the farewell by French been published here by one Asael Benham of Wallingford. I give you this info. because I think it my duty to do as I wd be done by."[14] Despite such views, Benham was apparently popular. The Reverend George Hood, writing about Benham in 1882, speaks of his "good mind and diligent reading," of his "noble face and fine address." He concludes, "With good sense and intelligence, correct morals and a kind heart, he retained the respect and love of his acquaintances."[15]

Where and when did Morgan's attentive inner ear first hear the music that appears in Benham's book? Was he following the plow when the tune "Amanda" came to him and fitted itself to the Ninetieth Psalm in the splendid Watts version? Was he following the plow in Vermont—or Massachusetts? How much did he write, beside the nine pieces that have survived? Other psalmodists wrote dozens, scores, hundreds of tunes, turning them out almost as one would pile cordwood or pare apples. Other psalmodists published fat books of their tunes. Morgan published no books, and how many of his compositions have been lost, one is not likely ever to know. It is possible that those that have survived, those that Benham and Adgate chose, were his finest.

One of Morgan's tunes, "Montgomery," is the only tune by a Vermonter to be included among the 100 psalm- and hymn-tunes "most frequently printed in American collections during the eighteenth century," as Richard Crawford has noted in giving these 100 tunes the title, "Core repertory."[16] After Benham's book came out, it did not take other compilers long to discover Morgan. Andrew Law himself, despite his feelings about anyone connected with Adgate, published "Amanda" and "Montgomery" in the third edition of his *Rudiments of Music,* issued in 1791. Jacob French, another well-known composer and compiler, included "Montgomery" in his tunebook of 1793, *The Psalmodist's Companion.* He, like several other compilers, did not acknowledge the composers of the tunes he included. Nehemiah Shumway's *American Harmony,* also published in 1793, included "Montgomery" and "Huntington." The next year Daniel Read—who had considered Benham's printing of an anthem by Jacob French irregular—included "Amanda," without acknowledgement, in his *The Columbian Harmonist, No. 2.* In 1797 Elias Mann included in his *The Northampton Collection of Sacred Music* both "Montgomery" and "Huntington"—and even credited Morgan with a third piece, "Ocean," which is usually credited to Timothy Swan or some other psalmodist, but which has many of the characteristics that one finds in Morgan's music.[17] *The New Jersey Harmony,* also published in 1797, included "Amanda," "Montgomery," "Huntington," and "Symphony"—with no acknowledgement. The popular *Village Harmony,* published in 1796 in Exeter, New Hampshire, by Henry Ranlet, included "Montgomery," as did David Merrill's *The Psalmodist's Best Companion,* published by Ranlet in Exeter in 1799. Amos Pillsbury's *The United States' Sacred Harmony,* another 1799 publication, included "Montgomery."

It is apparent that within a decade after Morgan's music was first published, a number of well-known and widely distributed tunebooks presented one or more of his compositions. It is equally clear that a number of musicians were aware not only of the tunes but also of the man who had created them. The Reverend Elkanah Kelsay Dare of Wilmington, Delaware, a Methodist clergyman and musician of some note, wrote a letter to Andrew Law[18] in which he defended American music by saying, "We can claim a Billings, a Morgan, a Swan, a Hall, etc., which claim no small share of merit. I know few tunes which excel in solemnity Billings' 'Brookfield,' Morgan's 'Amanda,' Swan's 'China,' and Hall's 'All Saints, New.'"[19] Morgan's longest work, "Judgment Anthem," drew from able and well-known Daniel Read a comment which at least shows the anthem's popularity. Writing to his brother Ezra, Read implies that the reason "the writings of John Bunyan are more read than those of Dr. Johnson,[20] and Morgans Judgement Anthem is so much more admired than that Anthem of Anthems as it has been called, *O give thanks & * by Dr. Arnold" is that Morgan's anthem, like Bunyan's *Pilgrim's Progress,* speaks directly and simply to the people. Read concludes, "It is however, I believe, best that in a worshiping assembly, the prayers, the sermon, the psalms and the music, should be in a language understood by the worshipers generally."[21]

When one turns from Morgan's reputation to the music

itself, one finds music that reflects both the English heritage of the first American compositions and also the distinctively "New World" qualities of these native compositions. One is dealing with a very small but very revealing body of music: seven hymn tunes (Sounding Joy, Symphony, Amanda, Montgomery, Pleasant Valley, Huntington, Wethersfield); one secular lament (Despair); and one anthem (Judgment Anthem, or "Hark, ye mortals, hear the trumpet").[22]

It may be fortunate that New England composers who reached adulthood about the time of the Revolution had had no opportunity to hear great orchestras, choirs, and organs perform the works of Bach and Handel before they themselves began to write music. The urge to imitate the works of such masters might well have been irresistible—and the results would very likely have been a pale reflection of the original. The crusading and reforming Wesleys of England, anxious to insure singing by entire congregations, impressed by the beauty of the German music that the Moravians brought to America, and open to all the musical influences that the England of their day had to offer, stressed types of music, including German hymn tunes, which in the end made Methodist congregational singing outstanding. One does not, however, compose in what might be called the musical language of another country, no matter how well he may sing in that language. One composes in his native tongue, whether in music or in words. It was among American Congregationalists and Baptists, rather than among Methodists influenced by the English Wesleys, that the school of composition to which has been given the too-narrow name of "American psalmody" developed. Responsive as they were to all the stimuli of the simple, strong early psalm tunes of the English psalters, to the more ornate hymn tunes (including fuging tunes) of the eighteenth-century English tunebooks, and to English folk tunes that they and their forebears had sung for generations, our first composers fashioned a musical idiom that was forthright, compelling, sometimes lively and sometimes plaintive, often rough-hewn. American music of the late-eighteenth-century bears something of the same relation to Handel's music, for instance, that a coin silver spoon fashioned by a New Englander of the period does to a spoon made by a Hester Bateman in London—or that a chair made by a New Englander does to the Sheraton or Chippendale chair that was in some tenuous way the model for the Yankee product.

Morgan is credited by musical scholars of today with being one of the most characteristic writers in the "new" American idiom of post-Revolutionary times. Wilfrid Howard Mellers, in a study entitled *Music in a New Found Land*,[23] declares, "In the music of Justin Morgan . . . the folk element is combined with other more sophisticated elements that still tend towards the archaic. 'Amanda' . . . has a very crude form of sixteenth-century false relation." Mellers adds that this "false relation" is used to express "death's nastiness."

It seems to me that Mellers is guilty of a particularly infelicitous twentieth-century misinterpretation both of the effect of the music and of the attitude of an eighteenth-century man of Morgan's stamp toward death. The devout Morgan saw death as part of God's plan, and never by any stretch of the imagination can he be suspected of having found any part of God's plan "nasty." The temporary parting from a loved one that Morgan believed death entailed might seem poignant—as indeed the plaintive melody of "Amanda" suggests; the shortness of human life, our plant-like birth and growth and decay and death, might seem one of the great mysteries. Such losses were to be felt, to be borne, and to be accepted.

As he began to compose "Amanda," Morgan's musical imagination seems to have been set to work by that stanza from Isaac Watts's long-meter setting of the Ninetieth Psalm that appears with the music in Benham's book and that reads:

Death like an overflowing stream,
Sweeps us away; our life's a dream,
An empty tale; a morning flow'r
Cut down and wither'd in an hour.

That same psalm, however, begins with:

Through ev'ry age, eternal God,
Thou art our rest, our safe abode;
High was thy throne, e'er heav'n was made,
Or earth thy humble footstool laid.

and ends with:

Teach us, O Lord, how frail is man;
And kindly lengthen out our span;
Till a wise care of piety
Fit us to die, and dwell with thee.

Any congregation singing "Amanda" in the 1790s would have sung all eight verses of the psalm—as Morgan expected them to do. They and he knew that death is a part of life and that God is "our safe abode."

Mellers is on sounder ground when he comments on the general effect of "Amanda" upon the hearer than he is when discussing "nasty death." He speaks of the "purely modal tune, with bare fifths and flat seventh cadences that are, like folk-song, melancholy yet resigned." He adds that this "folk-modalism" appears also in "Huntington," and was apparently Morgan's "natural musical idiom." In "Huntington," says Mellers,

the hymn section gains a rugged boldness from the parallel fourths and octaves, while the fuguing section makes an unsuccessful attempt at the European harmonist's sense of progression, for there is a long dominant pedal that "prepares" nothing. The fortuitous clashes of the passing notes and the driving energy of the descending scale phrase have, on the other hand, considerable power, making us aware of the slipperiness of the rocks and of the determination necessary to avoid their perils.

The text to which Mellers here refers is Watts's setting of Psalm 74:

> Lord, what a thoughtless wretch was I,
> To mourn, and murmur, and repine,
> To see the wicked, placed on high
> In pride, and robes of honour, shine!
>
> But, oh, their end, their dreadful end!
> Thy sanctuary taught me so:
> On slipp'ry rocks I see them stand,
> And fiery billows roll below.

In concluding his remarks on Morgan, Mellers says that those "primitives" who lacked "the deep imaginative instincts of Timothy Swan or Justin Morgan are apt, inevitably, to produce music that sounds to us quaint rather than affecting." He places in this category some of the music of Samuel Holyoke (of Massachusetts and New Hampshire), who in the eighteenth century certainly enjoyed a far wider reputation as a musician than did Morgan.

Other critics have found in Morgan's music not only the special characteristics of his school of composers but also special excellence in employing that idiom effectively. Allan C. Buechner has said of Morgan's most popular tune, "Montgomery," that "the fuging technique is handled with unusual skill, there being a second set of fugal entries once the 'fuge' proper has commenced. The tumultuous effect created is brought under control at the cadence points, giving the whole a wonderful sense of destination and vigor."[24] James Chapman has said of Morgan's "Sounding Joy," "The great rhythmic drive of this fuging tune and the strength resulting from the upward movement of its melodic lines more than compensate for any breeching of 'traditional' or 'correct' harmonic rules."[25]

Of Morgan's one long work, the popular "Judgment Anthem," the most extensive comment by a modern critic has been made by Ralph T. Daniels in his study, *The Anthem in New England before 1800*.[26] Speaking first of the distinctive qualities of all Morgan's music, Daniels remarks, "His many 'fuging-tunes,' his imaginative, if untutored, musicianship, his originality, and his attraction to texts of a somewhat vivid pictorial quality . . . are all strongly reminiscent of William Billings. Another similarity to his better-known contemporary is an implied patriotism in his disdain of Italian tempo and dynamic markings; he used only English indications such as 'slow,' 'lively,' . . . ." Of the anthem, "Hark, ye mortals, hear the trumpet,"[27] Daniels says that the most remarkable feature is "its tonal gravitation between two unrelated key centers, E minor and E-flat major, a gravitation made with no pretence at modulation."[28] He adds, "Two coloristic devices, apparently original with Morgan, occur several times during the course of the anthem. One is a sudden change of tessitura for the sake of graphic expressiveness. The other is achieved by having one or two voices continue to sound after the others have dropped out of a four-part chord."[29] All of these devices—the sudden changes of key, the great shifts in range, and the dropping out of voices to leave one insistent voice carrying its message directly to the hearer—emphasize the extent to which Morgan allowed his text to determine the musical structure of his anthem, as Daniels points out that eighteenth-century American writers of anthems customarily did.[30] Although this tendency may have been due partially to the composers' limited knowledge of musical structure, it must also have been caused by the composers' sense of the importance of the words.[31]

The text of Morgan's "Judgment Anthem" could not have failed to send a thrill of perhaps appalled attention through any congregation and choir in a New England church of the 1790s. It was not for nothing that Thomas of Celano's great Latin hymn of the thirteenth century, *Dies Irae*, had over the intervening centuries been translated by scores of poets into the various vernacular languages, English in particular. It was certainly not for nothing that *The Day of Doom*, written in 1662 by Michael Wigglesworth, "teacher" of the church at Malden, Massachusetts, became so well known in New England that as late as the early nineteenth century "many an aged person" could still repeat the entire long poem "by heart."[32] For the orthodox eighteenth-century churchman of Calvinistic hue, Doomsday was both fascinating and possibly at hand. It was the subject of poem after poem, hymn after hymn.[33]

Morgan's text begins with the same insistent, demanding, trochaic tetrameter that distinguishes Thomas of Celano's striking hymn, which was called the "high water mark" of Latin ecclesiastical poetry:[34]

> Thomas: Dies irae! Dies illa,
> Solvet saeclum in favilla,
> Teste David cum Sybilla.
> Morgan: Hark, ye mortals! Hear the trumpet,
> Sounding loud the mighty roar . . .

Much of the "Judgment Anthem" text is akin to the Wigglesworth poem, in word as in thought. In Wigglesworth the sinners are told to

> Depart to Hell, there may you yell,
> and roar Eternally.

In Wigglesworth "the Judge draws nigh, exalted high," while "the Mountains smoke, the Hills are shook, / the Earth is rent and torn."

Daniels speaks of "the doggeral character of the text" of Morgan's "Judgment Anthem."[35] Most of the text is far from doggerel, however, and what it is and how Morgan chose to use it tell much both of his artistic aims and of the tastes of the people who found the "Judgment Anthem" to be "the glory of the front gallery," as one member of a choir of the era later called it.[36]

Note how the beginning of Morgan's "Judgment Anthem" differs from a similar passage in Handel. Morgan begins,

> Hark, ye mortals, hear the trumpet
> Sounding loud the mighty roar.
> Hark, the archangel's voice proclaiming:
> Thou, old time, shall be no more!

Handel's great bass solo in *The Messiah* proclaims the same theme: "The trumpet shall sound, the dead shall be raised incorruptible. . . . " The difference is clear: Handel's text, which is of course St. Paul's (I Corinthians 15:52), speaks in the third person, describing, as from a prophetic observer's vantage point, what will come to pass. The Morgan text reaches out in a command in the second person, grabbing by the throat the perhaps reluctant listener and compelling him to pay heed.

Although most anthems written by the New England psalmodists were set to words taken directly from the poetic prose of the Bible, Morgan chose to draw on the poets of his era. His opening stanza is from a hymn that first appeared in *A Choice Collection of Hymns and Spiritual Songs*, compiled by the Reverend Samson Occom and published in 1774.[37] It is quite possible that the hymn was written by Occom, who was an ordained Presbyterian clergyman—and a Mohican Indian. Thus a hymn by one of the most native of native Americans may have provided the opening stanza of Morgan's anthem. It is known that Occom's collection, containing as it does many direct, compelling hymns aimed at making intelligible to the simplest people the way of the religious life, was popular on the New England frontier.[38]

With the second stanza Morgan begins to pick up lines from a well-known hymn of English origin, John Cennick's "Lo, He Cometh."[39] When he arrives at the stanza that begins, "Hark, the archangel swells the solemn summons

loud,/ Tears the strong pillars of the vaults of heaven . . .",
Morgan shifts suddenly to a work by one of the most distinguished of hymn writers. At last one learns why, of all
possible books of poetry, Isaac Watts's *Horae Lyricae* was
among Morgan's books when he died.[40] In that work of 1706,
the thirty-two-year-old English poet, hymnist, and clergyman attempted to place in the irregular verse form known as
"English Sapphic" his concept of "The Day of Judgment."
Unfortunately Morgan leaves out of his anthem some of the
finest lines from the Watts ode ("When the fierce North Wind
with his airy forces/ Rears up the Baltick to the foaming Fury
. . ."), but the lines that he does include are those that Daniels
describes as having a "vivid pictorial quality."[41] Doubtless
Daniels has in mind such lines as

> Hark, the shrill Outcries of the guilty wretches!
> Lively bright Horror, and amazing Anguish,
> Stare thro' their eye-lids, while the living Worm lies
> Gnawing within them.

Vivid these lines are—but doggerel they are not. Watts
provides in this poem a free, somewhat irregular rhythmic
pattern that allows the composer much room in which to
maneuver and yet offers him striking images. Morgan knew a
good image when he saw one. The combination as set forth in
Morgan's arresting music of the direct, uncompromising
challenge of "Hark, Ye Mortals" with Watts's vivid language
and the consolation of "Lo, He Cometh" made the "Judgment Anthem" a "favorite of the front gallery" and of the
congregation until changing musical, religious, and social
styles swept the anthem out of fashion in the second decade of
the nineteenth century.[42]

A final bit of evidence as to Morgan's concern for the words
being sung is the fact that he seems to have chosen voices to
introduce solo passages with special care as to the appropri-
ateness of such voices to the content of the verse. Thus the
counter (alto), which was normally sung by boys' voices in

Morgan's day, introduces most passages that deal with "Christ victorious," and the high treble (women's voices) sounds the first trumpet-like warning of an impending judgment that will lead both to heaven and to hell.

Earlier critics who faulted Morgan and his contemporaries for writing anthems that lacked the musical backbone of English anthems of the period[43] were apparently criticizing the Americans for failing to do something that they were in fact not attempting to do: to give form to their works primarily through musical patterns. It was, as Daniels remarks, the words that gave form to the works, in Morgan's anthem as in others by the New England psalmodists. In this anthem, at least, Morgan might well be called a "rhapsodist" rather than a psalmodist.[44]

The texts that Morgan selected for his seven hymn—or psalm—tunes suggest what one would be led to expect from the text of the "Judgment Anthem": all emphasize the Calvinistic doctrine of the sovereignty of God; four of the seven deal with death; and two of those four with the Last Judgment. The remaining three sing of the glory of God and the wonder of his Universe. All seven employ texts taken from Isaac Watts's metrical version of the psalms, which by Morgan's time had supplanted the Bay Psalm Book, Sternhold and Hopkins, and even the "New Version" of Tate and Brady in all but the most conservative New England Congregational churches. Thus Morgan had at his command metrical versions of the psalms written by one of the great masters of hymnody, that form of poetry of which Tennyson said, "A good hymn is the most difficult thing in the world to write."[45]

"Montgomery" (Psalm 63) is of course one of the three tunes that sing most insistently of the glory of God:

> Early, my God, without delay,
> I haste to seek thy face . . .
> I've seen thy glory and thy pow'r
> Through all thy temple shine . . .

"Sounding Joy" (Psalm 95) shouts its message of belief:

> Come, sound his praise abroad,
> And hymns of glory sing;
> Jehovah is the sov'reign God,
> The universal King.
> He formed the deeps unknown;
> He gave the seas their bound;
> The wat'ry worlds are all his own,
> And all the solid ground.

"Wethersfield" (Psalm 148) calls upon the "tribes of Adam" to join with "heav'n and earth and seas" in offering "notes divine/ To your Creator's praise." The psalm concludes:

> The shining worlds above
> In glorious order stand,
> Or in swift courses move,
> By His supreme command.
> He spake the word,
> And all their frame
> From nothing came,
> To praise the Lord.

"Symphony" (Psalm 50), like "Huntington" (Psalm 73), seems a preliminary statement of the message of the "Judgment Anthem." It begins, "Behold the Judge descends" and includes the line "But gather first my saints (the Judge commands)"—a line echoed in the "Judgment Anthem's" "Come ye ransom'd sinners home." "Pleasant Valley" presents the familiar 119th Psalm: "My soul lies cleaving to the dust;/ Lord, give me life divine." Like "Amanda," it treats of death but also of life, and of God's dominion over both life and death.

Only in "Judgment Anthem," with its inclusion of verses by Cennick and possibly Occom, does one find mention of Jesus in the works of Morgan. Even here, the emphasis is upon the Christ who "ransom'd sinners," not upon Jesus, "lover of my soul." When Morgan's daughter Emily Egerton died in 1828, she asked to have sung at her funeral the hymn, "While on the verge of life I stand," by the English non-conformist clergyman Philip Doddridge.[46] The "I" of the Doddridge poem anticipates the "blissful interview" he or she will have with Jesus in the afterlife, when he will be "raised in His arms to view His face." Although the Great Awakening of Jonathan Edwards's time had been centered around the concept of Jesus, as all religious revivals in

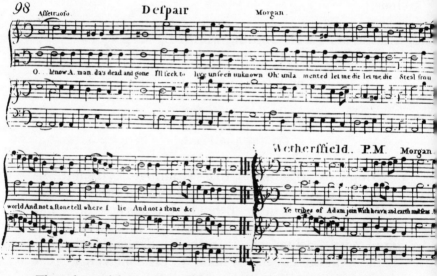

The only surviving secular piece by Justin Morgan is "Despair," shown here in the form in which it first appeared in Andrew Adgate's *Philadelphia Harmony*, third edition, Part Two, published in 1791. The text, altered from Alexander Pope's "Ode to Solitude," is apparently an elegy for Martha Morgan, Justin's wife, who died in March of 1791. The engraving, taken here from an 1803 edition of Adgate's tunebook, is the one that was used in earlier editions of the work. *Courtesy of Clements Library, University of Michigan, Ann Arbor, Mich.*

America have been, there was an important difference between the attitude of Edwards's age and that of the revivalists of the "Second Great Awakening" in the early nineteenth century. The Romantic Movement, with its subjectivism, had done its work by the dawn of the new century. Edwards and his followers had wished to "lose themselves in Christ," while those who experienced religious "awakening" during the wave of early-nineteenth-century revivals wished to "find themselves in Christ."[47] Justin Morgan had grown up while the Edwards influence was still strong in western Massachusetts; the subjectivism and intimacy of his daughter's religious attitude, at least as they are portrayed by her memorialist, the Reverend Rufus Nutting, seem alien to the spirit that celebrates the sovereignty of God in Morgan's compositions.

There remains one tune, "Despair," to be discussed. As early as 1811 a tunebook—Benjamin Leslie's *The Concert Harmony*—declared that "Amanda" was "composed by Morgan, to be sung at the funeral of his wife, of that name."[48] The comment indicates how well "Amanda" and its composer were known, even by one who did not know that Morgan's wife was named Martha, not Amanda. The idea that "Amanda" was written as an elegy to Martha Morgan persists in our own time. In 1960 musicologist Irving Lowens wrote that the song was "inspired by the death of [Morgan's] wife."[49] "Amanda," however, was included in the first edition of Benham's *Federal Harmony*, which bears the publication date 1790, and which was being advertised in Bennington's *Vermont Gazette* by 3 January 1791.[50] Martha Morgan did not die until the twentieth of March in 1791. It is entirely possible, of course, that "Amanda" was written when Martha Morgan's health already seemed in a precarious state, and that, as he composed "Amanda," Morgan was drawn to thoughts of the transitory nature of life.

"Despair," the only surviving Morgan tune that was not included in Benham's book, made its first appearance in

Andrew Adgate's *Philadelphia Harmony*, third edition, part two, in 1791.[51] It was in the fall of that year that Morgan may have been teaching singing someplace along the Susquehanna River and may have met either Adgate or his collaborator Spicer.[52] In any case, "Despair" is the only Morgan tune to use a secular text, and it mentions "Amanda." When one remembers that the name *Amanda* means "worthy to be loved," and when one reads the stanza that was printed with the music of "Despair," there is no doubt that this song was indeed an elegy for Martha Morgan. The stanza reads:

> Oh! now Amanda's dead and gone
> I'll seek to live unseen, unknown.
> Oh! Unlamented let me die,
> Steal from the world, and not a stone
> Tell where I lie.

For the words of this stanza Morgan turned to the poet Alexander Pope, drawing the stanza from the "Ode to Solitude" that Pope wrote when he was a schoolboy and that was frequently printed in editions of *An Essay on Man*. Agnes Marie Sibley, in *Alexander Pope's Prestige in America, 1727-1835*,[53] has shown that most Americans considered the famous poem not deistic, but an expression of "cosmic faith"—"the best that *reason* could do to justify the moral government of God."[54] Pope's "whatever is, is right" seemed even to most orthodox church members an expression not of fatalism but of faith "in the over-all wisdom of God." The many editions of this poem published in America frequently included Pope's "Universal Prayer" and his "Ode to Solitude" as poems thought to be harmonious with the long *Essay on Man*, and doubtless it was in such an edition that Morgan found the ode.[55]

When Pope wrote the ode in his schoolboy days, he was obviously under the influence of the Latin poets who sang so often of the joys of simple rural life. Pope's poem therefore is a hymn to the simple life, and only by changing the first line radically could Morgan make it into an elegy. The Pope stanza reads:

> Thus let me live, unseen, unknown;
> Thus unlamented, let me die,
> Steal from the world, and not a stone
> Tell where I lie.

Whatever else can be said of "Despair," it is obvious that it can be claimed as a genuinely "Vermont" composition, written after Morgan came to Vermont. The titles of some of his other tunes give at least a hint that they were composed in Massachusetts. There is no indication of place in the tunes whose names suggest a mood or a method of performance: "Sounding Joy," "Amanda," "Despair," and "Symphony."[56] Morgan uses fewer place names as titles for his tunes than do many of his contemporaries, but four of his tunes do bear place names: "Montgomery," "Pleasant Valley," "Huntington," and "Wethersfield." Frequently singing masters named their songs after places where the tunes were composed and after towns in which they conducted—or hoped to conduct—singing schools. The four towns that gave Morgan titles for compositions could be towns in Vermont, but when one considers the state of civilization in those towns in 1790, it seems far more likely that the titles refer to towns in Massachusetts and Connecticut. One discovers that Montgomery is a town lying less than fifteen miles northwest of Morgan's hometown, West Springfield, and that the town just above Montgomery is Huntington. A horseman of Morgan's caliber could have had a pleasant and easy ride up the Westfield River to Montgomery, could have conducted a singing school there, and then ridden on to Huntington to complete a winter's circuit of instruction. To discover the other two town-related tune names, one need only work his way down the well-traveled Connecticut River to Hartford, Connecticut. Five miles south of Hartford is Wethersfield, renowned as a music center almost equal to Hartford at the dawn of the nineteenth century. It attracted the attention of the redoubtable Andrew Law and Timothy Olmstead, the latter described by one devotee as "the Mozart of America."[57] Perhaps before these worthies became the musical leaders in the area, Morgan may have visited Wethersfield and possibly taught there. To find Pleasant Valley, one turns west from Hartford to New Hartford, birthplace of Morgan's publisher, Benham, and locates Pleasant Valley on the Farmington River, just a mile or two north of the village of New Hartford.

Justin Morgan composed one anthem and eight psalm tunes that are known. Among them are three compositions that were widely acclaimed, even among the works of able men who wrote scores and in some cases hundreds of tunes, and who disseminated them in a flood of tunebooks that were published during what Alan Clark Buechner has called "the golden age of choral music in New England," 1760 to 1800.[58] How much recognition Morgan the musician received among his fellow townspeople is not known, but that music shaped and contained his inner life and that it set its stamp upon him and therefore to some extent left its impress upon his public life, one cannot doubt.

Notes

1. Andrew Law, Alexandria, Va., to his brother, William Law, Cheshire, Conn., 11 November 1791, in the Andrew Law Papers, Clements Library Collection, University of Michigan, Ann Arbor, Mich., quoted by permission of the Clements Library.

2. Richard A. Crawford, *Andrew Law, American Psalmodist*, Pi Kappa Lambda Studies in American Music (Evanston, Ill.: Northwestern University Press, 1968).

3. Law Papers, L 18, quoted by Crawford, *Andrew Law*, p. 75, with a footnote comment that the letter "implies that Benham's purpose was to pry into the brothers' musical enterprise." The system of numbering for the Law Papers, Clements Library Collection, was devised by Professor Crawford and is described by him on p. xvii of *Andrew Law, American Psalmodist*.

4. Crawford, *Andrew Law*, pp. 62 ff.

5. Ibid., pp. 64 ff.

6. Ibid., p. 65.

7. Details of Harmon's life will be recounted in a subsequent study.

8. Margaret Gardiner, "The Great Justin Morgan Pedigree Controversy," *The Chronicle of the Horse* 23 December 1966, p. 27.

9. See below, pp. 166-67.

10. Samuel Blair, *A Discourse on Psalmody, Delivered by the Reverend Samuel Blair, in the Presbyterian Church in Neshaminy, at a Public Concert, Given by Mr. Spicer, Master in Sacred Music, under the Superintendency of the Rev. Mr. Erwin, Pastor of That Church, with an Appendix, Containing the Addresses of Mr. Erwin, and Mr. Spicer, on the Occasion* (Philadelphia, Pa.: Printed and sold by John M'Cullough, 1789).

11. Wallingford (Conn.) Probate Records, 4:13 ff. The estate of Ambrose Doolittle was presented for probate at a court held 21 October 1793.

12. William Law, Cheshire, Conn., to his brother Andrew in Philadelphia, 10 March 1802, in the Andrew Law Papers, Clements Library Collection, quoted by permission of the Clements Library.

13. Now in the possession of the New Haven Colony Historical Society in New Haven, Conn.

14. Letter No. 38, to Jacob French of Uxbridge, 10 June 1793, in Daniel Read's Letter Book, quoted by permission of the New Haven Colony Historical Society Library, New Haven, Conn.

15. Article by George Hood in September 1882 issue of *Musical Herald,* quoted by Frank J. Metcalf, *American Writers and Compilers of Sacred Music* (New York and Cincinnati, Ohio: Abingdon Press, 1925), pp. 90-91.

16. Richard A. Crawford, "Connecticut Sacred Music Imprints, 1778-1810," *Music Library Association Notes* 27 (1971):679.

17. I am indebted to Nym Cooke, a graduate student at the University of Michigan, for calling my attention to Morgan traits in "Ocean."

18. The letter was written in 1811, but reflects the attitudes of the 1790s more than it does the attitudes of 1810—by which time European and especially English church music was all the fashion.

19. Crawford, *Andrew Law,* pp. 210-11.

20. Presumably Read refers to the Reverend Samuel Johnson, clergyman and educator who was first president of King's College, now Columbia University.

21. Irving Lowens, *Music and Musicians in Early America* (New York: W. W. Norton & Co., 1964), pp. 170-71.

22. All of Morgan's compositions, with accompanying texts, are in Appendix A of this study.

23. Wilfred Howard Mellers, *Music in a New Found Land* (London: Barrie and Rockliff, 1964). In speaking of the entire school, Mellers writes (p. 7),

The half-inituitive composers, thinking modally, like folk-singers, did not know how to achieve the highly civilized equilibrium between horizontal polyphony and vertical homophony that characterized their European forebears. Yet their rawness was their authenticity. Their "mistakes" in harmony and part-writing could be at times inspired; indeed, they were not mistakes at all, since they were a creative manifestation of their identities. For the first time we thus hear, in their music, the accent of the New World; their "guileless truth," like that of Natty Bumpo, is inseparable from their barbarism.

It is interesting to note that American music seems to have preceded poetry and poetic-prose in the use of a distinctively American idiom. Ola Elizabeth Winslow in her biogrgaphy of Jonathan Edwards *Jonathan Edwards, 1703-1758* [New York: Macmillan Co., 1940] comments on the fact that the great preacher's figures of speech came from the Bible rather than from his "farm boyhood" (p. 146). She adds that American poetry of the same period spoke of heather and gorse, yew and skylarks, instead of whippoorwills, goldenrod, and gentians (p. 147). Even a century later, Winslow comments, Emerson shocked Harvard audiences by speaking of "meal in the firkin, milk in the pan."

24. Allan C. Buechner, program note (p. 21) for Folkways Record Album No. FA 2377, *The New England Harmony*, a collection of early American Choral music presented by the Old Sturbridge Singers, directed by Floyd Corson, singing master, and members of the Harvard Wind Ensemble, recorded in the Meeting House at Old Sturbridge Village, Mass., in May 1964.

25. Program notes for Philo Record 1000, *Vermont Harmony*, recorded by the University of Vermont Choral Union, directed by James Chapman, with notes by Chapman and Betty Bandel, 1973.

26. Ralph T. Daniels, *The Anthem in New England before 1800* (Evanston, Ill.: Northwestern University Press, 1966), pp. 127-28.

27. The first line of the anthem is used as its title in several collections.

28. A recent study by Karl Douglas Kroeger, "The Worcester Collection of Sacred Harmony and Sacred Music in America, 1786-1803" (Ph.D. diss., Brown University 1976), pp. 286-87, argues that this shift is meant to indicate merely a change from E-minor to E-major, and back again, with the singers remaining at the same pitch level when they encounter the change in mode. Kroeger, citing theoretical introductions in influential eighteenth-century tunebooks to support his contention, argues that to the "fasola" singer the notes F#-G#-A in three sharps and F-G-A-flat in four flats, for instance, would both be read as la-mi-fa and would therefore be considered identical sequences.

29. Daniels, *The Anthem in New England*, pp. 127-28.

30. Ibid., p. 47.

31. Allen Perdue Britton ("Theoretical Introductions in American Tune-Books to 1800" [Ph.D. diss., University of Michigan, 1949], p. 249) points out that Morgan's publisher, Asahel Benham, who himself composed "in as pure as American idiom as can anywhere be found," spoke out "sharply . . . against those singers who insisted on [purely musical] accent in all cases." In the introduction to his tunebook (p. 10, 5th ed.) Benham declared, "Many singers, indeed I may say many young teachers are so biggoted in favour of accenting the first and third crotchets in a bar of common time (without paying any regard to the word) that they entirely destroy the design of accenting, and make their singing go like a person with one leg shorter than the other."

32. Michael Wigglesworth, *The Day of Doom* (New York, 1867), from the 6th ed. of 1715, quotation in the introduction to Francis Jenks's essay in the *Christian Examiner* of November 1828.

33. A story is told of a group of "Calvinistic Close Communion Baptists" who settled in the northwest corner of Randolph, very near to the spot where Justin Morgan is said to have made his home, and who, when an earthquake occurred in the summer of 1780, decided that the Day of Judgment was not far off. One night, two months after the earthquake, there came a particularly vivid appearance of the Aurora Borealis. "Mr. Hebard" sprang to horse and galloped to his neighbors, screaming "The Day of Judgment has come! Awake! Awake!" Two women were temporarily deranged. A child was born prematurely and died the next day. (Mrs. Sarah H. Rowell, "Samuel Flint," in section on Randolph in Abby Maria Hemenway, *The Vermont Historical Gazetteer* [Burlington, Vt.: Privately printed, 1871], 2:1012.)

34. Theron Brown and Hezekiah Butterworth, *The Story of Hymns and Tunes* (New York: American Tract Society, 1906), p. 62.

35. Daniels, *The Anthem in New England*, p. 128.

36. "B," writing to the *Connecticut Courant* from New York in 1854 (quoted by N. H. Allen, "Old Time Music and Musicians," *The Connecticut Quarterly* 3 [1894] :288), from the distance of half a century makes fun of the "front gallery" for thinking "Judgment Anthem" and its like fine music; but it is evident that both choir and congregation found the anthem compelling before changing tastes brought often second-rate European church music into fashion in American churches.

37. Reverend Samson Occom, comp., *A Choice Collection of Hymns and Spiritual Songs* (New London, Conn.: Timothy Green, 1774). The writer is indebted to the late Rev. Dr. Charles L. Atkins of Merrimack, N.H. for calling to her attention this source of a portion of the text of the "Judgment Anthem."

38. Two other Vermont psalmodists made use of Occom's "Hark Ye Mortals" hymn. Jeremiah Ingalls's "Angel's Hymn" uses this text (Ingalls, *The Christian Harmony*, [Exeter, N.H.: Henry Ranlet, 1805], p. 132). "Solemn Close," by Joel Harmon, Jr. (*The Columbian Sacred Minstrel* [Northampton, Mass.: Andrew Wright, 1809], p. 76) employs the same hymn.

39. Of special interest in "Judgment Anthem" is Morgan's weaving together of lines from many sources, sometimes changing wording slightly to fit his purposes. See Appendix B for analysis of his text and the sources from which he drew.

40. See above, p. 59.

41. Daniels, *The Anthem in New England*, p. 127.

42. As late as 1810 the anthem was printed by Herman Mann of Dedham, Mass. for David Belknap of Framingham, as a ten-page pamphlet—with no acknowledgement given to Morgan as composer. A copy of this scarce pamphlet is in the Brown University Library in Providence, R.I.

43. J. Murray Barbour (*The Church Music of William Billings* [East Lansing, Mich.: Michigan State University Press, 1960], p. 133) quotes Hamilton C. Macdougall (*Early New England Psalmody* [Brattleboro, Vt.: Stephen Daye Press, 1940] as a particularly severe critic of Billings "and his followers" for failure to master the musical structure of anthems.

44. I am indebted to Howard G. Bennett, professor emeritus of music at the University of Vermont, for suggesting the term *rhapsodist* as an appropriate one to describe the Morgan of "Judgment Anthem."

45. Tennyson made this remark in the last year of his life, 1892. He was speaking with Herbert Warren, president of Magdalen College, Oxford, and Tennyson's son Hallam took notes on the conversation. Tennyson went on to say, "in a good hymn you have to be commonplace and poetical. The moment you cease to be commonplace and put in any expression at all out of the common, it ceases to be a hymn." He expressed a preference for Heber's "Holy, Holy, Holy," saying that it was "better than most," and had "a fine metre too." Tennyson then went on to speculate "What will people come to in a hundred years? Do you think they will give up all religious forms and go and sit in silence in the Churches listening to the organs?" It is noteworthy that the Heber hymn that Tennyson, a master of prosody, favored employs a somewhat irregular and by no means simple trochaic meter, rather than the often deceptively simple common or ballad meter used so successfully by Watts. (Hallam Tennyson, *Alfred Lord Tennyson, A Memoir by His Son* [New York: Macmillan Co., 1898], 2:401.)

46. Rufus Nutting, *Memoirs of Mrs. Emily Egerton, an Authentic Narrative* (Boston: Perkins and Marvin, 1832), p. 138.

47. I am indebted to a student of nineteenth-century evangelistic religious history, Helen Pease Long of Keeseville, N.Y., for suggesting this distinction.

48. This early reference to "Amanda" as an elegy was called to my attention by Nym Cooke. *The Concert Harmony* was published in Salem, Mass.

49. Program note for the record, *The American Harmony*, sung by the Chapel Choir of the University of Maryland, conducted by Fague Springmann, Washington Records WLP 418. The date *1960* is indicated in the notes.

50. *Vermont Gazette*, 3 January 1791, p. 4: "Just received, and now ready for sale, *Federal Harmony*, containing the Rudiments of Psalmody, in a Familiar Manner; together with a Collection of Music (Most of which are entirely new) composed by Asahel Benham. Price 36 s. per dozen—3/6 single. Apply to Jonathan Robinson, Bennington, December 1790."

51. See above, p. 138, for the titles of the various editions of this work.

52. See above, pp. 139-40.

53. Agnes Marie Sibley, *Alexander Pope's Prestige in America, 1727-1835* (New York: King's Crown Press, 1949), p. 26 and passim.

54. Ibid., p. 28.

55. The edition of *An Essay on Man* published in Bennington, Vt. in 1785 by Haswell and Russell includes "Universal Prayer" but does not have "Ode to Solitude."

56. A primary meaning of the word *symphony* in the eighteenth century was a composition to be sung or played with all parts sounding harmoniously and simultaneously, rather than with one part answering another as in the "fuges" of which Morgan and his contemporaries were so fond. "Symphony," unlike all other Morgan compositions, is a four-part harmonization such as one finds in older psalm settings or in nineteenth-century hymns, with only the merest hint of fuging to lend variety.

57. The anonymous "B," writing in the *Connecticut Courant* of 1854, describes Law and Olmstead as the masters who rescued Hartford and Wethersfield from musical barbarism. It is "B" who places upon Olmstead's head the Mozartian crown.

58. Alan Clark Buechner, "Yankee Singing Schools and The Golden Age of Choral Music in New England, 1760-1800" (Ph.D. diss., Harvard Graduate School of Education, 1960).

—— 9 ——

Figure Again

SINCE the primary business of this inquiry has been to determine the place and importance of music in the life of Morgan and the impact of his musical life upon the New England frontier, it may seem strange to end as one began, with that well-known horse Figure. Yet the two things that stand out at the end of Morgan's life are the books that are listed in the inventory of his estate, and the stallion Figure.

It is quite unnecessary to tell again the often-repeated story of "the horse Justin Morgan." There have been detailed, sometimes excellent, and often fanciful accounts of that horse's ancestry, life, and descendants ever since D. C. Linsley began the fashion by writing *Morgan Horses: A Premium Essay*, in 1857. Perhaps the best accounts are those which the indefatigable Joseph Battell wrote between 1894 and 1911 when, as has been said, he devoted three stout volumes to *The Morgan Horse and Register* and two similar volumes to *The American Stallion Register*.[1] In the 1790s there were thirteen stallions in the new United States that rejoiced in the name of Figure; and it was Joseph Battell who proved to the satisfaction of all reasonable people that the Figure which founded the Morgan breed of horses was a colt foaled probably in 1789, its sire being the horse True Briton (often written Britain) or Beautiful Bay, its dam a mare owned by Justin Morgan, the daughter of Diamond, the stallion that Morgan advertised at stud in 1783—said Diamond being "of the Wild Air stock."[2] It will be recalled that Morgan also kept True Briton at stud in 1785; and Morgan's cousin John Morgan, Jr., of Springfield, in April of 1788 advertised the horse, stating that Justin Morgan had kept him "three seasons ago." True Briton, it seems, had been owned during the Revolution by Colonel James DeLancey of the Westchester Light Horse, British Army, and had been liberated in 1779 or 1780 at White Plains, when some American scouts happened upon him and made off with him. The scouts sold him to Joseph Ward, merchant, of Hartford, Connecticut. Several years later Ward sold the horse to Selah Norton of East Hartford; it was apparently for Norton that the Morgans kept the horse at stud during the 1780s.[3]

It is when True Briton's son Figure enters the scene that the picture becomes clouded. From the 1840s through the 1880s many men, including Morgan's son and grandsons, were recounting in various periodicals the only true story of Figure's life, the difficulty being that the accounts differ one from another.[4] Battell, going back to the actual newspaper advertisements of the horse at stud, cleared up much of the difficulty. Figure, bred in 1788 and foaled in 1789, when Morgan was already in Vermont, was advertised in May of 1792 as being at stud in Hartford. The *Connecticut Courant* in its May 7 to May 21 issues of that year advertised, "Figure, a beautiful bay horse 15 hands high will cover this season at the stable of the subscriber at 20 shillings the season or $2 the single leap. Samuel Whitman. Hartford (West Division), May 5." It will be noted that this first advertisement of Figure indicates a height of fifteen hands, which takes him well out of the "little" and "runt colt" class persistently emphasized by the legends.[5] It will also be seen that if the three-year-old horse was being used at stud before Morgan saw him, Figure was not trained by Justin Morgan. All accounts agree that Morgan went to his home territory to collect a debt and accepted the young horse in payment. Battell notes that

Samuel Whitman's advertisement for Figure was terminated May 21, although such advertisements were customarily maintained through July. Battell speculates that Morgan arrived in Hartford in late May, bought Figure (or accepted him in payment of a debt), and brought him back to Randolph before the twentieth of June. He bases the latter date on the fact that in the Randolph Grand List, which was made up annually on the twentieth of June, Justin Morgan suddenly jumps from ten pounds (his 1791 rating) to twenty-three pounds. In 1791 Vermont had passed a law, to take effect in 1792, requiring the listing, for tax purposes, of any stallion of two years or more at twenty pounds.[6]

One account of the coming of Figure to Vermont gives a fleeting glimpse of Justin Morgan actually saying something. In a story told by Jude Moulton of Chelsea, grandson of Justin Morgan's sister Eunice, Moulton says that when Justin Morgan arrived in Randolph, with Figure, he stopped overnight at his sister's house, "about a mile from the center toward the East Branch." In the morning Morgan called the next-door neighbor, Jude Moulton, to see his new horse, and asked his opinion of him. Moulton "said he saw a little runt that did not look to be worth ten dollars and said so. Mr. Morgan tapped the horse on the shoulder and said, 'A good deal there, sir; a good deal there, sir.'" It was this Jude Moulton who married Eunice Miller's daughter Eunice, and it was their son Jude who later said that his father had "told him these facts."[7]

If , after the death of his wife, Morgan spent part of 1791 traveling in his capacity as musician, it seems evident that he spent part of 1792 traveling in his capacity as breeder of horses. The latter activity must have been stressed for the next three years, since one finds Justin Morgan advertising his stallion in 1793, 1794, and 1795. On the eighth of April in 1793 *Spooner's Vermont Journal,* published in Windsor, carried an advertisement that reads:

Will cover this season at Captain Elias Bissell's stable in Randolph, and at Captain Josiah Cleveland's stable in Lebanon (N.H.), the famous *Figure Horse,* from Hartford, in Conn.—, at 15 shillings for the season if paid down, or 18 shillings if paid in the fall, in cash or grain at cash price. Said horse's beauty, strength, and activity, the subscriber flatters himself the curious will be best satisfied to come and see. Said Horse will be in Lebanon the second Monday in May next, there to continue two weeks, and then return to Randolph; so to continue at said Cleveland's and Bissell's, two weeks at each place through the season. Justin Morgan, Randolph, April 8th, 1793.

The same newspaper carries an advertisement in the 1794 spring issues in which Morgan advertises "the beautiful horse *Figure*" at "$1 the single leap; $2 the season, or 16 shillings if not paid by 1 Sept." The horse was being kept at Ezra Edgerton's stable in Randolph and at Lieutenant Durkee's or Elkanah Stevens's in Royalton, with "constant attention . . . at each of the above places." It will be seen that the price for Figure's services had declined. Since six shillings equaled a dollar, two dollars for "the season" was less than fifteen shillings for the same length of time. As has been noted earlier, the advertisement of May 1795 appeared in the *Rutland Herald.*[8] It reveals that Figure had moved to a new area of the state—"Figure will cover this season at the stable of Samuel Allen in Williston, and at a stable in Hinesburgh, formerly owned by Mr. Munson. Figure sprang from a curious horse owned by Col. DeLancy of New York, but the greatest recommendation I can give him is, he is exceedingly sure, and gets curious colts." The advertisement, signed by Justin Morgan, was dated Williston, 30 April 1795.

Thus far Joseph Battell traced the story, ferreting out fact, not hearsay, in old and doubtless fragile copies of newspapers with what must have been unshakable patience and determination. One small piece of the puzzle escaped him—a piece that readily comes to hand in this day of microfilmed runs of early American newspapers made available in most large

THE BEAUTIFUL HORSE
FIGURE,

WILL cover this feafon, at the moderate price of *One Dollar* the fingle leap, *Two Dollars* the feafon, if paid down, or by the firft of September next; if not paid at that time, it will be *Sixteen Shillings.*——Said Horfe will be kept at the ftable of *Ezra Edgerton,* in *Randolph,* and Lieut. *Durkee's* or *Elhanah Stevens',* in *Royalton.*——He will be kept at Randolph til the fecond Monday of May, when he will be taken to Royalton, there to be kept every Monday Tuefday, and Wednefday; then return to Randolph, where he will continue Thurfday, Friday and Saturday; and fo alternately during the feafon.——The fubfcriber flatters himfelf that the Horfe's ftrength, beauty, and activity, will bear examination by the curious.

JUSTIN MORGAN.

☞ Conftant attention will be paid at each of the above places.

Randolph, April 21, 1794

Justin Morgan's own words describe his horse, Figure, the founding sire of the Morgan horse breed, in this advertisement that Morgan placed in *Spooner's Vermont Journal* (Windsor, Vt.) in April and May of 1794. Morgan refrained from making exaggerated claims about the horse's ancestry, and concentrated on Figure's own "strength, beauty, and activity." *Courtesy of the University of Vermont Morgan Horse Farm, Weybridge, Vt.*

libraries. Battell thought the 1795 advertisement of Figure the last one that had a bearing on the story of Justin Morgan. There is, however, one more. As has been said, in the 1 April 1796 issue of the *Burlington (Vt.) Mercury*,[9] one finds an advertisement, this one signed by Samuel Allen of Williston, which reads:

> Figure will cover this season, at the stable of Peter Benedict, Esq., in Burlington—at 12 shillings the single leap—4 dollars the season—and 6 dollars to ensure a foal. I shall omit the customary encomiums in advertisement of this kind—Suffice it to say—He is a beautiful Bay—15 hands three inches high, and grandson to the famous imported horse, Wild-Air. I would wish every Gentleman, that has a mind to put their mares to him, to call and see him. He is high spirited and remarkably good natured—Has covered two seasons at Hartford, in Connecticut, and two at Randolph, in this state, to great satisfaction, as he is very sure, and his colt's has proved Fine. Good pasturing for Mares, and constant attendance given by Samuel Allen. N.B. The pay will be expected next January, in cash or any kind of country produce. February 29, 1796.

The height of the horse seems surprising, since the Whitman advertisement of 1792 made Figure three inches shorter; and the evidence seems to be that Figure was at stud one season in Hartford and three in the Randolph area. Much more important than either of these statements, however, is the light that the advertisement may throw on the murky problem of where and when Justin Morgan parted from his horse.

Turning once more to the inventory of Morgan's estate, one finds listed no horse, but one piece of real estate: one hundred acres of land in Moretown, valued by the appraisers at $50.00. Moretown, lying halfway between Randolph and Williston, had 24 inhabitants by 1790, and by 1795 not many more, some of them doubtful that they could make a living in the town's mountainous terrain. A number of proprietors let their land go when the state legislature in 1791 laid a halfpenny per acre land tax on all Vermont lands in order to raise money for roads and similar necessities. Thus at a "public vendue" held in Burlington 3 January 1794 Samuel Allen of Williston bought the entire rights of five of the town's original proprietors, amounting to many hundreds of acres, for less than four pounds.[10] This procedure, common throughout sparsely settled Vermont in the 1790s, allowed Allen to realize 272 pounds on an investment of less than four pounds by the time that he had sold the last two hundred acres on 5 October 1796. His buyers paid sums ranging from three to thirty-seven pounds for varying amounts of acreage.

Justin Morgan fell somewhere in the middle. By a deed dated 28 May 1795 (Moretown Land Records, 1: 34) he paid twenty pounds for one hundred acres, it being "the original right of John Wright Jun'r."

A glance back at Morgan's advertisements for Figure will confirm the fact that in April of 1795 Morgan advertised his horse as standing at stud "at the stable of Samuel Allen in Williston." The following April 1796, Allen himself was advertising the horse.

Many and varied have been the stories of how and when Morgan parted from Figure. His own son said that a short time before Morgan died he "made the horse over" to William Rice, then living in Woodstock, to pay his bills.[11] Others claimed that this one or that one bought the horse, and some even said that Morgan owned the horse when he died, although it is obvious from the probate of his estate that he did not.

It appears that the advertisement of 1796 and the Moretown land records speak for themselves: where else could a man reduced in circumstances as Morgan was by 1795 find twenty pounds with which to pay for a hundred acres, except by the sale of his prized horse? The Grand List is clear: Morgan was listed at twenty-three pounds in 1792, twenty-seven in 1793, twenty in 1794—and thereafter not at all. By June of 1795 he possessed no property in Randolph that would place him on the Grand List. Since undeveloped land was not placed on the Grand List, presumably Morgan would not have been listed in Moretown. Surely Morgan sold the horse to Allen, and Allen paid Morgan in land. Less than a year later Jonathan Shepard of Montpelier bought the horse, paying, he said, two hundred dollars—" a very large price at that time."[12] The twenty pounds in land that Morgan received from Allen equaled $66.66.

Why did Morgan sell his great stallion, his "remarkably good natured" horse who may well have been a companion and friend? It is possible that Morgan could no longer afford to keep the horse properly; but if he had been in desperate need of actual money, surely he could have sold such a horse for cash. There may have been another reason for the sale. By 1795 Morgan was presumably aware of the progress of his illness, which, according to some accounts, had been noticed in his early manhood.[13] When he died less than three years after making the land purchase, Morgan had a half ounce of opium (value thirty-three cents) among his few possessions.

David F. Musto, M. D., historian and psychiatrist at Yale University and an authority on the history of the use of drugs in the United States, answered a query regarding the possession of this amount of opium at the time of Morgan's death in the following way:

> 'Lung fever' could have been a chronic lung infection other than tuberculosis. . . . In any event, the opium was probably taken for pain and to depress the cough reflex. . . . Half an ounce of opium was not a large amount if he was on the frontier, had a chronic condition and might need some at any time. The form was probably crude opium, since if it were a tincture or other form, it would probably have been noted. . . . He may have learned from experience what sized pinch to take. There were almost no efficacious medicines in the 18th and early 19th centuries other than opium; nearly everything else was ineffective, even dangerous, and perhaps foul tasting as well. . . . There was no Federal law in 1798 controlling opium and I doubt any Vermont state

or local laws affecting the sale of opium at the time. . . . In sum, it appears that this opium user was within the bounds of accepted medical practice for 1798.[14]

In examining a number of other estate inventories of Morgan's time and place, the writer has failed to find any mention of medicine. It would seem that Morgan, against whose estate there was a charge of $4.69 by Ezekiel Bissell "for doctoring in last sickness" and a further charge of $1.20 "for nursing and attendance in last sickness," had known illness for some months or more probably years before his death.

What could a man, so reduced in worldly possessions, so deprived of a helpmate, so ill, do for his young children? The eldest daughter was married and was busy with her own growing family. A boy of nine and three young girls could certainly not manage a stallion, nor could they profit from his stud fees. In eighteenth-century agrarian America, land was wealth. Every yeoman farmer of them all dreamed of leaving a thriving "home farm" to his heirs.

Justin Morgan, it seems, gave up his fine horse in order to buy land—the only security that he might conceivably pass on to his children.

His plan almost worked. The appraisers of Morgan's estate valued that estate at $308.32—a small amount when compared to the holdings of owners of large and expanding farms of the Randolph area, but by no means the estate of a town pauper. Among Morgan's assets were listed, as has been said, a cash note against William Rice for $94.24 and a stock note against him for $25.00. There was a stock note against Peter Edson for $41.60, and a "due bill" on Stiles Sherman for $5.00. There was a "book account" against Morgan's wife's brother-in-law, Aaron Smith, for $3.00, and similar book accounts against Joel Smith and Israel Converse. In a word, at the time of his death Morgan was still dealing with various men and believed that people owed him money, just as he owed people money. In the ensuing probate court actions the

charges against Rice and various other debtors were dis-
allowed, for reasons not explained. In 1800 Ezra Edgerton, the
administrator, sold the Moretown land for $66.66—exactly
what Morgan had paid for it. By the time the case was
concluded, on 4 March 1802, Ezra Egerton had died, Andrew
Steel had accepted his post, and the estate had dwindled to
$41.48. Expenses, it seems, also totaled $41.48, and the case
was closed. One may perhaps be excused if he is reminded of
the famous case of Jarndyce vs. Jarndyce in Dickens's *Bleak
House.*

Presumably Morgan thought that his hundred acres in
Moretown would provide at least a little security for his
children. The land was by no means useless. It passed from
Egerton to Porter Converse of Randolph for $66.66, and
Converse in 1806 sold it to Issachor Mayo, Jr. of New
Hampshire, for $400. In 1812 Issachor sold half the acreage to
Calvin Williams for $210.00. Calvin sold the fifty acres to
William Prentiss for $230.00—in 1813. And in 1822 Prentiss
sold the land to his son for $700. Morgan had not bought a
swamp or the rocky peak of a mountain.

And so Morgan died, on March 22, 1798, and Dunbar and
Ralston were allowed $3.13 "for articles in last sickness and
funeral charges." Horace Day was allowed fifty cents for
funeral charges. There is no record of what was sung at
Morgan's funeral, if indeed anything was sung.

His fellow townsmen placed over Morgan's grave the same
kind of carefully carved stone that marked the graves of most
New Englanders of the eighteenth century, whether they were
rich or poor, judges or farm hands. The profile bust of a man
that appears at the top of the stone is encircled by the wreath
of victory, and just below the wreath are two six-sided rosettes. Such rosettes, common on many gravestones in New
England, are assumed by scholars to be symbols of stars, and
by extension of souls mounting to heaven.[15] Taken in con-
junction with the wreath, they seem to repeat the message of
Morgan's "Judgment Anthem": "Oh, Death, where is thy
sting? O grave, where is thy victory?"

Justin Morgan's gravestone shows the rosettes and wreath of victory that were often used on New England gravestones in the eighteenth century. The rosettes are believed to represent souls mounting to Heaven; the wreath suggests victory over death. The gravestone is now in the Randolph Historical Society museum, Randolph, Vt. *Photo by Jack Rowell.*

This is the way that the life ended of Justin Morgan, husbandman, yeoman, briefly "esquire"—of Justin Morgan, in everything but the narrowly legalistic sense of the word, gentleman.

Notes

1. Cf. above, p. 50. Battell—philologist, author, editor, publisher, and philanthropist—who was born in Middlebury, Vt., in 1839 and was graduated from Middlebury College, was editor and publisher of *The Middlebury Register,* owner of an inn on Bread Loaf Mountain in Ripton (near Middlebury), and owner of a large farm at Weybridge, on the outskirts of Middlebury. In 1905 Battell gave to the United States government his 500-acre Weybridge Farm to serve as a center for the breeding of Morgan horses. He also made generous gifts of forested land to the state of Vermont, and of his Bread Loaf property to his alma mater, Middlebury College. The Morgan Horse Farm at Weybridge is now owned and managed by the University of Vermont.

The *Morgan Horse and Register* was published in Middlebury between 1894 and 1915 and *The American Stallion Register* was published in Middlebury between 1909 and 1911. Battell died in Washington, D.C., in 1915.

2. For details of these advertisements, see above, pp. 90-91.

3. Battell, *The American Stallion Register,* 2: xcii ff.

4. See Appendix C for details of these varying and interesting accounts.

5. It is interesting that Battell, who made an exhaustive study of the origin of "the Morgan horse," himself came to question the statements by Linsley and others that the horse was only fourteen hands high. In *The Morgan Horse and Register,* 1: 112, he quotes a letter written by John Woodbury in 1857 that states that "the original Morgan, as I best recollect, was in weight not more than one thousand pounds, and maybe one hundred pounds less; height, about same as Backman horse. . . ." Battell adds that the Backman horse was described as fifteen and a half hands high and declares that either the height of the Backman horse had been exaggerated "or Justin Morgan was taller than he has been reported. This is one of many suggestions that leads us to believe that Justin Morgan was considerably more than fourteen hands high." Battell was unaware of the 1796 advertisement for Figure (given above, p. 170) that states that he is fifteen hands three inches high.

6. Battell, *The American Stallion Register,* 2: ccviii.

7. Jude Moulton's story is recounted in the long article in *The Middlebury Register* of 23 January 1885 (see above, p. 123), which Battell attributes to Allen W. Thomson of Woodstock. It is interesting to note that in that same article, but in a section that does not quote Moulton, Thomson remarks, "Judge Griswold was Mr. Morgan's nearest neighbor. The judge's statement is, 'That early morning after Mr. Morgan got home, Mr. Morgan came to his house and wanted he should go over and see a colt he had taken home from where he used to live. The judge went over and was showed the colt in the pasture.'" It would seem that by the time Messrs. Moulton, Griswold, and Cottrell (see above, p. 46), as aging men, were asked what they remembered about "the original Justin Morgan horse," everyone wanted to believe, and did believe, that he had seen the horse at the very dawn of his great career.

8. See above, p. 48
9. See above, p. 45 and p. 49, n. 3. A microfilm copy of this newspaper is in the Wilbur Collection, University of Vermont's Bailey Library.
10. Town of Moretown, Land Records, 1: 61, deed dated 14 January 1795 and recorded 4 July 1796.
11. This story is told by Allen W. Thomson in the 9 October 1885 issue of *The Middlebury Register,* p. 8; but in the same article Thomson declares that Justin Morgan, Jr. "told his son, H. D. Morgan, now of Stockbridge, that he has made some wrong statements in regard to his father's horse," when he was first interviewed about the horse in 1842.
12. Battell, *The Morgan Horse and Register,* 1: 104. Battell quotes various chroniclers who state that Shephard purchased the horse from "a man in Woodstock," and this man soon became, in various accounts, William Rice. It is entirely possible, of course, that Figure passed from Morgan to Allen to Rice to Shepard within one year, in that day of fervent horse-trading.
13. See above, p. 45.
14. David F. Musto, M.D., Department of History, Yale University, to the author, 27 March 1972.
15. The highly symbolic nature of many gravestones erected by New England Puritans, who were firmly opposed to "graven images" in their meeting houses, has been described in detail by Allen I. Ludwig in his *Graven Images: New England Stonecarving and its Symbols, 1650-1815* [Middletown, Conn.: Wesleyan University Press, 1966]. For Ludwig's discussion of star and rosette images as symbols for the soul, see his p. 189.

10

Postlude

THE story of Justin Morgan did not end with his death, just as it did not begin with his birth. It went on—and goes on—in the lives of his descendants, in the performances of Morgan horses, and in the beauty of his music, which surfaced here and there during the nineteenth century and which is enjoying a revival in the late twentieth century.

The frail health that apparently dogged Morgan's steps also limited the number and age of his descendants. While many men of his era had so many children and grandchildren that one cannot even count their descendants in the 1970s, Morgan's line produced relatively few grandchildren and great-grandchildren. There was his obviously able daughter Emily, married to Asa Egerton, tavernkeeper, early widowed and early required to follow in her father's footsteps by sending her children out to other homes to provide them with adequate sustenance and education. The memoir of Emily's short but remarkable life tells of her fitting herself to teach, of her serving as teacher and Sunday-school teacher in the Randolph area until, after eleven years of separation from her children, she could call the three of them (Justin had died in babyhood) back to her home. It tells of how her daughter Martha, also a teacher, married a missionary, Asher Wright, and went to Buffalo, New York, only to die there at the age of twenty-three, in 1832. It tells the beginning of the story of her son, Albert Mirabeau, who was graduated from Dartmouth in 1829, went south to Georgia to teach, and died there in 1839, when he was thirty-two. It tells of how Emily herself, aged 44, died in 1828. The hymn of Doddridge, "While on the Verge of Life," which she asked to have sung at her funeral,[1] stressing as it does the nineteenth-century emphasis upon Jesus the Savior rather than the eighteenth-century emphasis upon God the Sovereign, might have seemed strange to Justin Morgan; but doubtless he would have accepted it as he did the Occom hymn that begins his "Judgment Anthem"— and as presumably he would have accepted any sincere statement of religious conviction. When Emily Egerton's estate was probated, one finds evidence of the love of fine things that one would expect of Justin Morgan and his descendants.[2] There are the two Britannia teapots valued at two dollars and the two silver tablespoons valued at $3.50. Most interesting, there is an "old bass viol" valued at five dollars— and one thirsts to jump to the conclusion that it was Justin Morgan's, until one reads in Emily's memoir that her husband was a devotee of the bass viol and played it assiduously.[3] The bass viol was left to the youngest of the three children, Asa, and with one-third of an account against Ebenezer Parkhurst, Jr. and M. H. Cady for $65.12, and a note against William Nutting for $29.98, was acknowledged by Asa, through his guardian Libbeus Egerton, as "his third" of Emily's estate.

Of the other descendants of Justin Morgan, it is easiest to trace those who bear his surname and who are of course descendants of his one son, Justin, Jr. This son, who lived out his life in Rochester and Stockbridge, Vermont, and died in Stockbridge in 1853, served briefly as a volunteer in the War of 1812; was a storekeeper in Rochester, where "Briggs and Morgan" in 1822 sold some brimstone and pearlash to Jeremiah Ingalls, another of the Vermont psalmodists; was town representative from Stockbridge to the Vermont House of Representatives in 1840 and senator from Windsor County in 1844-45; and represented Stockbridge at Vermont's constitutional convention of 1850. Justin, Jr. is spoken of as a fine musician, as are his children.[4] In the Helen Harkness Flanders Ballad Collection at the Middlebury College Library are two items that were presented to the library in the 1940s by Walter B. Mahony, a great-grandson of Justin Morgan, Jr. One is a copy-book of favorite tunes apparently prepared by Timothy B. Egerton of Randolph sometime around 1800, which contains three Morgan tunes; the other is a copy of the *Middlesex Collection of Church Music*, published in Boston in 1807. Stamped on the titlepage of the *Middlesex Collection* is the name *Justin Morgan*, in letters that look as if they may have been made by a rubber handstamp. Since the book was published nine years after Justin Morgan's death, the "Justin Morgan" marked on the titlepage may have been Justin Morgan, Jr. If so, Justin, Jr. was leaning heavily toward the often second-rate English hymn tunes that were becoming the fashion by 1807 and that were driving the very original American tunes of Morgan's day out of the popular hymnbooks. The *Middlesex Collection*, which was prepared for the Middlesex Musical Society in Massachusetts, contains no Morgan tunes but plenty by A. Williams, Tansur, Dr. Worgan, and other English composers whose works have not survived the test of time.

Of Justin, Jr.'s five children, four were sons; but of those four only one is known to have had descendants who in turn produced descendants. One of the four, Charles, who settled in Rochester, Vermont, was a dealer in hops, wool, and valerian root; and when he was interviewed by the editor of *The Middlebury Register* 8 January 1886, the interviewer spoke of him as "a gentleman of large means and an extensive dealer in wool and hops, both in this region and the West."

If one steps sideways in tracing the lines of Morgan descent, he finds other interesting persons. There is, for instance, Col. Jonathan Peckham Miller, son of Heman Miller and grandson of Morgan's sister, Eunice Miller. Jonathan, born in

Randolph in 1797 and early orphaned, grew up to win renown both as a soldier and as a citizen. Leaving the University of Vermont in 1824 to go to Greece and take part in the Greek war for independence, Miller won for himself, at the siege of Missolonghi, the title of "the American Daredevil." He returned to Vermont with Lord Byron's sword—and with a war orphan whom he adopted, Lucas Miltiades Miller. Thereafter Miller settled down in Montpelier to a distinguished career as lawyer, member of the state legislature, and anti-slavery champion.

Today, in the 1970s, one direct descendant of Justin Morgan is executive editor of a nationally known magazine and others are teachers; still others, living in Vermont, are farmers and businessmen. As late as 1908, one descendant of Justin Morgan, Justin Thatcher of Nashville, Tennessee, was said to possess a fine baritone singing voice.[5]

As to the Morgan horses—who needs to be told about them? There is hardly a horse show in the country that does not feature some members of that hardy, adaptable, brave, intelligent breed. They are, as they have always been, ready to carry a rider, to pull a plow, to draw a smart phaeton or a mundane wagon. They are as American as Yankee Doodle in their willingness to work, their hardy never-say-die attitude, their clever ability to figure out what to do next. Horse enthusiasts have written reams about them, describing how they brought an entire Vermont regiment down to Washington and the theater of the Civil War with no evidence of fatigue, or how they outlast other horses in the grueling trail rides of the twentieth century. Suffice it to say—the Morgan horse is today a prized catch of the horse fancier, as he has been for 170 years.

Morgan's music, once out of fashion, had to wait until American ears caught up with it again. When Culture with a capital *C* invaded America about 1810 and foreign music masters named Signor This and Mademoiselle That became prominent in American villages, music such as Morgan's disappeared very suddenly from the standard tunebooks used in the larger churches and singing schools and societies of New England. People started to make fun of the fuging tunes, with their repetitions of words that, if distorted, could be very funny indeed. Only rustics, it was soon implied, would favor such music. Samuel Griswold Goodrich, who as "Peter Parley" won fame as a writer of children's books, in the 1850s recalled that "Montgomery" had been the favorite of Molly Gregory, who came to the Goodrich house in Ridgfield, Connecticut, in the early years of the century, to help with the spinning. Molly would spin and sing in the attic, taking all four parts of "Montgomery" so that young Goodrich could hear "Oh, for a cooling . . . oh, for a cooling . . . oh, for a cooling" wherever he went, indoors or out. Goodrich told how in the church choir "Molly took upon herself the entire counter, for she had excellent lungs." He added that the fuging tunes "had then run a little mad."[6] Then there is the unknown "B" who, writing in 1854, made fun of the "Judgment Anthem" as "the glory of the front gallery" and of "Oh, for a cooling" ("Montgomery") that "chased itself round the circle like a dog after his tail, to the amusement of all the mischievous boys present, especially on a July Sabbath." "B" was speaking here of what he viewed as the nadir of church music, taught in "an obscure parish of Connecticut in 1803" under the instruction of "Jenks and Griswold" before Law and Olmstead rescued that and other parishes from such barbarity.[7] A more serious attack upon the fuging tune was made very early in the nineteenth century by John Hubbard, professor of mathematics at Dartmouth College, a composer of music and first president of the Handel Society of Dartmouth (founded in 1807 "to improve and cultivate the taste and promote true and genuine music and discountenance trifling unfinished pieces").[8] Hubbard read an *Essay on Music* before the Middlesex Musical Society, Dunstable, Massachusetts, in 1807, in which he fulminated against fuging tunes partly because their "chaos of words" could not "affect the heart, nor inform the understanding."[9] He assumed that if the treble was singing "your songs invite. . ." while the counter was singing "Let the high heav'ns. . ." and the tenor "Those spacious fields . . .," no one could make anything of the composition as a whole. One would need to be furnished "with ears as numerous as the eyes of Argus." Hubbard also objected to appropriating tunes "from the midnight revel, from the staggering bachanal, from the profane altar of Comus" to couple with hymns offered "in the temple of Jehovah." He suggests that the *Beggars' Opera* provided many of the "modern tunes" offered as suitable for psalm- and hymn-singing by some of his contemporary American tunebook compilers.[10]

By the time that Thomas Hastings, a prolific composer and prominent singing master of the nineteenth century, wrote on the history of American music in his *Musical Magazine* in 1836, he could feel justified in classifying Morgan and Benham among nine composers whom he singled out as peculiarly inept. He declares:

> Morgan is a name of more [than Jacob French's] notoriety. His Huntington and Montgomery were universal favorites among the lovers of the fuguing style. His Judgment Anthem was quite famous. Had he really intended it as a burlesque, he could scarcely have invented a worse thing. But public taste was then extensively perverted. The man, as we well recollect, was in good standing when he wrote the piece, and he doubtless did his best to produce good music. The words were awfully solemn, and this circumstance gave for a while, great celebrity to the tune.[11]

A few rugged individualists stood out against the rising tide of disapproval of our first American composers. Attention has already been invited to the stout defense of Morgan and his fellows by the Reverend Elkanah Kelsay Dare of Wilmington, Delaware, clergyman and musician who in a letter of 1811 boldly argued with the redoubtable Andrew Law on the merits of native American music.[12] Throughout the nineteenth century there were occasional attempts in New England to recognize the work of the early psalmodists. Thus G. W. Fargo and Jesse Pierce in 1847 brought out *Ancient Harmony Revived,* publishing their tunebook in Hallowell, Maine, and including in it works by Morgan and many of his fellows. They stoutly insisted that they need not offer apology "for sending forth our Aged Harmony to contend with the almost indefinite number of singing books that flood our country with their scientific, cold and heartless chords that make no lasting impression of devotional feelings." Again in 1879 Simeon Pease Cheney of Vermont brought out his *The American Singing Book* (Boston) and included in it not only many of the favorite tunes by Morgan and his contemporaries but also invaluable biographical notes collected by Cheney, his brother Moses Ela Cheney, and others who had known at first or certainly at second hand the subjects of their biographies.

As recently as 1940 a letter written by David Dana Hewitt of Mechanicsville, New York, to Walter B. Mahony of Scarborough-on-Hudson, grandson of Justin Morgan III, bears witness to the fact that Morgan's "Judgment Anthem" was not entirely forgotten in the Northeast during the nineteenth century.[13] Mr. Hewitt declares that "My grandmother, before her marriage in 1805, sang a difficult part in the soprano of the 'Judgment Day' Anthem in such a manner that she was the admiration and envy of her young companions." He goes on to say that in 1886 or 1887 he belonged to a Choral Club that "sang the 'Judgment' Anthem, and there was only one soprano singer that was able to take the difficult part in the Anthem. She was a girl of about 19 years of age."[14]

Morgan's music enjoyed its most continuous success, however, not in New England but in the West (Pennsylvania) and the South, where the country folk took it up and made it part of their standard repertoire. The "fasola" singers who embraced Law's "shape notes"—a device for aiding beginners by associating a given note with a given shape (a

triangular note for the tonic tone of a key, for instance)—also
embraced as their own "Montgomery" and the "Judgment
Anthem" in the camp meetings and singing schools of Pennsylvania and the piedmont of Virginia and farther south and
west. Unfortunately, these and other Morgan tunes can easily
be oversimplified and roughened so that they sound like the
most primitive folk tunes conceivable. It is in this form that
one hears them today sung by some of the "fasola" singers of
the southern mountain regions.[15] In one of the most popular
books used by the "fasola" singers, *The Original Sacred
Harp*,[16] one finds Morgan's "Montgomery" attributed to
"the Rev. David Morgan" (a man who lived a generation or
more after Morgan's time); his "Sounding Joy" attributed to
B. F. White; his "Symphony" attributed to R. D. Munson of
Williston, Vermont; and his "Huntington" attributed to no
one in particular.

When in 1949 one of the ablest of modern students of
American musical history, Allen Perdue Britton, wrote his
Ph.D. dissertation ("Theoretical Introductions in American
Tunebooks to 1800"),[19] it seemed to him that there was no real
awareness among Americans in general of just how good the
music of Morgan and his contemporaries was. "At this late
date," he wrote, "we can do little else than mourn the loss of
our first original art music. A sacrifice upon the twin altars of
good taste and correct harmony, it vanished from the knowledge of serious musicians." How great Britton felt this loss to
be was indicated in the conclusion:

> The American people, deprived of an art music based upon
> a native idiom of immediate appeal to their musical sen-
> sibilities, have ever since manifested an understandable
> suspicion of the essential validity of all serious music, or
> have come to support and perhaps even to enjoy it only
> from motives more social than artistic. . . . If a Billings or a
> Morgan could write anthems in the eighteenth century
> which seemed not to need a prior lesson in music apprecia-
> tion for their enjoyment by musically unsophisticated

colonial audiences, it might be that a contemporary composer could succeed in reaching the fairly well educated
modern public if his music was based upon a recognizable
idiom.[18]

Fortunately, since Britton wrote his thesis many musicians
and music lovers have discovered the value of the works
written by Morgan and his fellows. In the past score of years
there has developed, in fact, genuine enthusiasm for the
compositions of the psalmodists. One finds, for instance, that
Thomas Canning, having discovered "Amanda," used it as
the basis of his "Fantasy on a Hymn Tune by Justin Morgan
for Double String Quartet and String Orchestra."[19] Critics
and historians have begun to analyze the contributions of
Morgan, as well as those of his contemporary composers. As
has been said, Alan Clark Buechner includes comments on
Morgan in his "Yankee Singing Schools and The Golden
Age of Choral Music in New England, 1760-1800", and Ralph
T. Daniel in *The Anthem in New England before 1800* makes
an extended analysis of the musical style and power of
"Judgment Anthem." Wilfrid Howard Mellers, it will be
recalled, in *Music in a New Found Land: Themes and
Developments in the History of American Music* treats Morgan as perhaps the most characteristic composer of his
school.

Recent recordings such as *The New England Harmony*
performed by the Old Sturbridge Singers and *The American
Harmony* presented by the Chapel Choir of the University of
Maryland include some of Morgan's best-known tunes, and
Vermont Harmony, a recording made in 1973 by the University of Vermont Choral Union, includes all of Morgan's
music that has come down to today.[20]

At the sesquicentennial celebration of the First Methodist
Church in Burlington, Vermont, held in the fall of 1973, at
the bicentennial celebration of Morgan's hometown, West
Springfield, Massachusetts, held in April of 1974, and at other
programs in other towns and churches—once again almost

two centuries after Morgan wrote tunes to the glory of God, men and women "sound His praise abroad, and hymns of glory sing" in the strong, soaring airs given us by Justin Morgan, yeoman.

Notes

1. See above, p. 156.

2. Randolph Probate District Records, 11: 21, record of probate court held 4 July 1828 at Brookfield, Vermont.

3. The fact that no one knows what instrument Justin Morgan played, although all singing masters seem to have played some instrument, is evidence of how fragmentary knowledge is regarding Justin's musical career.

4. An account book of Briggs and Morgan is in the Vermont Historical Society Library, Montpelier. The second Justin Morgan's fine tenor voice and musical accomplishments are remembered by Moses Ela Cheney in Simeon Pease Cheney, *The American Singing Book* (Boston, White, Smith and Company, 1879), p. 171.

5. Ella Janette Morgan Mahony, daughter of Justin Morgan III, to her daughter, Emma Goodrich Mahony, dated 29 August 1908 from Battle Creek, Mich. The letter is now in the possession of Mrs. Mahony's granddaughter, Janet Morgan Mahony Wilson of Washington, D.C., and is quoted with her permission.

6. Samuel Griswold Goodrich, *Recollections of a Lifetime* (Auburn, N.Y.: Miller, Orton and Mulligan, 1856), quoted in June Barrows Mussey, *Yankee Life* (New York: Knopf, 1947), p. 149.

7. N. H. Allen, "Old Time Music and Musicians," *The Connecticut Quarterly* 3 (1897): 288. The "Jenks and Griswold" of "B's" comment are Stephen Jenks and Elijah Griswold, whose tunebooks were extensively used in the early nineteenth century. Jenks's *The American Compiler of Sacred Harmony* (Northampton, Mass.: Privately printed, 1803) includes Morgan's "Huntington."

8. Louis Pichierri, "Music in New Hampshire, 1623-1800" (Ph.D., Syracuse University, 1956), p. 245.

9. John Hubbard, *Essay on Music* (Boston: Manning and Loring, 1808), p. 18.

10. Ibid., p. 19. Charles Wesley's great satire in hymn form on the idea that gay secular tunes are unsuitable for religious use ("Enlisted in the cause of sin, / why should a good be evil?") was given its first American setting by Vermont's Jeremiah Ingalls in his *The Christian Harmony* (Exeter, N.H.: Henry Ranlet, 1805). The tune that Ingalls married to the Wesley words is called "Innocent Sounds."

11. Thomas Hastings, ed., *The Musical Magazine* 1 (1835): 87.

12. See above, p. 145.

13. The writer is indebted to Mary Murray Brown (Mrs. Leland S. Brown) of Bedford, N. Y., for making available to her this letter written 18 June 1940 to Mrs. Brown's father, the late Walter B. Mahony. Mrs. Brown is a great-great-great-granddaughter of Justin Morgan.

14. In the conclusion of his letter Mr. Hewitt tells of how, in 1937, when the Presbyterian Church in Mechanicsville, N.Y., held its centennial celebration, he instituted a search for a copy of the "Judgment Anthem," and was successful in turning up a copy and interesting the choir in the work.

15. Compare, for instance, *Folk Music of the United States: Sacred Harp Singing*, ed. George Pullen Jackson, Library of Congress Music Division Recording Laboratory, AAFS L11.

16. *The Original Sacred Harp*, Denson rev. ed. (Cullman, Ala.: Sacred Harp Publishing Company, 1967).

17. Allen Perdue Britton, *Theoretical Introductions in American Tune-Books to 1800* (Ann Arbor, Mich.: University Microfilms, 1949).

18. Ibid., p. 366.

19. The fantasy is played by the Houston Symphony Orchestra, conducted by Leopold Stokowski on Everest Record LPBR 6070.

20. *New England Harmony*, Folkways Records FA 2377, is performed by the Old Sturbridge Singers with Floyd Corson as singing master and members of the Harvard Wind Ensemble. The music was selected and annotated by Alan C. Buechner and the recording done by Bill Bonyun with Arthur F. Schrader as coordinator.

American Harmony, Washington Records WLP 418, is performed by the Chapel Choir of the University of Maryland, Fague Springmann, conductor; the music selected and annotated by Irving Lowens.

Vermont Harmony, Philo 1000, is performed by the University of Vermont Choral Union directed by James G. Chapman, with notes by Betty Bandel and James G. Chapman.

Appendix A

The Music of Justin Morgan
Compiled and Edited by
James G. Chapman

All of Justin Morgan's music, except "Despair," first appears in Asahel Benham's *Federal Harmony, Containing in a Familiar Manner, The Rudiments of Psalmody, Together with a Collection of Church Music (Most of Which Are Entirely New)* (New Haven, Conn.: A. Morse, 1790). "Despair" first appears in Andrew Adgate's *Philadelphia Harmony, Part Two* [third edition], printed in Philadelphia by Westcott and Adgate in 1791, and bound with Adgate's *Rudiments of Music,* fourth edition, printed by John M'Culloch.

Unless otherwise indicated, the texts are from Isaac Watts's *The Psalms of David. Imitated in the Language of the New Testament, and Applied to The Christian State and Worship,* first published in England in 1719.

The counter (alto) voice, which appears in many of the pieces with the alto- or C-clef, has been transposed to the G-clef, used more frequently today. Meter signatures are those of the originals with one exception: the sign $\supset$, no longer in use, has been rendered ¢. According to writings of the period, the former is slightly faster than the latter (two seconds to the bar, as opposed to three); but musical and textual sense should override mathematical exactitude. Other than these changes, every effort has been made to reproduce the originals, faithfully and unedited, from what are believed to be the earliest sources. Printing errors there may be, but on the basis of the overall style of the genre one cannot be sure that many of the strange dissonances, unusual voice leadings, and so on, are not precisely what the composer intended.

Metrical indications at the headings of the pieces follow common practice: Short Meter, S.M. (66.86); Short Meter Double, S.M.D.; Common Meter, C.M. (86.86); Common Meter Double, C.M.D.; Long Meter, L.M. (88.88); Long Meter Double, L.M.D. Texts that differ from these frequently-used patterns are so indicated.

Comments on the texts are by Betty Bandel.

It is pointless to fault the psalmodists for not following the "rules" often thought of as "traditional" or "correct" harmonic procedures. Morgan is certainly not bothered by them in any of his music. The great rhythmic drive of this fuging tune and the strength resulting from the upward movement of its melodic lines more than compensate for any breech of rules.

SOUNDING-JOY

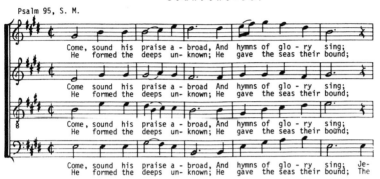

* There is no repeat sign in the 1790 edition.

The style here is similar to that of the preceding piece. The mere allusion to the fuging principle in what is predominantly a four-part harmonization emphasizes the importance of the principle itself in Morgan's approach to writing. A primary meaning of the word *symphony* in the eighteenth century was a composition to be sung or played with all parts sounding harmoniously and simultaneously, rather than with one part answering another as in the "fuges."

Psalm 50, 10 10.10 10.10 10

SYMPHONY

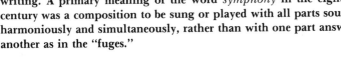

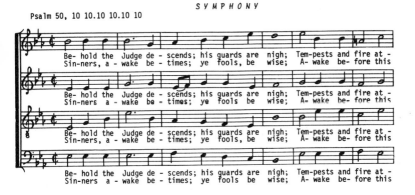

Be- hold the Judge de - scends; his guards are nigh; Tem-pests and fire at -
Sin-ners, a - wake be - times; ye fools, be wise; A- wake be- fore this

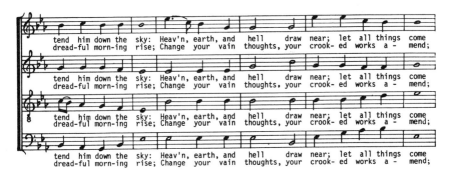

tend him down the sky: Heav'n, earth, and hell draw near; let all things come
dread-ful morn-ing rise; Change your vain thoughts, your crook- ed works a - mend;

To hear his jus-tice, and the sin - ner's doom:___ But gath-er first my
Fly to the Sav-ior, make the Judge your friend:___ Lest like a li - on

Psalm 90, L. M.

Death like an o - - ver - flow - ing stream, Sweeps us a - way;___ our
Through ev - 'ry age, e - - ter - nal God, Thou art our rest,___ our

life's a dream, An emp - ty tale, a morn - - ing flow'r,
safe a- bode; High was thy throne, e'er heav'n___ was made,

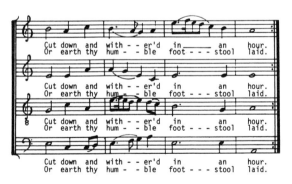

Cut down and with - - er'd in___ an hour.
Or earth thy hum - - ble foot - - - stool laid.

It has been assumed by some historians of music that this lovely, folk-like song was written by Morgan as an elegy to his wife, who died in March 1791 but the song was published the year before Martha Morgan died. "Despair," however, printed in 1791 after Martha's death, mentions "Amanda," and is the only Morgan work to use a secular text. It seems probable that "Despair" was written as a lament for the composer's wife.

The virtual absence from the melody (the tenor) of the defining sixth scale degree and the unraised seventh give the piece a strong Dorian quality. The sharp, simultaneous cross relation (f-sharp and f-natural) in the first measure is as uncompromising as death itself, while the open fifth at the beginning and at various cadences suggests its bleakness.

This vigorous work, praised by musicologist Alan C. Buechner for the "unusual skill" with which the fuging section is handled (there are actually two separate fuging sections), is one of the hundred psalm and hymn tunes "most frequently printed" in American tunebooks of the eighteenth century, according to Richard Crawford ("Connecticut Sacred Music Imprints," in *Music Library Association Notes, June 1971*). It is the only tune by a Vermonter to be so distinguished, and it remained a favorite through much of the nineteenth century. It is still in print in the *Original Sacred Harp* (1966 edition), a tune-book printed in Alabama.

MONTGOMERY

Psalm 63, C. M. D.

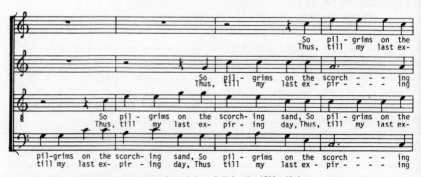

* The alto note may have been intended as "a" in the 1790 edition.

scorch-ing sand, Be- neath a burn-ing sky, Long for a cool-ing stream,
pir - ing day, I'll bless my God and King; Thus will I lift my hands,

sand, Be- neath a burn-ing sky, Long for a
day, I'll bless my God and King; Thus will I

scorch-ing sand, Be- neath a burn-ing sky,
pir - ing day, I'll bless my God and King;

sand, Be- neath a burn-ing sky,
day, I'll bless my God and King;

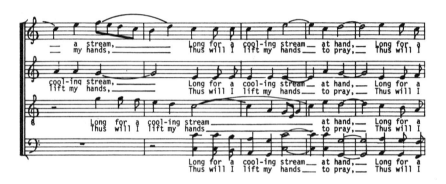

__ a stream, Long for a cool-ing stream__ at hand,__ Long for a
__ my hands, Thus will I lift my hands__ to pray; Thus will I

cool-ing stream, Long for a cool-ing stream__ at hand,__ Long for a
lift my hands, Thus will I lift my hands__ to pray, Thus will I

Long for a cool-ing stream __ at hand, Long for a
Thus will I lift my hands to pray, Thus will I

Long for a cool-ing stream__ at hand,__ Long for a
Thus will I lift my hands__ to pray, Thus will I

cool-ing stream at hand, And they must drink or die. die.
lift my hands to pray, And tune my lips to sing. sing.

cool-ing stream at hand, And they must drink or die. die.
lift my hands to pray, And tune my lips to sing. sing.

cool-ing stream at hand, And they must drink or die. die.
lift my hands to pray, And tune my lips to sing. sing.

cool-ing stream at hand, And they must drink or die. die.
lift my hands to pray, And tune my lips to sing. sing.

Morgan's only fuging tune to begin in triple meter also has elements of two "subjects" in the fuging section. There is even an attempt at inverting "subject" material, a rather sophisticated technique for the American frontier.

PLEASANT VALLEY

Psalm 119, C. M.

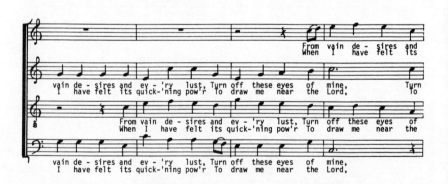

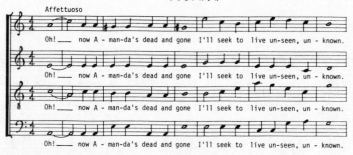

Text: Altered from the last stanza of Alexander Pope's *Ode on Solitude*.

See note on "Amanda." Morgan chose as the basis for his "Despair" the last stanza of Alexander Pope's "Ode on Solitude," written when the poet was a schoolboy. Pope, echoing the Latin poets whom he was studying, sang of the joys of simple rural life; but Morgan, by the addition of a first line quite different in tone from the pastoral tone of Pope's ode, made the poem into a lament. Pope's stanza reads:

> Thus let me live, unseen, unknown;
> Thus unlamented, let me die,
> Steal from the world, and not a stone
> Tell where I lie.

As in "Amanda," the Dorian mode is in evidence, and cross relations are effectively used ("unlamented" and "tell"). Notice also the haunting medial cadence, ". . . let me die."

As in "Montgomery," Morgan sets two verses of text to the somewhat extended musical structure. Unlike "Montgomery," however, "Huntington" has only one fuging section, which is effectively framed by the opening and closing portions. To signal the end of the "fuge" Morgan gradually thins his texture by dropping out upper voices over a pedal point in the bass, thus reversing the additive procedure with which a normal fuging section begins. Here, and in "Montgomery," splitting the bass voice into octaves emphasizes the importance composers attached to this voice. Vermont's Joel Harmon, Jr., like the Bostonian Billings, declares that "more than half of the strength of the voices ought to be on the bass."

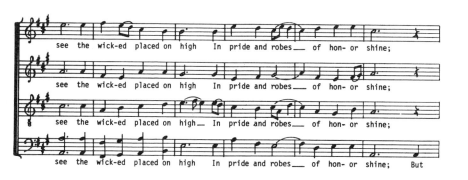

* The alto note might have been intended as a "b" in the 1790 edition.

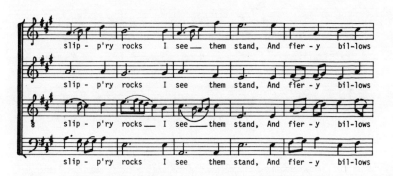

With "Sounding Joy" and "Pleasant Valley," "Wethersfield" is of the shorter, straightforward type of fuging tune. Morgan does, however, make another attempt at inverting his "subject" when the soprano enters the fuging fray.

worlds of light, Be- gin ___ the song. song.
no - thing came, To praise ___ the Lord. Lord.

worlds of light, Be- gin the song. song.
no - thing came, To praise the Lord. Lord.

worlds of light, Be- gin ___ the song. sung.
no - thing came, To praise ___ the Lord. Lord.

worlds of light, Be- gin the song. Ye song.
no - thing came, To praise the Lord. He Lord.

Most anthems written by the New England psalmodists were set to words taken directly from the poetic prose of the Bible (King James version). Morgan, however, drew on the poets of his era for his text, and in doing so coupled in one anthem an elaborate ode by Isaac Watts with one of the barest and most direct hymns of the young America. The American hymn, "Hark, Ye Mortals," may in fact have been written by an Indian, the Mohican who was an ordained Presbyterian clergyman, the Reverend Samson Occom, in whose *A Choice Collection of Hymns and Spiritual Songs*, published in 1774, the hymn first appeared. The Watts poem "The Day of Judgment," an ode in the irregular meter known as "English Sapphic," was included by the thiry-two-year-old poet and clergyman in his *Horae Lyricae*, published in 1706. Lines from a third well-known hymn, "Lo, He Cometh," by the English hymnist John Cennick, are also woven into the text of the anthem. The combination of the direct, uncompromising challenge of "Hark, Ye Mortals" with Watts's vivid language and the consolation of "Lo, He Cometh" seems to have helped to make Morgan's work one of the most popular anthems of its era.

Musicians have remarked that the early American psalmodists, with little formal musical training, knew too little of harmonic structure to give their longer works, the anthems, variety and form. Morgan apparently sought for variety by employing two unusual devices: he used a sudden change of range (tessitura) when the text invited such a change, and he also employed what on paper looks like an equally sudden and even startling shift to an unrelated key without preliminary modulation (e-minor to E-flat-major and back again). It has been argued by Karl Kroeger in "The Worcester Collection of Sacred Harmony and Sacred Music in America, 1786-1803" (Ph.D. Brown University, 1976, pp. 286-87), that eighteenth-century American musicians used this notation merely to indicate a shift from e-minor to E-major, and that singers continued singing on the same pitch level when they encountered the change in mode. Morgan also seems to have chosen voices to introduce solo passages with special care that the voice would be appropriate to the words being sung. Thus the counter (alto), which was normally sung by boys' voices in Morgan's day, introduces most passages that deal with "Christ victorious," and the high treble (women's voices) sounds the first trumpet-like warning of an impending judgment that will lead both to heaven and to hell. In effect, the message of the text was so important to Morgan that he allowed it to dictate the musical form of his composition. In his anthem, at least, he might well be called a "rhapsodist" rather than a psalmodist.

Hark, Hark, ye mor-tals hear the trum-pet sound-ing loud the might-y

Hark, Hark,

Hark, Hark,

Hark, sound-ing loud the might-y

roar. Hark the arch- an-gel's voice pro- claim-ing: Thou, old time, shall be no more!

Thou, old time, shall be no more!

Hark the arch- an-gel's voice pro- claim-ing: Thou, old time, shall be no more!

roar. Hark the arch- an-gel's voice pro- claim-ing: Thou, old time, shall be no more!

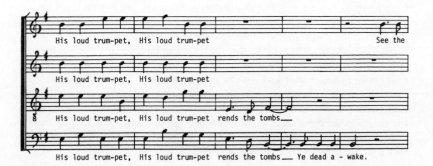

His loud trum-pet, His loud trum-pet See the

His loud trum-pet, His loud trum-pet

His loud trum-pet, His loud trum-pet rends the tombs

His loud trum-pet, His loud trum-pet rends the tombs Ye dead a - wake.

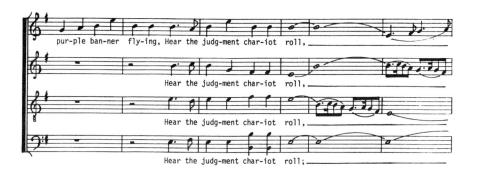

purple ban-ner fly-ing, Hear the judg-ment char-iot roll, ____

Hear the judg-ment char-iot roll, ____

Hear the judg-ment char-iot roll, ____

Hear the judg-ment char-iot roll; ____

roll; ____

roll; ____ Hear the sound of

roll; ____

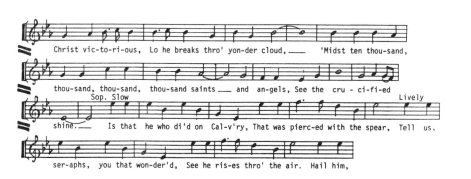

Christ vic-to-ri-ous, Lo he breaks thro' yon-der cloud, ____ 'Midst ten thou-sand,

thou-sand, thou-sand, thou-sand saints ____ and an-gels, See the cru - ci-fi-ed

Sop. Slow   Lively

shine. ____ Is that he who di'd on Cal-v'ry, That was pierc-ed with the spear, Tell us,

ser-aphs, you that won-der'd, See he ris-es thro' the air. Hail him,

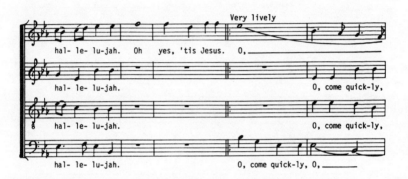

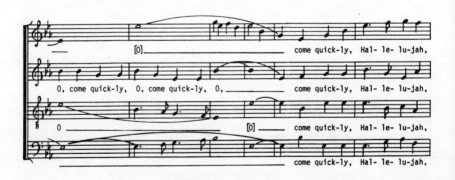

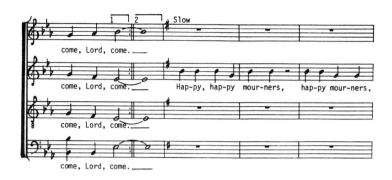

come, Lord, come. ___

come, Lord, come. ___ Hap-py, hap-py mour-ners, hap-py mour-ners,

come, Lord, come. ___

come, Lord, come. ___

Soft

hap - py mour-ners, Lo, ___ in clouds ___ he comes, he comes.

View him smil-ing,

All ye na-tions now shall sing him

All ye na-tions now shall sing him

Now de-ter-min'd ev-'ry e-vil to de-stroy.

songs of ev - -er-last-ing joy. Now re-demp-tion long ex-pec-ted, See the so-lemn

songs of ev - -er-last-ing joy. Now re-demp-tion long ex-pec-ted, See the so-lemn

Now re-demp-tion long ex-pec-ted, See the so-lemn

Now re-demp-tion long ex-pec-ted, See the so-lemn

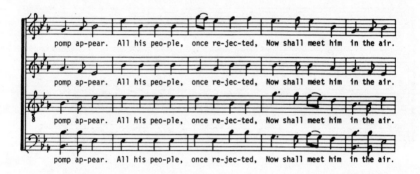

pomp ap-pear. All his peo-ple, once re-jec-ted, Now shall meet him in the air.

pomp ap-pear. All his peo-ple, once re-jec-ted, Now shall meet him in the air.

pomp ap-pear. All his peo-ple, once re-jec-ted, Now shall meet him in the air.

pomp ap-pear. All his peo-ple, once re-jec-ted, Now shall meet him in the air.

Hal-le- lu- jah, hal-le- lu- jah, wel-come, wel-come, bleed-ing Lamb. Now his

Hal-le- lu- jah, hal-le- lu- jah, wel-come, wel-come, bleed-ing Lamb. Now his

Hal-le- lu- jah, hal-le- lu- jah, wel-come, wel-come, bleed-ing Lamb. Now his

Hal-le- lu- jah, hal-le- lu- jah, wel-come, wel-come, bleed-ing Lamb. Now his

mer-it by the harp-ers, Thro' the e - ter-nal deep re- sounds.____ Now re-

mer-it by the harp-ers, Thro' the e - ter-nal deep re- sounds. Now re-

mer-it by the harp-ers, Thro' the e - ter-nal deep re- sounds. Now re-

mer-it by the harp-ers, Thro' the e - ter-nal deep re- sounds.____ Now re-

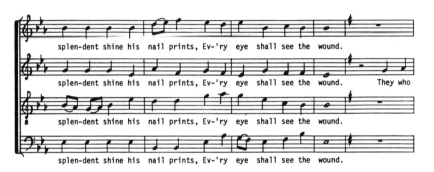

splen-dent shine his nail prints, Ev-'ry eye shall see the wound.

splen-dent shine his nail prints, Ev-'ry eye shall see the wound. They who

splen-dent shine his nail prints, Ev-'ry eye shall see the wound.

splen-dent shine his nail prints, Ev-'ry eye shall see the wound.

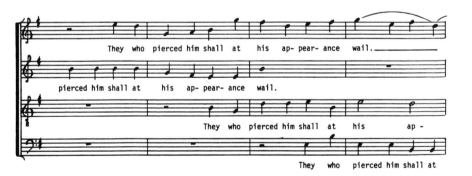

They who pierced him shall at his ap- pear- ance wail._____

pierced him shall at his ap- pear- ance wail.

They who pierced him shall at his ap -

They who pierced him shall at

pear-ance wail. _____ Ev-'ry is-land, sea and moun-tain,

his ap - pear - ance wail. _____

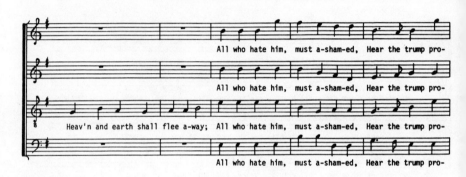

All who hate him, must a-sham-ed, Hear the trump pro-

All who hate him, must a-sham-ed, Hear the trump pro-

Heav'n and earth shall flee a-way; All who hate him, must a-sham-ed, Hear the trump pro-

All who hate him, must a-sham-ed, Hear the trump pro-

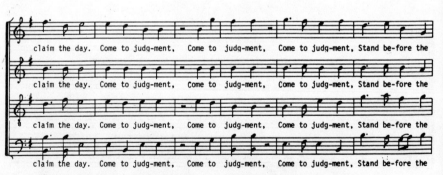

claim the day. Come to judg-ment, Come to judg-ment, Come to judg-ment, Stand be-fore the

claim the day. Come to judg-ment, Come to judg-ment, Come to judg-ment, Stand be-fore the

claim the day. Come to judg-ment, Come to judg-ment, Come to judg-ment, Stand be-fore the

claim the day. Come to judg-ment, Come to judg-ment, Come to judg-ment, Stand be-fore the

* Lower Bass note is clearly an "F"; I have taken it to mean an octave. "E."

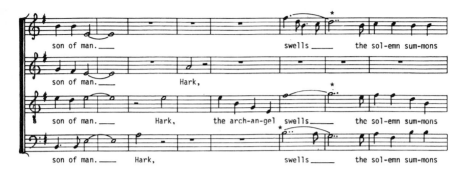

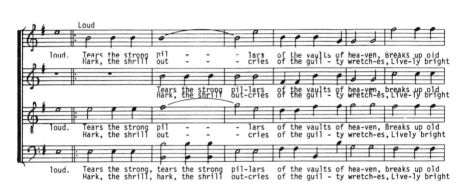

* Printed as ♩ ♩· in the 1790 edition.

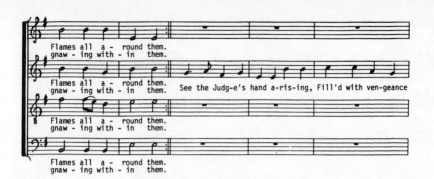

Flames all a - round them.
gnaw - ing with - in them.

Flames all a - round them.
gnaw - ing with - in them. See the Judg-e's hand a-ris-ing, Fill'd with ven-geance

Flames all a - round them.
gnaw - ing with - in them.

Flames all a - round them.
gnaw - ing with - in them.

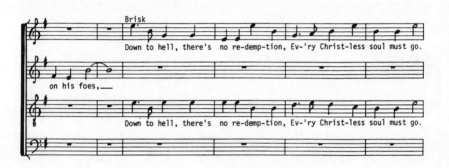

Brisk

Down to hell, there's no re-demp-tion, Ev-'ry Christ-less soul must go.

on his foes, ___

Down to hell, there's no re-demp-tion, Ev-'ry Christ-less soul must go.

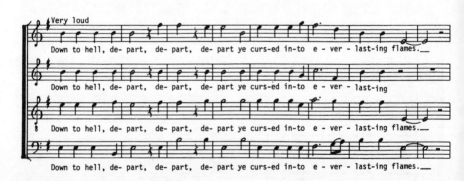

Very loud

Down to hell, de-part, de-part, de-part ye curs-ed in-to e - ver - last-ing flames. ___

Down to hell, de-part, de-part, de-part ye curs-ed in-to e - ver - last-ing

Down to hell, de-part, de-part, de-part ye curs-ed in-to e - ver - last-ing flames. ___

Down to hell, de-part, de-part, de-part ye curs-ed in-to e - ver - last-ing flames. ___

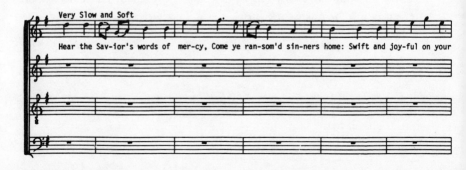

Very Slow and Soft

Hear the Sav-ior's words of mer-cy, Come ye ran-som'd sin-ners home: Swift and joy-ful on your

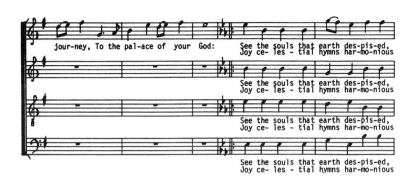

jour-ney, To the pal-ace of your God:

See the souls that earth des-pis-ed,
Joy ce- les - tial hymns har-mo-nious

See the souls that earth des-pis-ed,
Joy ce- les - tial hymns har-mo-nious

See the souls that earth des-pis-ed,
Joy ce- les - tial hymns har-mo-nious

See the souls that earth des-pis-ed,
Joy ce- les - tial hymns har-mo-nious

In ce - les-tial glo-ries move, Hal-le - lu- jah big with won- der, Prais- ing Christ's e -
In soft sym-pho- ny re - sound; An-gels, ser-aphs, harps and trum-pets, Swell the sweet an-

In ce - les-tial glo-ries move, Hal-le - lu- jah big with won- der Prais- ing Christ's e -
In soft sym-pho- ny re - sound; An-gels, ser-aphs, harps and trum-pets, Swell the sweet an-

In ce - les-tial glo-ries move, Hal-le - lu- jah big with won- der, Prais- ing Christ's e -
In soft sym-pho- ny re - sound; An-gels, ser-aphs, harps and trum-pets, Swell the sweet an-

In ce - les-tial glo-ries move, Hal-le - lu- jah big with won- der, Prais- ing Christ's e -
In soft sym-pho- ny re - sound; An-gels, ser-aphs, harps and trum-pets, Swell the sweet an-

ter-nal love; Hal- le- lu - jah, hal- le- lu - jah, ech - o through the realms of light.
gel-ic sound; Hail Al-migh- ty, hail Al-migh- ty, Great e-ter - nal

ter-nal love; Hal- le- lu - jah, hal- le- lu - jah, ech - o through the realms of light.
gel-ic sound; Hail Al-migh- ty, hail Al-migh- ty, Great e-ter - nal

ter-nal love; Hal- le- lu - jah, hal- le- lu - jah, ech - o through the realms of light.
gel-ic sound; Hail Al-migh- ty, hail Al-migh- ty, Great e-ter - nal

ter-nal love; Hal- le- lu - jah, hal- le- lu - jah, ech - o through the realms of light.
gel-ic sound; Hail Al-migh- ty, hail Al-migh- ty, Great e-ter - nal

Lord, A - men.

Lord, A - men.

Lord, A - men.

Lord, A - men.

Appendix B

Text and Sources of the "Judgment Anthem"

The "Judgment Anthem" gives evidence of Justin Morgan's independence and originality in his choice of texts, as well as in his musical style. Preferring poetry to the poetic prose of the King James version of the Bible (which was customarily used by writers of anthems in his day), Morgan drew most of his text from three sources: Isaac Watts's English Sapphic ode, "The Day of Judgment" (first published in *Horae Lyricae* in 1706); John Cennick's hymn, "Lo, He Cometh" (1752); and the American hymn, "Hark, ye mortals, hear the trumpet," which first appeared in the book of hymns and spiritual songs collected, edited, and presumably partially written by the Reverend Samson Occom, and published in 1774. It is probable that "Hark, Ye Mortals" was written by Occom, the Mohican Indian and Presbyterian clergyman whose collection of hymns, many of them direct and compelling in their manner of presentation, enjoyed considerable popularity and ran through several editions. Morgan's "Judgment Anthem" picks up lines from two other hymns, "The Great Assize" and "On the Resurrection," both of which appear in Occom's book. Cennick's "Lo! He Cometh" also appears in Occom. Indeed, Watts's "The Day of Judgment" is in Occom, just as it was in the copy of *Horae Lyricae* that Morgan owned at the time of his death. When one discovers that the Occom book emphasizes hymns in trochaic meter and realizes that the "Judgment Anthem" is almost entirely trochaic, except for the lines that use the dactylic and anapestic feet of Watts's English Sapphic ode, one is led to suspect that Morgan had a copy of Occom at hand as he composed his anthem.

Morgan allows the message—theological and musical—which he wishes to convey, to take precedence over all such minor matters as the rhythmic pattern and rhyme scheme of the poetry appropriated for his purpose. It will be seen that in some cases he tears a line out of one stanza in a given hymn and marries it to lines from another stanza, without regard to the carefully worked out rhyme scheme of the original hymn. In the analysis given below, lines from "Hark, ye mortals" are identified as "Occom"; those from "The Day of Judgment" as "Watts"; those from "Lo, He cometh" as "Cennick"; those from "The Great Assize" (in Occom) as "Assize"; and those from "On the Resurrection" (in Occom) as "Resurrection."

"Judgment Anthem"

1	Hark, ye mortals, hear the trumpet	Occom
2	Sounding loud the mighty roar,	Occom
3	Hark, the archangel's voice proclaiming	Occom
4	Thou, old time, shall be no more!	Occom
5	His loud trumpet	Assize
6	Rends the tombs—Ye dead awake	Assize
7	See the purple banner flying,	Occom
8	Hear the judgment chariot roll.	Occom
9	Hear the sound of Christ victorious	unidentified
10	Lo he breaks thro' yonder cloud	Resurrection
11	Midst ten thousand thousand saints and angels	Cennick
12	See the crucified shine.	Cennick
13	Is that he who died on Calv'ry	Resurrection (Stanza 5)
14	That was pierced with the spear	Resurrection (Stanza 5)

15 Tell us, seraphs, you that wonder'd,	Resurrection (Stanza 2)
16 See he rises thro' the air.	Resurrection (Stanza 5)
17 Hail him, hail him—Oh yes, 'tis Jesus	unidentified
18 Hallelujah, Hallelujah—Oh yes, 'tis Jesus	unidentified
19 O come quickly, O come quickly	Cennick (Stanza 6)
20 Hallelujah, come, Lord come.	Cennick (Stanza 6)
21 Happy, happy mourners, happy mourners,	Cennick (Stanza 4)
22 Lo, in clouds he comes, he comes.	Cennick (Stanza 4)
23 View him smiling, now determin'd	Cennick (Stanza 6)
24 Ev'ry evil to destroy.	Cennick (Stanza 6)
25 All ye nations now shall sing him	Cennick (Stanza 6)
26 Songs of everlasting joy.	Cennick (Stanza 6)
27 Now redemption long expected	Cennick (Stanza 5)
28 See the solemn pomp appear.	Cennick (Stanza 5)
29 All his people, once rejected	Cennick (Stanza 5)
30 Now shall meet him in the air.	Cennick (Stanza 5)
31 Hallelujah, hallelujah,	Cennick (Stanza 5)
32 Welcome, welcome, bleeding Lamb.	unidentified
33 Now his merit by the harpers	Cennick (Stanza 2)
34 Thro' the eternal deep resounds.	Cennick (Stanza 2)
35 Now resplendent shine his nail prints,	Cennick (Stanza 2)
36 Ev'ry eye shall see the wound.	Cennick (Stanza 2)
37 They who pierced him	Cennick (Stanza 2)
38 Shall at his appearance wail.	Cennick (Stanza 2)
39 Ev'ry island, sea and mountain,	Cennick (Stanza 3)
40 Heav'n and earth shall flee away;	Cennick (Stanza 3)
41 All who hate him, must ashamed,	Cennick (Stanza 3)
42 Hear the trump proclaim the day.	Cennick (Stnaza 3)
43 Come to judgment, come to judgment,	Cennick (Stanza 3)
44 Stand before the son of man.	Cennick (Stanza 3)
45 Hark the archangel	Occom
46 Swells the solemn summons loud,	Occom
47 Tears the strong pillars of the vault of heaven	Watts
48 Breaks up old marble, the repose of princes;	Watts
49 See the graves open and the bones arising,	Watts

50 Flames all around them.	Watts
51 Hark the shrill outcries of the guilty wretches,	Watts
52 Lively bright horror and amazing anguish,	Watts
53 Stare through their eyelids, while the living worm lies	Watts
54 Gnawing within them.	Watts
55 See the Judge's hand arising,	unidentified
56 Fill'd with vengeance on his foes,	unidentified
57 Down to hell, there's no redemption	unidentified
58 Ev'ry Christless soul must go.	unidentified
59 Down to hell, depart, depart,	variants of Philip Doddridge lines in
60 Ye cursed into everlasting flames.	"And will the judge descend?"
61 Hear the Saviour's words of mercy,	Occom
62 Come ye ransom'd sinners home:	Occom
63 Swift and joyful on your journey,	Assize
64 To the palace of your God.	Assize
65 See the soul that earth despised,	Occum
66 In celestial glories move,	Occom
67 Hallelujah, big with wonder,	Occom
68 Praising Christ's eternal love;	Occom
69 Hallelujah, hallelujah	Occom
70 Echo through the realms of light.	Occom
71 Joy celestial, hymns harmonious,	Occom
72 In soft symphony resound;	Occom
73 Angels, seraphs, harps, and trumpets,	Occom
74 Swell the sweet angelic sound	Occom
75 Hail Almighty, Hail Almighty,	Occom
76 Great eternal Lord, Amen.	Occom

"The Day of Judgment"—Isaac Watts
"An ode, attempted in English Sapphic"

When the fierce north wind with his airy forces
Rears up the Baltic to a foaming fury;
And the red lightning, with a storm of hail comes
  Rushing amain down,

How the poor sailors stand amazed and tremble!
While the hoarse thunder, like a bloody trumpet,
Roars a loud onset to the gaping waters,
     Quick to devour them.
Such shall the noise be, and the wild disorder,
(If things eternal may be like these earthly)
Such the dire terror when the great archangel
     Shakes the creation;
Tears the strong pillars of the vault of heav'n,
Breaks up old marble, the repose of princes;
See the graves open, and the bones arising,
     Flames all around 'em!
Hark, the shrill outcries of the guilty wretches!
Lively bright horror, and amazing anguish,
Stare through their eyelids, while the living worm lies
     Gnawing within them.
Thoughts, like old vultures, prey upon their heartstrings,
And the smart twinges, when the eye beholds the
Lofty Judge frowning, and a flood of vengeance
     Rolling afore him.
Hopeless immortals! how they scream and shiver,
While devils push them to the pit wide yawning
Hideous and gloomy to receive them headlong
     Down the centre.
Stop here, my fancy: (all away, ye horrid
Doleful ideas) come, arise to Jesus,
How he sits godlike! and the saints around him
     Thron'd, yet adoring!
O, may I sit there when he comes triumphant,
Dooming the nations! then ascend to glory,
While our hosannas all along the passage
     Shout the Redeemer,

    Amy L. Reed in *The Background of Gray's Elegy* (1924), as
quoted in Arthur Paul Davis, *Isaac Watts, His Life And
Works* (New York: Dryden Press, 1943), p. 166, speaks of the
"enormous popularity" of Watts's "Day of Judgment" in the
eighteenth century. She suggests that the poem's popularity
shows continuing interest in "the vanity of life and the
horrors of death and judgment"—a favorite theme of such
seventeenth-century poems as Wigglesworth's "The Day of

Doom." Miss Reed points out that in many poems Watts "consistently offsets these ideas by the thought of the saving power of Jesus and the bliss of the good in heaven," but she believes that the average reader was more stirred by the horrors than by the beatific vision. It will be observed that Morgan, by picking up much of "Lo, He Cometh" and all the conclusion of "Hark, Ye Mortals" to balance against Watts, stresses the rewards of the saved very strongly.

Appendix C

Accounts of the Origin of the "Justin Morgan Horse"

The first attempt to trace the ancestry of the original Morgan horse was apparently made in the periodical, the *Albany Cultivator,* in 1841, beginning with the October issue. All the *Cultivator* articles dealing with "the Justin Morgan horse" were reprinted, in whole or in part, in Daniel C. Linsley's *Morgan Horses: A Premium Essay on the Origin, History, and Characteristics of This Remarkable American Breed of Horses.* . . . (New York: C. M. Saxton and Company, 1857). Linsley added information that he had gathered personally. In 1885 Joseph Battell's *Middlebury Register and Addison County Journal* ran a series of articles, later attributed by Battell to Allen W. Thomson of Woodstock, which gathered reminiscences from a number of men not mentioned in earlier accounts. Thomson had, according to the *Register,* originally written his account for *Turf, Field, and Stream* in 1883. Finally in the 1890s Battell brought out the first two volumes of *The Morgan Horse and Register,* in which, as in his later *American Stallion Register* (1909-11), he contributed much added information based on his own research, notably in the newspapers that advertised "Figure" in the 1790s. The excerpts given here are placed as nearly as possible in the chronological order in which the original articles appeared, so that the reader may follow the development of the "Justin Morgan" legend, especially the part that emphasizes the horse's diminutive size. When documentary evidence contradicts points made in the various narratives, that fact is noted in editorial comments placed in brackets. All "Battell" quotations are from *The Morgan Horse and Register,* volume one.

George Bernard, Sherbrook, P.C., letter dated August 1841, printed in *The Cultivator* (Albany) 8 (October 1841): 162:

> The original Morgan horse, called also the Goss horse, is well known to have appeared in Randolph and in St. Johnsbury (Vt.) some forty years since, and to have been kept as a stallion, at first with but little and subsequently with very great patronage, some five and twenty years, or until he was thirty years old or more. Various accounts are current as to his origin; many think it quite distinct from the Canadian breed of Norman-French extraction, and consider the horse to have been of Dutch blood, and to have been introduced from some of the settlements on Hudson river, southward of Albany. Stories are told of a traveller's blood mare having got with foal by a Canadian or Indian pony, at various places north and west, and having brought forth this horse; all these accounts are improbable, and appear to be unauthenticated.
>
> For the last dozen years . . . I have believed that the original Morgan horse was of French Canadian origin. . . .

Barnard appends an affidavit signed by John Sterns, "sworn before me at Charleston village, this 14th of August, 1841, David Connell, J.P.":

> I was about 13 yrs of age when the Morgan horse was 1st brought to St. Johnsbury, in Vermont, where my father lived. As I am now fifty, it must have been about 1804. . . . At my uncle David's [Goss], we found uncle John [Goss] from Randolph, with a little, heavy, handsome, active bay horse. . . . Uncle John said that he was a Canadian horse that he had just got from Justin Morgan of Randolph, who had lately brought him from Montreal. . . . [Justin Morgan died

in 1798. Justin Morgan, Jr., 18 in 1804, never owned the
Morgan horse.] Uncle John had lent Morgan the sum of
forty dollars on occasion of the latter's going a journey to
Montreal in Canada. Morgan obtained the horse, then four
years old, at Montreal, and being unable to repay the
money on his return, disposed of him to uncle John, to pay
the debt. . . .

Justin Morgan, Jr., Stockbridge, Vermont, letter dated 1
March 1842, printed in the June issue of *The Cultivator* 9
(1842):99:

. . . I have read the affidavit of the said Sterns attentively,
and know that he is entirely mistaken. . . . My father owned
said horse to the day of his death [cf. Justin Morgan probate
inventory, p. 170 above], and, in the settlement of my
father's estate, said horse passed into the hands of William
Rice, then living in Woodstock, Vt., since deceased.
. . . My father, Justin Morgan, brought said horse, or
rather, said colt, into Randolph, Vt., in the summer or
autumn of 1795. Said colt was only two years old when my
father brought him to Randolph, Vt., and never had been
handled in any way, not even to be led by a halter. [Cf.
advertisements of Figure at stud, 1792 and following, pp.
168 ff.] My father went to Springfield, Mass., the place of
his nativity, and the place from which he removed to
Randolph, in the spring or summer of 1795, after money
that was due to him at that place, as he said; and, instead of
getting money as he expected, he got two colts—one a three
years old gelding colt, which he led, the other, a two years
old stud colt, which followed all the way from Springfield
to Randolph; having been, as my father said, always kept
with, and much attached to the colt he led. Said two years
old colt was the same that has since been known all over
New England by the name of the Morgan Horse.
My father broke said colt himself, and, as I have before
remarked, owned and kept him to the time of his decease,
which took place in March, 1798, and said horse was five
years old the spring my father died. . . . I know that my
father always, while he lived, called him a Dutch horse.

John Morgan, Lima, New York, letter printed in the July 1842 issue of *The Cultivator* 9, 110:

Mr. John Morgan informs us . . . that the two years old stud . . . 'was sired by a horse owned by Sealy Norton of East Hartford, Conn., called the True Briton, or Beautiful Bay; he was kept at Springfield one season, by the said Justin Morgan, and, two years after, I kept him two seasons.' This horse was said to be raised by Gen. De Lancey, commander of the refugee troops on Long Island, and rode by him in the Revolution. It was said that one Smith stole the horse from the General, at King's Bridge, while the General was in the tavern—ran him across the Bridge, and took him to the American army near White Plains, and sold him to Joseph Ward, of Hartford, Conn., for $300. . . . Ward . . . traded him off to Norton, and Norton kept him for mares while he lived.

"Mr. Weissinger," letter to "The Louisville Journal" quoted in *The Cultivator* 2, n.s. (Autumn 1845):

Mr. Cottrel, of Montpelier, Vt., who is as well acquainted with horses as any man in Vermont, says there is not the slightest doubt that the original Morgan was got by a Canada horse. He says the most probable account of his origin is this: 'A man by the name of Smith, of Plainfield, N.H., had a fine imported mare. He rode this mare to Canada on a courting expedition, and while there his mare got in foal. Smith regretted the accident, and laying no value upon the colt, he sold it to Morgan, a singing-master, who, when the colt was grown, rode him around on his singing circuit . . . '

Solomon Steele, Derby Line, Vermont, letter dated 12 March 1856 (in Linsley, *Morgan Horses*, p. 102):

. . . Justin Morgan brought him to Randolph, Vt., from Mass., in the autumn of 1795. Mr. M intended to apply him to the payment of a note held against him, but not being able to obtain what he considered a reasonable price for him, and having no keeping for him, he let him to a man by the name of Robert Evans, for one year, for the sum of fifteen dollars. Immediately after this, Evans undertook the job of clearing fifteen acres of heavy timbered land for a Mr. Fisk, and before the first of June following, had completed the job, with no other team but this colt. . . . While Evans was engaged in piling this timber, the remarkable powers of this horse, it would seem, were in a measure developed, as he was then found able to out-draw, out-walk, out-trot, or out-run every horse that was matched against him. . . . Thus early in the history of the Morgan horse it was an admitted fact that however small, he could not be beaten, where strength, speed, and endurance were the test.

Linsley, *Morgan Horses,* p. 131:

The original, or Justin Morgan, was about fourteen hands high, and weighed about nine hundred and fifty pounds. . . . He was a fleet runner at short distances. Running horses short distances for small stakes was very common in Vermont fifty years ago. Eighty rods was very generally the length of the course, which usually commenced at a tavern or grocery, and extended the distance agreed upon, up or down the public road. . . . After Mr. Morgan's death, he was sold by the estate to William Rice, of Woodstock, Vt. Mr. Rice used him in the ordinary work of his farm for about two years, or until 1800 or 1801, when Robert Evans . . . bought him. . . . Mr. Evans kept him three or four years, or until 1804, when he was sued for debt; Col. John Goss became his bail, took the horse for security, and finally paid the debt and kept him. Mr. John Goss was not much of a horseman, and therefore took the horse to his brother, David Goss, of St. Johnsbury, who . . . kept him seven years, or until 11811, and it was while owned by him that the Hawkins, Fenton, and Sherman horses were sired.

D. P. Thompson, *The History of Montpelier,* published 1860, (quoted in *Battell, The Morgan Horse and Register,* p. 104): "Jonathan Shepard of Montpelier . . . sold his [blacksmith] shop and custom to James Hawkins, taking his (Hawkins') farm, and letting Hawkins have, too, the first

Morgan horse ever known in Vermont or elsewhere." Note by Thompson: "Mr. Shepard's statement in regard to the horse is that he purchased him of a man in Woodstock for about two hundred dollars, a very large price at that time. The man in Woodstock had the horse of one Justin Morgan, a man of that section who reared him from a colt. Mr. Shepard states of his own knowledge that Justin Morgan owned the mare that brought the colt. . . ."

Allen W. Thomson of Woodstock, Vermont, article in *Turf, Field, and Farm*, 1883 (quoted in Battell, *The Morgan Horse and, Register*, p. 105): "Mr. Shepard's son, George C., now of Montpelier, writes that the town records show that his father took a deed of Mr. Hawkins' farm, February 14, 1797, and that it must have been then that his father sold the horse. Mr. Shepard does not remember the name of the man his father had the horse of in Woodstock. . . ."

Letter dated 22 July 1857 from John Woodbury to Hon. J. P. Kidder, owner of Woodbury Morgan, printed in *The Spirit of the Times*, 1874, and quoted by Battell, *The Morgan Horse and Register*, p. 112: "The original Morgan, as I best recollect, was in weight not more than one thousand pounds . . . height about same as Backman horse. . . ." Battell adds that the Backman horse was called fifteen and a half hands high, and concludes, "As Mr. Woodbury calls the Justin Morgan about the same height, it is evident either that he was mistaken, or the height of 'Charley' [the Backman horse] has been exaggerated, or Justin Morgan was taller than he has been reported. This is one of many suggestions that leads us to believe that Justin Morgan was considerably more than fourteen hands high." [Compare 1792 and 1796 advertisements for Figure, pp. 166 and 170 above.]

Allen W. Thomson of Woodstock, article in *The Middlebury Register*, 23 January 1885: "Judge Griswold was Mr. Morgan's nearest neighbor. The judge's statement is, 'That early the morning after Mr. Morgan got home, Mr. Morgan came to his house and wanted he should go over and see a colt he had taken home from where he used to live. The judge went over and was showed the colt in the pasture.'"

Later in the same article Thomson tells the story [see p. 167 above] of Morgan's bringing the horse first to the house of his sister Eunice, and of Eunice's nextdoor neighbor Jude Moulton being the first to have the honor of viewing the new colt. When Battell repeats this story in *The Morgan Horse and Register,* he deletes the one speech that any of the story-tellers allowed Morgan to make. The speech (his answer to Jude Moulton's comment that the new colt was a "little runt that did not look to be worth ten dollars") was, "A good deal there, sir; a good deal there, sir."

Again in this article Thomson tells of a difference of opinion between Jude Moulton's grandsons: "One of them thinks his grandfather said the four-year-old horse was gray, but the other said not, that he said bay. . . ."

Thomson then says that William Rice "lived at Randolph when Mr. Morgan did; he removed to Woodstock about 1796; he was a dishonest man, and it is believed that he cheated Mr. Morgan out of what he had. Some say he had the four-year-old horse and took him to Woodstock, and some say the horse was sold and taken to Williston." [Battell in *The Morgan Horse and Register* deletes the comment regarding William Rice's alleged dishonesty.]

In speaking of the connection of Jonathan Shepard of Montpelier with the Morgan horse, Thomson writes: "The time (Feb. 14, 1797) that Mr. Shepard sold the horse shows it could not have been 'the Justin Morgan,' as Mr. Morgan owned him at that time. [See above, pp. 171-73, for account of Morgan's probable sale of his horse in 1795.] There cannot be any doubt but that Mr. Shepard's horse was a horse tnat Justin Morgan once owned, and that it was the one he advertised the seasons of 1793 and 1794, and was, too, the one he took from Springfield with the two-year-old colt . . ."

Thomson quotes Charles L. Lamb, attorney at South Royalton, Vermont, to the effect that "the color of 'the Justin

Morgan in mare time, was a dark dappled bay, inclining to the brown, nose brown or mealy, had no white on him, about fourteen hands high, and never weighed over nine hundred pounds."

In a later article in *The Middlebury Register*, 2 October 1885, Thomson remarks, "Without knowing more, it is hard now to say what horse the Figure horse was. He may have been the horse Justin Morgan, but we think not. It is claimed on good authority that the three-year-old gelding colt was a grey stud colt, and was the Figure horse and was taken north from Randolph. Grey Figure was advertised to stand at Williamstown, Vermont, in 1795." [Although "Grey Figure" of Williamstown was advertised in the *Vermont Gazette* of 17 April 1795, two years later the 28 May 1797 issue of the *Rutland Herald* carried an advertisement for "Bay-Figure", placed at stud by Asa Graves of Rutland. In neither case do the ancestry and description of the horse match those of the horse that Morgan apparently received from Samuel Whitman of Hartford, Connecticut, in 1792.]

In the 2 October story Thomson also remarks that in 1842 Justin Morgan, Jr. said his father brought the horse to Vermont in 1795, and adds: "He [Justin, Jr.] told his son, H. D. Morgan, now of Stockbridge, that he had made some wrong statements in regard to his father's horse. . . . Mr. Weir says that Mr. Morgan did not own the horse at the time of his death and there cannot be much doubt that it was the spring of 1795 that Mr. Morgan sold the horse. . . . That is why Mr. Morgan's son made the mistake he did. He remembered that there was something done in 1795 in regard to the horse, and gave it that that was the year he was taken to Vermont, when it was the year that his father sold him."

After concluding that the horse went from Morgan to William Rice, Thomson says, "Mr. Linsley states that Mr. Rice let Robert Evans of Randolph have the horse in 1801 and that he let John Goss have him in 1804 and that Mr. Goss let his brother David at St. Johnsbury have him; that he was taken back to Randolph in 1811 and kept there and in the vicinity until his death. . . . He died at Chelsea in February 1819, or was killed. The cause of his death was a kick that he received from a mare hitched in the barn beside him. . . ."

Interview with Charles Morgan, grandson of Justin, written by W. H. Bliss 16 January 1885 and published in *The Middlebury Register* 28 October 1886: "Mr. Charles Morgan . . . understands that Justin Morgan went back to Springfield to collect his pay of a man for whom he had worked, and, not getting money, took a yearling colt, the Justin Morgan horse. He never heard of the Figure horse, never heard that Justin Morgan owned or handled more than one horse in Vermont. . . ." (Quoted by Battell, *The Morgan Horse and Register*, p. 97.)

Interview in 1885 with Selim French, aged seventy-five, proprietor of a hotel at Barnard, Vermont, given in ibid., p. 99: "The original Morgan horse came from Hartford, Connecticut, to Randolph. I never saw him." [Mr. French thus gains the distinction of being one of the two men, alive and living in Vermont before the death of Figure in 1819 or 1821, who were sure that they never saw the horse, and said so.]

Interview in 1885 with J. E. Davis, seventy-three years old, also of Barnard, given in ibid., p. 99: "I never saw the Justin Morgan but was well acquainted with Jonathan Shepard, of Montpelier, who said that he, at one time, owned the old Justin Morgan horse. . . . Figure Eagle was a bay horse, fifteen and one-fourth hands, 1100 to 1200 pounds. . . ." Battell adds, "The substitution of the word Figure for Morgan, in Figure Eagle, is also very significant, as the horse referred to is without question the one so well known as Morgan Eagle. . . ."

Ibid., p. 105 (1894): "It is clear that the horse passed out of Morgan's possession in the fall of 1795. It is very probable that he was in the hands of Evans the following winter. At all events, when Morgan finally disposed of the horse, he passed to William Rice of Woodstock. This is universally conceded, save that, until the records were examined, it was supposed from the statement of Justin Morgan, 2d, that Rice had the horse from the estate, after Justin Morgan's death. The records show that Justin Morgan did not own him at his death. . . . William Rice . . . took the horse for a debt, moved to Woodstock, and apparently disposed of him as soon as he found a customer. . . ." [As has been indicated above in chapter 10, "Figure Again," this student of Morganiana believes that Figure went from Justin Morgan to Samuel Allen of Williston, probably then to William Rice to Jonathan Shepard to James Hawkins to Robert Evans, and so on and on.]

Ibid., p. 118: Battell traces the stud career of Figure: 1795, kept by Justin Morgan at Williston and Hinesburgh; 1796, kept by Jonathan Shepard at Montpelier, and perhaps earlier in the season by William Rice at Woodstock [Substitute Samuel Allen of Hinesburg for Rice?]; 1797, passed to James Hawkins of Montpelier, "and it is not known where kept until purchased, probably 1801, by Robert Evans, Randolph, who sold him, probably 1804, to John Goss, Randolph." Battell states that Figure died in 1821 at the age of 32, and that his last owner was Levi Bean of Chelsea.

As his final comment regarding the two friendly colts that had been boon companions in the Morgan story ever since Justin Morgan, Jr. wrote his letter of 1 March 1842 to *The Cultivator*, Battell concludes (p. 118): "It seems very probable that the two colts brought in . . . were the three or four-year-old stallion, Figure (or "Justin Morgan"), and another colt, instead of a three-year-old gelding and two-year-old stud. . . ." [Then again, as Charles Morgan suggested, the two colts may have been one colt—Figure, the non-pareil.]

The Legend in Memorials

Justin Morgan, man and horse, in bronze and stone: West

Springfield, Massachusetts: At 455 Birnie Road, just off Morgan Road, there is a large stone marker supporting a bronze tablet that reads: "Here lived Justin Morgan/ Born in West Springfield 1747/ Died in Randolph, Vt., 1798./ From this farm came the stallion/ Justin Morgan/ Progenitor of that useful breed/ Known as Morgan horses." (The marker was erected by the city of West Springfield.)

Randolph Center, Vermont, historical marker on Main Street: "Randolph, home of Justin Morgan. In 1791 Schoolmaster Justin Morgan brought to Vermont the Colt that was to bear his name and to make them both famous. This Morgan Horse which Justin Morgan took as payment of a debt became the ancestor of one of the greatest breeds of horses ever established in America."

Randolph Center cemetery, marker over Justin Morgan's grave: "Justin Morgan 1747-1798. This man brought to Vermont the colt from which all Morgan horses are descended." This very modern marker in highly polished granite was erected by the American Morgan Horse Association, and the fine old gravestone that featured the man rather than the horse was removed when the marker was put in place. The gravestone is now in the custody of the Randolph Historical Society. The stone shows the profile of a man's bust, in eighteenth-century dress, and reads simply, "Justin Morgan/ Died March/ 22nd A.D. 1798/ in the 51st year/ of his Age." A grave marker standing near the Morgan grave reads, "Martha Morgan/ Wife of Justin Morgan/ Died 20 March 1791/ About the 40th year of her age." The stone is identical in type and design to the one that formerly marked Justin's grave.

Woodstock, Vermont, historical marker on Central Street: "On this site the progenitor of the famous Morgan breed of horses was owned by Sheriff William Rice about 1800. Justin Morgan took his name from that of the singing schoolmaster who originally brought him to Vermont, but who lost possession of the later famous horse to Sheriff Rice in payment of a debt."

Chelsea, Vermont, memorial stone placed by the Morgan Horse Club [now the American Morgan Horse Association] on the farm, now owned by Mr. and Mrs. Harold Childs, where Figure died: "On This Farm Lies/ The Body of/ Justin Morgan/ Foaled 1789, Died 1821/ Progenitor of the/ First Established American/ Breed of Horses."

Weybridge, Vermont, at the University of Vermont's Morgan Horse Farm: imposing heroic-sized statue of "the Justin Morgan horse," said to be one of the few statues in the world to feature a riderless horse. The bronze statue is mounted on a granite base on which is written, "1921/ Given by/ The Morgan Horse Club/ to the/ United States/ Department of Agriculture/ in Memory of/ Justin Morgan/ Who Died in/ 1821." The sculptor was Frederick Roth, whose sculptures featuring animals included the very well-known "Roman Chariot" done for the Pan-American Exposition in 1901, and who was at one time president of the National Sculpture Society. A group of small bronzes by Roth are now in the Metropolitan Museum of Art in New York.

Note: Many of these markers contain inaccuracies. Indeed, Justin Morgan's own gravestone may be in error, if the Springfield, Massachusetts, vital records are correct in stating that Morgan was born 28 February 1747. By this reckoning he would by the date of his death, 22 March 1798. have already attained the age of fifty-one and would therefore have been in the fifty-second year of his life. (See above, p. 84.) Despite the errors, however, the markers attest to strong interest in "the Morgan horse." There is still room, it would seem, for a marker to memorialize Justin Morgan, American composer.

Bibliography

The principal sources of information regarding Justin Morgan are public documents and newspapers of his day. These have been described in the Introduction, pp. 9-11.

Abbott, Jacob. *New England and Her Institutions.* Hartford, Conn.: S. Andrus and Son, 1847.

Adgate, Andrew. *Philadelphia Harmony, Part Two.* 3d ed. Philadelphia, Pa.: Westcott and Adgate, 1791.

Allen, N. H. "Old Time Music and Musicians." *Connecticut Quarterly* 1 (1895): 274-79.

Ann Arbor, Mich. University of Michigan. Clements Library. Andrew Law papers.

Atkins, Gains Glenn, and Fagley, Frederick L. *History of American Congregationalism.* Boston and Chicago: Pilgrim Press, 1942.

Atwill, Thomas H. *The New York [and Vermont] Collection of Sacred Harmony.* Lansingburgh, N. Y.: the author, 1795. Later editions include "and Vermont" in the title.

Bagg, J. N., comp. *Account of the Centennial Celebration of the Town of West Springfield, Mass.* West Springfield, Mass.: Published by the town, 1874.

———. "Marriages in West Springfield, 1774-96." *New England Historical and Genealogical Register* 29 (1875): 54-59.

Bagg, Lyman H. "Early Settlers of West Springfield." *New England Historical and Genealogical Register* 29 (1875): 283-89.

Bandel, Betty. "End of an Argument." *The Morgan Horse* 28 (April 1968): 41.

Barbour, J. Murray. *The Church Music of William Billings.* East Lansing, Mich.: Michigan State University Press, 1960.

Battell, Joseph. *American Stallion Register.* 2 vols. Middlebury, Vt.: American Publishing Co., 1909-11.

——. *The Morgan Horse and Register.* 3 vols. Middlebury, Vt.: Register Printing Company, 1894-1915.

Benham, Asahel. *Federal Harmony, Containing, in a Familiar Manner, The Rudiments of Psalmody, Together with a Collection of Church Music (Most of Which Are Entirely New).* New Haven, Conn.: A. Morse, 1790.

Blair, Samuel. *A Discourse on Psalmody, Delivered by the Reverend Samuel Blair, in the Presbyterian Church in Neshaminy, at a Public Concert, Given by Mr. Spicer, Master in Sacred Music, under the Superintendency of the Rev. Mr. Erwin, Pastor of That Church, with an Appendix, Containing the Addresses of Mr. Erwin, and Mr. Spicer, on the Occasion.* Philadelphia, Pa.: John M'Cullough, 1789.

Booth, Henry A. "Springfield during the Revolution." *Papers and Proceedings of the Connecticut Valley Historical Society* 2 (1904): 285-308.

Britton, Allen Perdue. *Theoretical Introductions in American Tune-books to 1800.* Ann Arbor, Mich.: University Microfilms, 1949.

Brown, Theron, and Butterworth, Hezekiah. *The Story of Hymns and Tunes.* New York: American Tract Society, 1906.

Buechner, Alan Clark. "Yankee Singing Schools and the Golden Age of Choral Music in New England, 1760-1800." Ph.D. dissertation, Harvard Graduate School of Education, 1960.

Burnham, Eleanor Waring. *Justin Morgan, Founder of His Race.* New York: Shakespeare Press, 1911.

Chapman, James G., ed. "Vermont Harmony: A Collection of Fuging Tunes, Anthems, and Secular Pieces by Vermont Composers of the Period 1790 to 1810, Including the Complete Works of Justin Morgan." Music transcribed by James G. Chapman, notes written by Betty Bandel and James G. Chapman. Burlington, Vt. 1972.

Chase, Gilbert. *America's Music from the Pilgrims to the Present.* New York: McGraw-Hill Book Co., 1955.

Cheney, Simeon Pease. *American Singing Book.* Boston: White, Smith, & Co., 1859.

Child, Ebenezer. *The Sacred Musician and Young Gentlemen's and Ladies' Practical Guide to Musick.* Boston: Manning and Loring for the author, 1804.

Chipman, David. *The Life of Hon. Nathaniel Chipman, LL.D.* Boston: Charles C. Little and James Brown, 1846.

Cooley, Harry H. Article on Justin Morgan. In *White River Valley Herald,* 15 December 1959.

Crawford, Richard A. *Andrew Law, American Psalmodist.* Pi Kappa Lambda Studies in American Music. Evanston, Ill.: Northwestern University Press, 1968.

———. "Connecticut Sacred Music Imprints, 1778-1810." *Music Library Association Notes* 27 (1971): 445-52 and 671-79.

Curwen, Spencer. *Studies in Worship Music.* 1st series, 3d ed. London: J. Cunnen and Son, n.d.

Dana, Henry Swan. *History of Woodstock, Vt.* Boston and New York: Houghton Mifflin Co., 1887 and 1889 editions.

Daniel, Ralph T. *The Anthem in New England before 1800.* Pi Kappa Lambda Studies in American Music. Evanston, Ill.: Northwestern University Press, 1966.

Davis, Arthur Paul. *Isaac Watts, His Life and Works.* New York: Dryden Press, 1943.

Doolittle, Eliakim. *The Psalm Singer's Companion.* New Haven, Conn.: printed for the author, 1806.

Eaton, Allen H. *Handicrafts of New England.* New York: Harper, 1949.

Edson, Carroll Andrew, ed. *Edson Family History and Genealogy: Descendants of Samuel Edson of Salem and Bridgewater, Mass.* Ann Arbor, Mich., n.d.

First Congregational Church of West Springfield. *History of the First Parish and the First Congregational Church of West Springfield, Mass.* West Springfield, Mass.: printed for the church, n.d.

Fisher, Dorothy Canfield. *Vermont Tradition.* Boston: Little, Brown, & Co., 1953.

Foote, Henry Wilder. *Three Centuries of American Hymnody.* 1940. Reprint. New York: Anchor Books, 1968.

Ford, Emily Ellsworth Fowler. *Notes on the Life of Noah Webster.* 2 vols. New York: privately printed, 1912.

Freeman, Samuel. *The Town Officer.* Boston: Thomas and Andrews, 1808.

Gardiner, Margaret. "The Great Justin Morgan Pedigree Controversy." Part 1. *Chronicle of the Horse.* 23 December 1966, pp. 26-27.

Graham, John Andrew. *A Descriptive Sketch of the Present State of Vermont.* London: Henry Fry, 1797.

Green, Mason A. "The Breck Controversy in the First Parish in

Springfield in 1735." *Papers and Proceedings of the Connecticut Valley Historical Society, 1876-1881* 1 (1881): 8-16.

Harbage, Alfred. *Conceptions of Shakespeare.* Cambridge, Mass.: Harvard University Press, 1967.

Harmon, Joel Jr. *The Columbian Sacred Minstrel.* Northampton, Mass.: Andrew Wright for the author, 1809.

Hart, Albert Bushnell, ed. *Commonwealth History of Massachusetts.* New York: States History Co., 1927-28.

Hastings, Thomas, ed. *The Musical Magazine* 1 (1835).

Hazard, Lucy Lockwood. *The Frontier in American Literature.* N.p., privately printed, 1927.

Hemenway, Abby Marie, ed. *The Vermont Historical Gazetteer: A Magazine, Embracing a History of Each Town, Civil, Ecclesiastical, Biographical, and Military.* 5 vols. Burlington, Vt., A. M. Hemenway, 1868-91.

Henry, Marguerite. *Justin Morgan Had a Horse.* New York: Rand McNally & Co., 1954.

Hill, Uri K. *The Vermont Harmony.* Northampton, Mass.: Andrew Wright for the compiler, 1801.

Holland, Josiah Gilbert. *History of Western Massachusetts.* Springfield, Mass.: Samuel Bowles, 1855.

Hollister, Hiel. *Pawlet for One Hundred Years.* Albany, N.Y.: J. Munsell, 1867.

Hood, George. *A History of Music in New England.* Boston: Wilkins, Carter & Co., 1846.

Hubbard, John. *Essay on Music.* Boston: Manning & Loring, 1808.

Hubbell, Seth. *A Narrative of the Sufferings of Seth Hubbell and Family, in His Beginning a Settlement in the Town of Wolcott, in the State of Vermont.* Danville, Vt.: E. and W. Eaton, 1826.

Ingalls, Jeremiah. *The Christian Harmony.* Exeter, N.H.: Henry Ranlet for the compiler, 1805.

Jenks, Francis. Essay on Michael Wigglesworth's *The Day of Doom.* In *Christian Examiner,* November 1828.

Jenks, Stephen, comp. *The American Compiler of Sacred Harmony.* Northampton, Mass.: privately printed, 1803.

Kroeger, Karl Douglas. "*The Worcester Collection of Sacred Harmony* and Sacred Music in America, 1786-1803." Ph.D. dissertation, Brown University, 1976.

Lamson, Genieve. *The Heritage of Bethany Church.* Randolph, Vt., n.p., 1955.

Lancaster, Mass. *The Birth, Marriage, and Death Register, Church*

Records, and Epitaphs of Lancaster, Massachusetts. Edited by Henry S. Nourse. Lancaster, Mass.: Clinton, 1890.

[Lathrop, Joseph.] *A Miscellaneous Collection of Original Pieces: Political, Moral, and Entertaining.* Springfield, Mass.: John Russell, 1786.

Lathrop, Joseph. "Memoir." In *Sermons by the Late Rev. Joseph Lathrop, D.D., Pastor of the First Church of West Springfield.* n.s., pp. xi-lxx. Springfield, Mass.: A. C. Tannatt, 1821.

———. *Sermons on Various Subjects.* 2 vols. Worcester, Mass.: Isaiah Thomas, 1796.

Leslie, Benjamin. *The Concert Harmony.* Salem, Mass.: the author, 1811.

Linsley, Daniel Chipman. *Morgan Horses: A Premium Essay on the Origin, History, and Characteristics of This Remarkable American Breed of Horses.* New York: C. M. Saxton & Co., 1857.

Longmeadow, Mass. Richard Salter Storrs Library. Diary of Reverend Stephen Williams.

Lovejoy, Evelyn. *History of Royalton, Vermont.* Burlington, Vt.: Town of Royalton and the Royalton Woman's Club, 1911.

Lowens, Irving. *Music and Musicians in Early America.* New York: Norton, 1964.

Ludwig, Allen I. *Graven Images: New England Stonecarving and Its Symbols, 1650-1815.* Middletown, Conn.: Wesleyan University Press, 1966.

McCorison, Marcus A. *Vermont Imprints, 1778-1820.* Worcester, Mass.: American Antiquarian Society, 1963.

Macdougall, Hamilton C. *Early New England Psalmody.* Brattleboro, Vt.: Stephen Daye Press, 1940.

Martin, Margaret A. *Merchants and Traders of the Connecticut River Valley, 1750-1820.* Smith College Studies in History 24, nos. 1-4. Northampton, Mass.: Smith College Department of History, 1938-39.

Mather, Cotton. *The Diary of Cotton Mather.* New York: Frederick Ungar Publishing Company, [1957].

Mellers, Wilfred Howard. *Music in a New Found Land.* London: Barrie & Rockliff, 1964.

Mellin, Jeanne. *The Morgan Horse.* Brattleboro, Vt.: Stephen Greene Press, 1961.

Metcalf, Frank J. *American Writers and Compilers of Sacred Music.* New York and Cincinnati, Ohio: Abingdon Press, 1925.

Minot, George Richards. *The History of the Insurrections in*

Massachusetts in the Year 1786 and the Rebellion Consequent Thereon. 2d ed. Boston: James W. Burditt & Co., 1810.

Montpelier, Vt. Vermont Historical Society. Royall Tyler Collection.

Moors, Hezekiah. *The Province Harmony.* Boston: J. T. Buckingham for the author, 1809.

[Morgan, Justin.] *Judgment Anthem.* Dedham, Mass.: Herman Mann for David Belknap, 1810.

Morris, Henry. "Miles Morgan." *Papers and Proceedings of the Connecticut Valley Historical Society, 1876-1881* 1 (1881): 250-62.

———. "Slavery and the Connecticut Valley." *Papers and Proceedings of the Connecticut Valley Historical Society, 1876-1881* 1 (1881): 207-18.

Morison, Samuel Eliot. *The Intellectual Life of Colonial New England.* 2d ed., 1956. Reprint. Ithaca, N.Y.: Cornell University Press, 1965.

Morse, Jedediah, and Parish, Elijah. *A Compendious History of New England.* 3d ed. Charlestown, Mass.: S. Etheridge, 1820.

Mussey, June Borrows. *Yankee Life, by Those Who Lived It.* 1st Borzoi ed., rev. 1937. New York: Knopf, 1947.

Nash, Ray. *American Writing Masters and Copybooks.* Boston: Colonial Society of Massachusetts, 1959.

New Haven, Conn. New Haven Colony Historical Society. Daniel Read's Letter Book.

Nickerson and Cox, comps. *The Illustrated Historical Souvenir of Randolph, Vermont.* Randolph, Vt.; n.p., 1895.

Nutting, Rufus. *Memoirs of Mrs. Emily Egerton, an Authentic Narrative.* Boston: Perkins and Marvin, 1832.

Occom, Samson, comp. *A Choice Collection of Hymns and Spiritual Songs.* New London, Conn.: Timothy Green, 1774.

The Original Sacred Harp. Denson rev. ed. Cullman, Ala.: Sacred Harp Publishing Company, 1967.

Patrick, Millar. *Four Centuries of Scottish Psalmody.* London: Geoffrey Cumberlege, Oxford University Press, 1949.

Perkins, Nathan. *A Narrative of a Tour through the State of Vermont.* 1789. Reprint. Rutland, Vt.: Tuttle, 1964.

Pichierri, Louis. "Music in New Hampshire, 1623-1800." Ph.D. dissertation, Syracuse University, 1956.

Pope, Alexander, *An Essay on Man.* Bennington, Vt.: Haswell and Russell, 1785.

Powers, Grant. *Historical Sketches of the Discovery, Settlement, and Progress of Events in the Coos County and Vicinity, Principally Included between the Years 1754 and 1785.* Haverhill, N.H.: J. F. C. Hayes, 1841.

Reed, Amy Louise. *The Background of Gray's Elegy: A Study in the Taste for Melancholy Poetry, 1700-1751.* New York: Russell & Russell, 1962.

Rourke, Constance. *American Humor.* 1931. Reprint. New York: Doubleday, 1953.

———. *The Roots of American Culture.* 1942. Reprint. Port Washington, N.Y.: Kennikat Press, 1965.

Seybolt, Robert Francis. *The Private Schools of Colonial Boston.* Cambridge, Mass.: Harvard University Press, 1935.

Sibley, Agnes Marie. *Alexander Pope's Prestige in America. 1736-1846.* New York: King's Crown Press, 1949.

Smith, Frances Grace. "The American Revolution Hits Church Music." *New England Quarterly* 4 (1931): 783-88.

Smith, Henry Nash. *Virgin Land.* 1950. Reprint. New York: Vintage, 1957.

Smith, William L. "Springfield in the Insurrection of 1786 (Shays's Rebellion)." *Papers and Proceedings of the Connecticut Valley Historical Society, 1876-1881* 1 (1881): 72-90.

Starr, Frank Farnsworth. *The Miles Morgan Family of Springfield, Mass.* Hartford, Conn.: n.p., 1904.

Stebbins, Rufus P. *An Historical Address Delivered at the Centennial Celebration of the Incorporation of the Town of Wilbraham.* Boston: George C. Rand & Avery, 1864.

Sternhold, Thomas; Hopkins, John; and others. *The Whole Booke of Psalms, Collected into English Meetre.* London: John Windet for the assignee of Richard Daye, 1601. [1st printing 1562.]

Stevenson, Robert. *Protestant Church Music in America.* New York: W. W. Norton & Co., 1966.

Sturtevant, Warner B. "Colonial Education in Western Massachusetts." Typescript in Springfield, Mass., Public Library.

Sullivan, Nell Jane Barnett, and Martin, David Kendall. *A History of the Town of Chazy, Clinton County, New York.* Burlington, Vt.: George Little Press, 1970.

Swift, Esther M. *West Springfield, Massachusetts.* West Springfield, Mass.: West Springfield Heritage Association for the Town of West Springfield, 1969.

Taylor, Robert J. *Western Massachusetts in the Revolution.* Providence, R. I.: Brown University Press, 1954.

Tennyson, Hallam. *Alfred Lord Tennyson: A Memoir by His Son.* New York: Macmillan Co., 1898.

Thompson, Daniel Pierce. *History of the Town of Montpelier, from the Time It Was First Chartered in 1781 to the Year 1860.* Montpelier, Vt.: E. P. Walton, 1860.

Tupper, Frederick, and Brown, Helen Tyler, eds. *Grandmother Tyler's Book.* New York and London: Putnam's, 1925.

U. S. Bureau of the Census. *Heads of Families at the First Census of the United States: Taken in the Year 1790.* Washington, Government Printing Office, 1907-8.

Walton, E. P., ed. *Records of the Council of Safety and Governor and Council of the State of Vermont.* Vol. 1. Montpelier, Vt.: J. & J. M. Poland, 1873.

Watts, Isaac. *Horae Lyricae: Poems Chiefly of the Lyric Kind.* London, 1706.

———. *Hymns and Spiritual Songs, in Three Books: with an Essay towards the Improvement of Christian Psalmody, by the Use of Evangelical Hymns in Worship, as well as the Psalms of David.* London: John Lawrence, 1707.

———. *The Psalms of David, Imitated in the Language of the New Testament, and Applied to the Christian State and Worship.* London: J. Clark, 1719.

Wells, Frederick P. *History of Newbury, Vermont.* St. Johnsbury, Vt.: Caledonian Co., 1902.

Wertenbaker, Thomas Jefferson. *The Puritan Oligarchy.* 1947. Reprint. New York: Grosset and Dunlap, n.d.

West, Elisha. *The Musical Concert.* Northampton, Mass.: Andrew Wright for Elisha West and John Billings, Jr., 1802. 2nd ed. by Andrew Wright for the compiler, 1807.

Winslow, Ola Elizabeth. *Jonathan Edwards, 1703-1758.* New York: Macmillan Co., 1940.

Sound Recordings

Canning, Thomas. *Fantasy on a Hymn Tune by Justin Morgan for Double String Quartet and String Orchestra.* Played by the Houston Symphony Orchestra conducted by Leopold Stokowski. Everest Record, LPBR 6070.

The American Harmony. Chapel Choir of the University of Maryland conducted by Fague Springmann. Washington Records WLP 418.

Jackson, George Pullen, ed. *Folk Music of the United States: Sacred Harp Singing.* Library of Congress Music Division Recording Laboratory, AAFS L11.

New England Harmony. Old Sturbridge Singers with Floyd Corson as singing master and members of the Harvard Wind Ensemble. Music selected and annotated by Alan C. Buechner. Folkways Records FA 2377.

Vermont Harmony. University of Vermont Choral Union conducted by James G. Chapman. Notes by Betty Bandel and James G. Chapman. Philo Records 1000.

Index

Cooke, Henry (master of the Children of the Royal Chapel), 30
Cottrell, Maylon, 46, 225
Counter voice, 182, 189
Court of General Sessions of the Peace for Hampshire County, licenses Justin Morgan as liquor dealer, 91
Courts of Common Pleas, hampered during Shays's Rebellion, 112, 113
Crane, Ichabod, 37 n
Crawford, Richard, 137, 144
Creativity, artistic, 13, 27, 38 n, 48, 74
Cromwell, Oliver, 74
Crown Point, 86
Cultivator, The (Albany, N.Y.), 46

Dana, Henry Swan, 18, 27
Daniels, Ralph T.: analyzes "Judgment Anthem," 150; calls its text "doggerel," 151
Dare, Reverend Elkanah Kelsay, defends American music, including Morgan's, 145, 183
Davenport, Isaac, 100
Day, Ebenezer: father of Luke and Thankfull, 70; grandfather of Justin Morgan, 70; marries Mary Hitchcock, 70; will mentions grandson Justin Morgan, 84-85, 120
Day, Luke (born 1706): father of Martha (Day) Morgan, 87; husband of Jerusha Skinner, 87; son of Ebenezer and Mary Day, 70
Day, Luke (1743-1801), 111, 116; in Vermont during Shays's Rebellion, 119 n; leader in Shays's Rebellion, 113; Luke Day, Gent., cousin and brother-in-law of Justin, sued by Morgan and others for defrauding them of their "volunteer" for Revolutionary War service, 106-9

Day, Martha. *See* Morgan, Martha (Day)
Day, Mary (Hitchcock): mother of Luke and Thankfull, 70; wife of Ebenezer Day, 70
Day, Thankfull. *See* Morgan, Thankfull (Day)
Day of Doom, The (Michael Wigglesworth), 151
Day of Judgment: belief in, 162 n; favorite theme, 220-21
"Day of Judgment, The" (Isaac Watts), 153, 216, 219; great popularity, 220
Death, emphasis upon in education, 56-57
Declaration of Independence, 90
Deerfield, Mass., 71
DeLancey, Colonel James, 166
Descriptive Sketch of the Present State of Vermont . . . , A (John Andrew Graham), 24-25
"Despair," 146, 155, 200; as first published, 156; elegy to Martha Morgan, 157-58; only Morgan tune with secular text (Alexander Pope), 158; "Vermont" composition, 159
"Dialogue between Christ, Youth, and the Devil," 28
Dick the Butcher, 112
Dick Whittington, 43
Dickinson College, 141
Dies Irae (Thomas of Celano), 65, 150
Dilworth, Thomas, 57, 86
Discourse on Psalmody, A (Reverend Samuel Blair), 142
Disney, Walt, film on Morgan, 50 n
Doddridge, Philip, 156
Doolittle, Ambrose: father of Eliakim, Eunice (wife of Joseph Morgan), and Lois (wife of Uri Benham), 143
Doolittle, Eliakim: *The Psalm Singer's Companion,* 36 n; Ver-